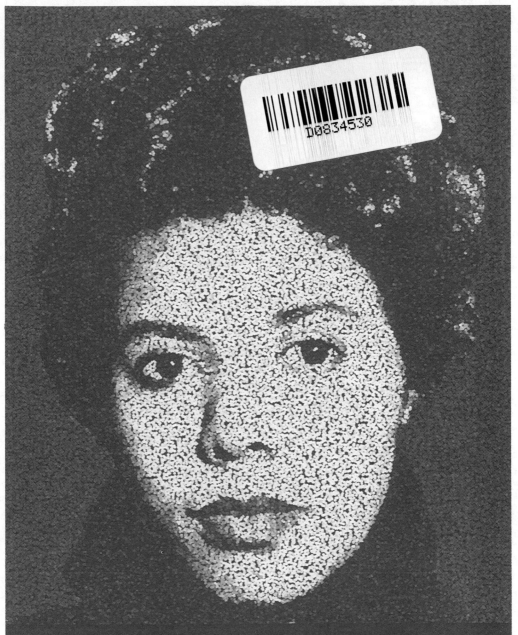

D0834530

THE LORRAINE HANSBERRY PLAYWRITING AWARD
An Anthology of Prize-Winning Plays

≈ • ≈

Foreword by Lloyd Richards

Introduction by Dr. Winona Fletcher • Afterword by Dr. Margaret Wilkerson

The Kennedy Center

THE JOHN F. KENNEDY CENTER FOR THE PERFORMING ARTS

Lawrence J. Wilker, *President*
Derek E. Gordon, *Associate Managing Director for Education*
John Lion, *Senior Program Director, KC/ACTF and Youth and Family Programming*

Copyright © 1996 The John F. Kennedy Center For The Performing Arts

All rights reserved. No part of this book may be reproduced in any form or by any means electronic or mechanical, including photocopying, recording, or by any information retrieval system, without permission in writing from the copyright holder.

For permission to use copyrighted material, our warmest thanks are given to the copyright holders listed on the credits page at the end of this book, which is to be considered a continuation of this copyright page.

Published by Clark Publishing, Inc.
P.O. Box 19240
Topeka, KS 66619
(913) 862-0218

Cover and Design by Todd R. Kinney

First Edition, First Printing

ISBN 0-931054-45-1

Proudly printed in Kansas by Gilliland Printing

Dedicated To:

Roger L. Stevens
Chairman Emeritus of the
John F. Kennedy Center for the Performing Arts
and Founding Father, KC/ACTF

and

Michael Kanin, in memorium
and Fay Kanin
Founders of the
Michael Kanin Playwriting Awards Program
for the
Kennedy Center American College Theater Festival

Acknowledgments

The genesis of this book involves the foresight of Derek E. Gordon, Associate Managing Director of Education at the Kennedy Center, who approached me with the kind and generous offer of Diana Carlin, owner of Clark Publishing, to publish a book on The Lorraine Hansberry Award, sponsored by the Kennedy Center American College Theater Festival. From the beginning, this was to be a non-profit venture with proceeds to support the on-going Lorraine Hansberry Award. The book could not have been possible without the sizable contribution of editor Dr. Winona Fletcher, who for the better part of two decades, served as the archivist, scholar, and spiritual advisor of the Award, and who, in addition, has contributed an introduction which grounds us squarely in the material. Special thanks for her afterword also goes out to Dr. Margaret Wilkerson whose research and writing on Lorraine Hansberry rank her as the top authority on this brilliant playwright's life and work. Director Lloyd Richards, has contributed a unique and personal preface on the atmospherics of the original Broadway production of Hansberry's masterpiece, A *Raisin in the Sun*.

This book is essentially a compilation of the work of the many fine award winning playwrights who are the very reason for the volume's existence, but the credit for the long hours spent assembling, proofing, pursuing legible copy, and successfully mediating between all parties involved is laid directly at the feet of my colleague, Susan Shaffer, whose goodwill, cheer, and wit kept the project percolating along. A special thanks should also be extended to Todd Kinney of Clark Publishing, who exhibited the patience of Job in dealing with our many requests and inquiries and to Ron Himes, Artistic Director of the St. Louis Black Repertory Theatre, who assisted with the final selection of material. A final thanks is extended to Lawrence J. Wilker, President of the Kennedy Center for his on-going support of this project in particular and of the Kennedy Center American College Theater Festival in general.

John Lion
Director, Kennedy Center American College Theater Festival
March 1996

Table Of Contents

Foreword

by

Lloyd Richards

You probably met Lorraine as I did, thru her writing.

It was the fall of 1957. The phone rang. It was Sidney Poitier. He was ecstatic. He laughed as he spoke in that joyous manner that is so distinctly Sidney.

Years before, we talked one night after an acting class where I had been the teacher and Sidney the student. Sidney had said that if he ever did a major play in New York, on Broadway, he wanted me to direct it. We were two struggling Artists sharing thoughts, perceptions, and dreams in the magic of the night. These were not contracts, just hopes that for some, are more binding than a contract. This was the call, the consequences of our work together, in class and of our sessions afterward in a place where they would let at liberty Artists linger over a cup of coffee.

The Play was called A *Raisin In the Sun*. It was by a woman who I had never heard of, Lorraine Hansberry. It was her first play. It would go into rehearsal the next September, after Sidney had finished filming *Porgy and Bess*. I should read the play and determine that I wanted to do it, then meet with the Producer, Philip Rose. If that went well, I should meet Lorraine. The rest was up to us.

Sidney sent the play over and that evening my wife Barbara and I sat or lounged on our queen size bed, with a pink marble mantle as a headboard, and read A *Raisin In the Sun*. We laughed aloud. We were moved. We cried. And we were silent when there was nothing to be said, when Lorraine had said it first and best.

Indeed I wanted to direct the play. Barbara wanted me to direct it.

Philip Rose is a dear man. Soft spoken but sharp, sensitive and bold, daring to believe that he could take a play about a Black family to Broadway. Naïve to think that he could find the funding to do it. I liked him immediately. We hit it off. I am short, Phil is short. We seemed to see the world from the same perspective. Short men and very tall men, I suppose, have to see swirling humanity differently. They are forced to. Sometimes this can form the basis for a bonding. Without speaking of it, I believe that Phil and I bonded.

Try as I might, I cannot recall the specifics of my first meeting with Lorraine. That generally means to me that it went well. There were no snags to relive over and over and to think of all the things one might have said. I know that we talked of theatre and of plays and playwrights. I know that we shared a love for Chekhov and Ocasey. We talked a lot about them and how much they had influenced her work and my life in theatre. At the end of the conversation there seemed to be no need to ask if I would be directing the play. It just seemed to be the natural step.

We had begun. Lorraine was my first living playwright. I had directed many of the greats, Shaw, Shakespeare, Williams, O'Neill, Miller, the Greeks. But they had never been in the room to approve or to object. This would be novel, this would be new to have the originating imagination there over your shoulder to evaluate what my imagination brought to illuminate and extend hers.

It would also be the first play that I directed that stemmed from my culture, that reflected me.

It would be more than a year before we went into rehearsal. There was so much to do. The play had to be rewritten and the creative artist, the designers selected and the designs completed. The actors had to be auditioned and cast. We had to secure a Broadway theatre where we could ultimately bring the play, out of town theaters where we could try the play out, and importantly, where we could find a possible (negro) audience and convince them to begin a new habit, (going to the theatre). We had to develop publicity and a marketing scheme. All this and much, much more had to be done. And we were neophytes, babes in the woods. I think that Sidney had been on Broadway once, in a small part and I had been twice, as an actor. Philip and Lorraine, never.

The production was budgeted at forty-three thousand dollars (I believe) with seventy-five thousand necessary to get us into New York and hold us for a few weeks and advertise, in hopes of catching on and staying there awhile. Every week we went into theatre owners' offices and sat, in hopes that they might have an opening next October or November for us. But it was going to be a busy, tight season and there just didn't seem to be a spot for this play about a negro family who wanted a decent home in a white neighborhood to live in. The smart money didn't consider our project one that would give them an acceptable return on their investment. There didn't seem to be much that made us attractive to the people who made Broadway happen. We were on hold. Come back next week. We were in that strange and uncomfortable position that play producers find themselves in sometimes, of needing someone else to fail so that you might get a chance. And yet you dare not tempt the fates by rooting for another project's failure. We could only wait and occasionally watch the powers play darts on a very attractive board on the office wall.

Lorraine was doing a complete rewrite on her play and I would meet with her every week to work on it. In the previous draft the family was in the new house by the second act and the play developed around the problems of the new neighborhood.

It was suggested to Lorraine that the real core of her play was in the family and how they developed toward the decision to make the move. Lorraine had accepted that suggestion. She was structuring the next version. The core of the play was changing. Walter was emerging as the protagonist. He had previously been a much less important character. Lorraine would write a new scene and read it to me. Phil Rose and Lorraine's husband, Robert Nimerof, often sat in on those meetings. The wonderful and relaxing thing about giving notes and suggestions to Lorraine was in knowing that she would never take a suggestion verbatim but would digest the thought, make it her own then give it back, use it in a different way than suggested. The work was good, but slow.

There was no glamour on the horizon, only a year of insurmountable problems that we would have to surmount to get into rehearsal at the appointed time, and guts, perseverance, tough decisions and hard, hard work that would ultimately get us to opening night at the Barrymore in New York, on Broadway. We were never conscious that we were making history, but we were. We were only conscious of working hard to make a good play the wonderful play it deserved to be.

Read it and enjoy it. Enjoy the results. The struggle is in the past, or at least in another book.

But for now, let us go on in this book. Let us see what these new playwrights have created that might challenge, stimulate or provoke us. "Let us see", as Mama would say, "what the new world has finally wrought". I think that Lorraine would be proud.

Lloyd Richards
February 1996

Introduction

by

Dr. Winona Lee Fletcher

If anything should happen before 'tis done, may I trust that all commas and periods will be placed and someone will complete my thoughts — the last should be the least difficult, since there are so many who think as I do. Good luck to you. This Nation needs your gifts. Perfect them!

— Lorraine Hansberry

At one time, publication of black works was viewed primarily as a way to fulfill African Americans' need to gain access to the mainstream; more and more African Americans are recognizing a need for the mainstream to have access to the arts of minorities. Through the arts, and particularly theatre a better understanding of those unlike ourselves can be gained.

Producer Robert Nemiroff, with sponsorship support of the McDonald's Corporation, established the Lorraine Hansberry Playwriting Award in memory of his wife in 1976.

The award was established for the best play on the black experience in America, produced in the Kennedy Center American College Theater Festival Michael Kanin Playwriting Awards Program. The award was to stimulate young playwrights to take up the challenge left by Hansberry when she died of cancer at age 34. She had written: "Look at the work that awaits you!. Write about our people: tell their story. You have something glorious to draw on begging for attention. Don't pass it up. Use it..." (from *To Be Young, Gifted, and Black*)

More than anything else this collection of plays and scenes is a testimony to Hansberry's wisdom and vision as stated in the above quotations, a tribute to the legacy she left and to the young writers who dared "to take up her pen." Hansberry would be justifiably proud of the winning authors who have produced works of considerable promise and quality.

Five representative winning plays are presented in their entirety in this first volume; others are represented by scenes from the plays. Brief comments on the winning scripts collectively, and singularly are provided with occasional references to other writers and scripts submitted for the award. The primary goals of the introduction are: to provide a history of the award; to assist the reader in determining how well young playwrights have accepted the challenge left by Hansberry and ACTF; and to ascertain the kind and quality of the dramatic literature resulting from their efforts. The words of Hansberry (in italics) and the playwrights speak for themselves here as much as possible; editorial comments connect and supplement these words.

Plays rooted in the African American experience seldom are included in the popular collections that come off the press; when an African American play is selected it is nearly always one of the "proven and tested" drama, almost never a play by a new and unknown writer regardless of talent. This anthology devoted to new winning plays on the black experience should encourage teachers and students to further explore the development of black images, foster more study of racial/ethnic heritage, shed light on the truth and reality of black life and encourage reading and production of the plays. It should inspire others to create plays that deal with the commonalties of the human experience and yet that emerge from and reflect values, forms, and styles indigenous to black culture.

The volume is also designed to serve classroom teachers and theatre students searching for new plays, scenes, and audition pieces from the black experience. Suggested scenes from the full-length dramas are italicized for quick reference. Brief introductions are provided for the scenes selected from other representative plays.

Facts and Demography

Winners receive monetary awards of $2,500, (1st Place), $1,000., (2nd Place) with grants of $750, and $500, to the departments producing the first and second place plays. In addition to the individual awards, the first place winner receives a full fellowship to attend the Shenandoah Valley Playwrights Summer Retreat in Staunton , Virginia. In some years additional recognition comes from The Dramatist Guild, The William Morris Agency and The New Dramatist of New York City. In 1993, The Dramatic Publishing Company began publishing the first place script. For eight of its ten years of existence, McDonald's supported the Hansberry Award. In 1985 McDonald's withdrew its support, and the Kennedy Center's National Committee on Cultural Diversity in the Performing Arts, under the leadership of Dr. Archie Buffkins, agreed to support the contest while efforts to obtain another corporate sponsor were undertaken. The Pennsylvania State University supported the award from 1989-1994.

The Award is the only known annual national award for college student playwrights for full length plays of the black experience that has endured for twenty consecutive years. The first ACTF/Hansberry Award was made in the Spring of 1977 to Judi Ann Mason, a 22-year old student at Grambling College in Louisiana who had already exhibited her gift for writing by winning the ACTF Norman Lear Award for best Comedy in 1975 (Livin' Fat).

At the time of this writing there are 34 winning scripts (ties for first place in 1979 and for second place in 1980. Of the winning playwrights, 20 are female and 12 are male; there are 25 black winners and 6 non-black winners. They come from: the South — Louisiana, North Carolina, Mississippi; the East-Pennsylvania, Maryland; the Mid-West — Indiana, Iowa, Missouri, Minnesota, Illinois; the West — California, Washington, Oregon.

Several winners have also won other ACTF awards simultaneously:
The David Library Award for the best play on American freedom (Houston, Gordon Pinnix); The Norman Lear Award (Mason, C. Houston). The 1984 first place play, *Eleven Zulu* by Patrick Clark made ACTF history by winning the National Student Playwrighting Award, the David Library Award and the Hansberry Award — all selected by a different set of adjudicators.

A number of past Lorraine Hansberry award winners have gone on to achieve success in the professional world of theatre and television. For example, Farrell Foreman, 1978 winner, received a National Endowment for the Arts Playwriting Fellowship in 1982, had a new play selected by New Dramatist for a premier reading featuring James Earl Jones, and has been produced professionally in Chicago. Gordon's *Bulldog and the Bear* received a workshop production at New Dramatist and was revised through the collaborative efforts of Gordon and Irvin Bauer who directed it. Mason has worked with Alex Haley and the Negro Ensemble Company. Vincent Smith, 1979 second place winner, enjoyed success with his play/musical revue, *Williams and Walker*. Velina Houston, 1982 first place winner, had her drama American Dreams produced by NEC Theatre Four in New York in 1984. Christine Houston, whose play 227 won the 1978 award, worked as a writer with Embassy Television; the NBS Television hit 227 is based on Christine's scripts. Endesha Holland, 1981 winner, completed the Ph.D. at the University of Minnesota and is now a professor at the University of Southern California. Several of the winning playwrights have served as adjudicators for the Hansberry competition in subsequent years.

As can be assumed from this sketchy demography, the Hansberry contest has identified a group of promising playwrights who can be expected through "caring and hard work" to insure the continuation of dramas of the black experience for years to come.

Jim Leonard, (ACTF award winner for *They Dance Real Slow in Jackson*) in making a plea for more productions once wrote: "Plays are written to be produced, not to be talked about." With apologies to Jim, these plays must be talked (and written) about if they are to become known and produced.

Some Collective Observations

1. There are no musicals and revues among the winning dramas. (One has subsequently been re-written as a musical revue — *Williams and Walker.*)

2. All the playwrights attempt serious treatments of what it means to be black in America, with varying degrees of seriousness and levity, to be sure. It is clear that this body of literature is a continuation of the "consciousness raising" of the '60s without pronounced revolt and/or protest and of the search for self and self-determination of the '70s.

3. Following the model set by A *Raisin in the Sun*, most of the dramas are realistic with the black family at their core. Almost none select "integration" as their primary theme, (except, of course, the drama on Martin Luther King), reflecting changes in attitude in the past 20 years, perhaps. One effort to write about school integration (*Patterns by Lilly*, 1990) may be signaling another change (in both society and the thoughts of playwrights) in the last decade of this century. This change may have been predicted as early as 1981 in Mitchell's "anti-integration" arguments cleverly woven into *Big Bucks*.

   Actually, there is no singularity of theme nor of place. The families vary from rural, uneducated Southern families to black urban, male dominated ones. There are two historical treatments: Martin Luther King and Bert Williams of Williams and Walker team; two Southern folk dramas: one Southern middle-class family drama; one feminist drama; and one documentary type on the Vietnam War.

4. Two dramatists chose absurdist treatments, and several of the writers incorporate impressionistic, expressionistic, and surrealistic elements/ devices into their realism.

5. Most dramas should be classified as "serious dramas," but a few are tragedies; one declares itself a tragi-comedy and, if the success of the television series 227 can be used as a yardstick, one lent itself more to comedic treatment with a message than to anything else.

The themes are as varied as the writers who chose them and support the diversity and complexity which Lorraine had the wisdom and foresight to see:

1. Significance of education for young blacks.

2. Recognition of responsibilities which come with "freedom in the family" — male and female and their interactions.

3. Continuing search for black identity and black manhood.

4. Problems facing Blacks in society in the inner city — drugs, crimes, existence of street people.

5. Black dreams, hopes, and despairs — in and outside the family structure.

6. Persistence of black stereotypes and their resulting evils.

7. American injustices and their effects on Blacks; murder, incest.

8. Effects of war, racism, colorism, male chauvinism, family deaths.

9. Discovery of black roots, images, life styles.

10. Religion and old fashioned morality; Aging and problems of seniors.

11. Interracial and inter-cultural relationships; Father-son relationships.

Indeed, without collaboration, these young writers of the black experience seem to be writing about *all the things that men have written about since the beginning of writing and talking* as Lorraine asked them to do in order to complete her unfinished thoughts! Paraphrasing Nikki Giovanni's explanation of Hansberry as a visionary writer:

> "these young people seem to have "the courage to say what (has) to be said to those who (need) to hear it. Lorraine "made it possible for (them) to look deeper."

(Freedomways 19.4 (1979): 282)

Focus on Specific Plays Introduced in this Anthology

One of the previously published winning plays is included in this collection; it represents a winner of other awards, presents opportunities for non-black casting, treats subjects not treated by other playwrights, and, will probably, appeal to a wider audience. Richard Gordon's *The Bulldog and the Bear* is a sentimental treatment of two aging men (one black and one white) forced by poverty to become roommates in a bleak two-room apartment. *The Washington Post* called it "rather touching and charming. Perhaps the kind of thing William Saroyan might have written if he hadn't become old and bitter."

Two of the women playwrights take the simplest of Southern rural folks for their protagonists and fashion two distinctly different dramas from them. In *A Star Ain't Nothing But A Hole in Heaven*, Judi Ann Mason has a young Louisiana girl hang on to her dream for a good education in the face of persistent obstacles. Endesha Ida Mae Holland's own life in the troubled South of the pre-'60s revolution, forms the basis for much of her writing. Her realistic play on mid-wifery, *Second Doctor Lady*, transforms the stage into rural Mississippi through authentic Southern dialect and spellbinding folklore. The "color problem" appears differently in Gayle Williamson's *Mirror, Mirror* (1993) as a very light complexioned black woman decides to stop "passing" and search for her real identity in the black community.

Farrell Foreman, a product of inner city Philadelphia, writes in the style of Ed Bullins. In Hansberry's words, his dramas are filled with *"the many truths that seem to be rushing at [him] as the result of things felt and seen and lived through."* *The Ballad of Charlie Sweetlegs Vine* (1978) is set in the pool hall of a black dope pusher and depicts the existence of inner city dwellers and their efforts to survive; his protagonist reminds us: "Don't nobody give you power, sweety, you take it." Foreman, and other writers, reinforce Hansberry's declaration that:

> *"all art is ultimately social . . . The question is not whether one will make a social statement in one's work — but only what the statement will say, for if it says anything at all, it will be social."*

(From The Negro Writer and His Roots: Toward a New Romanticism,
The Black Scholar, 12. 2. March/April 1981)

Brenda Faye Collie's 1980 winning drama, *Silent Octaves*, Erwin Washington's 1977) *Oh, Oh Freedom!*, Marta Effinger's *Union Station* and Olivia Hill's

Mother Spence (1992) are serious dramas of black working-class families. Collie builds her play around the most ordinary human being, a black father, erstwhile saxophone player, who cannot live in the present; she gives him an ambitious, but nagging wife, and a son who needs to prove himself to his Dad. The drama captures many of the profound truths of the black experience and proves Hansberry's observation that "*every human being is in enormous conflict about something.*" *Oh, Oh Freedom*, which critics called a tragi-comedy, depicts in chilling realism a black father emotionally trapped when his home life and promised job security collapse at the same time. The ingenious and hilarious tactics of survival forced upon the family provide the "comic" part of the tragi-comedy. Effinger writes her version of what happens to "deferred dreams" as an extended family share a single dwelling and the problems of survival In the Northeast section of Washington, D.C. The resolution of the drama reinforces the strength of African Americans under pressure. Olivia Hill's *Mother Spense* expands on the "pregnancy-abortion "issue introduced in *A Raisin in the Sun*. Tensions between the deeply religious matriarchal mother/grandmother and her pregnant daughter, who opts for an abortion, lead the audience into the tangled web of reality of many contemporary women and reveal some of the most controversial issues of the '90s.

The dramas of one male and one female playwright vary in structure from the "well-made play" of most of the Hansberry winners. *Strands* by, Eric Wilson, (1992), takes on the broad panorama of a pageant that traces the development of black manhood from the ceremonial birth ritual in Africa to the disenfranchised angry young man of the 1990s. The answer to the protagonist's plea for salvation is in the "strands that bind him to his African heritage." The play brings "total theatre" replete with music, dance, and drama to the stage in the development of its theme: "Life's journey is circular . . . returning us to our fathers." One is reminded of earlier efforts to tell the "whole story" as in Amiri Baraka's *Slave Ship* and George Wolfe's *Colored Museum* or the evolution of black music and dance traced in the spectacular Federal Theatre production of *Prelude to Swing*.

Shay Youngblood (1993) in *Movie Music*, creates a whimsical piece of theatre with surrealistic elements — lights, sounds, visual images, circular action and repetitive dialogue, that leads us on a complex journey into the world of three generations of strange women — women who hear voices of their ancestors. (Published as *Talking Bones*, The Dramatic Publishing Company, 1994.)

In the brief years between the critical acclaim of A *Raisin In The Sun* and her last days, Hansberry found herself explaining and defending much of her writing. In her words:

> "Art has a purpose and its purpose is action; it contains "the energy which can change things....Genuine heroism must naturally emerge when you tell the truth about people. This to me is the height of artistic perception and is the most rewarding kind of thing that can happen in drama."
>
> – Lorraine Hansberry

ACTF winners accepted this challenge and have found the potential for genuine heroism in the simplest of Southern rural folk to the poorest of inner-city dwellers. Even those characters who succumb to dying dreams (in the style of *Ceremonies in Dark Old Men*) cannot kill the purpose of their actions — and the truths continue to be told in energy-packed dramas filled with suspense and action.

The plays capture the "*commitment and celebration of the human spirit*," best exemplified perhaps in playwright Mason's young girl who hangs on to her dream of a good education; an act that moves the drama toward the universality which Hansberry assured could be achieved through the specificity of the black experience.

> "There are no simple men."
> (Hansberry)

Most of the plays in this body of literature *"presume to examine something of the nature of commitment"* — in Lorraine's opinion.

> "one of the leading problems before (her) generation: what to identify with, what to become involved in; what to take a stand on; what, if you will, even to believe In at all."
>
> (response to Chinese woman's letter, 1962)

Clearly, this part of the Hansberry challenge remains a treacherous area for young black playwrights, if the ACTF writers are typical. A critical examination of many of the scripts that were not chosen as winners reveals that shallowness of ideas and of characters and failure to recognize what constitutes "the black experience" (and certainly the best dramatization of it) have been major causes for reflection of the scripts. In Lorraine's words they **failed** to:

- Avoid oversimplification
- Create multi-dimensional characters, complex highly dramatic situations; to involve audience first with characters then with ideas.
- Abhor excessive concern with ideas to the detriment of other dramatic elements.
- Write honestly about the black experience.
- Show the truth of black people's lives — be a witness and to make blackness a window on the potential of the human race. (If Negroes could survive America, there was hope for the human race, indeed.)

Pronounced violation of all or most of Hansberry's advice can be found among the non-winning literature. Too frequently her admonition: "*The things you think you have to talk about!*" (*To Be Young, Gifted and Black*, 190) went unheard! The philosophies, ideas and messages of the ACTF playwrights reveal that this process of explaining and defending continues; at times their words and those of Lorraine leap back and forth across the decades as if only days have passed — and yet one can detect differences also. In their own words:

"I believe that one of the most sound ideas in dramatic writing is that in order to create the universal, you must pay very great attention to the specific. Universality, I think, emerges from truthful identity of what is... A reflection of the black experience is not real unless it transcends to reach all humanity. My strength as a writer comes from the courage it takes to present not a reflection, but the truth as it has been revealed to me."

(Judi Mason)

The antagonist in *Star* tries to discourage the protagonist's efforts to go to college:

Lemuel: All that education is for the white folks. They know what to do with it. They ain't got skills in they hands like us. They got to use they brains to make money. Colored man use his hands. A white man is in a bad fix, if he ain't got no brains cause he don't know how to use his hands.

(I, 1-Star)

"... In a very real way I'm just a tape recorder, maybe a gifted witness to all that's black around me, ... For me the road of experience has always been my surest route to what it is I want to learn."

(Farrell Foreman).

His 1970 job as a janitor in the NEC Building let him watch people like Robert Hooks at work and he began a dream to see his own writing come to life on stage. Seven years later the same Robert Hooks, as ACTF adjudicator, selected Foreman's *The Ballad of Chancy Sweetlegs Vine* as the 1978 Hansberry winner. In 1979 an interesting phenomenon occurred: all 3 winners were non-black and the results were a take-off on *The Caucasian Chalk Circle* (*The American Chalk Circle*), a feminist drama with the 2 black characters in supportive roles, *Hard Up,* and an absurdist drama on the New Orleans Mardi Gras with a 62-year old white woman as protagonist and two black stereotypical absurdist characters, (*Throw Me Something, Mister God.*) When asked what he considered his strengths as a playwright, one of the playwrights from this year responded:

"I would hope that it is a strength to be brave enough to attempt to portray characters of a different ethnic origin. It's certainly tougher than sticking to your own backyard."

He added:

"Winning the Lorraine Hansberry Award. . . reinforced my belief that it isn't impossible to empathize with another human being whose skin color is different from your own."

The words of the winning playwrights continue:

"I don't think about a particular audience when I'm writing a script. I only concentrate on what I'm writing, the characters I'm writing about, what I'm trying to get across."

(Brenda Faye Collie, 1980).

"Each of my plays has a definite universal appeal, though they were clearly aimed at Blacks. . . I'm very conscious of the audience — market — for each piece. ... I found it very difficult, if not impossible, to get Freedom produced anywhere...even though it had won the award and even though I had seen how powerfully it worked on audiences... Conclusion: You got to write and produce to be sure you see your works on stage..."

(Erwin Washington, 1977)

"My two short plays that were Hansberry winners were my first plays and I was influenced by two professors at the University of Minnesota to write. My plays are directed primarily at Blacks but with universal characters and situations. My strength, writing about the region that I know — the South and the use of authentic speech which makes characters alive and real."

(Endesha Holland, 1981)

In 1981, as if conscious of the need to establish the "differences" of a new decade, the first place drama was a social protest play about a young college couple — black male and white female in search of identity and acceptance. Until that time, it was the only play that dealt directly with racism and brought white characters to the center of the action. Like Hansberry, the writer and his characters were very aware of political and social issues both inside the black community and those impinging on it from the outside. However, the protagonist, in resisting his roommates' efforts to make him join a protest movement, reveals one of the several attitudes that reflect the "new thinking":

Jack: This is the '80s. The only change most people are interested in nowadays is the kind that jingles in your pocket.

(I, 1- *Big Bucks and 3 Piece Suits ' Til Kingdom Come, Amen!*)

Mitchell's drama, unlike the black protest and social drama of the '60s argues, quite effectively, both sides of the issues he raises ("anti-integration," "defiance of Black separatism," and "self-determinism." Unlike the introspective dramas of the '70s, his drama must be classified as both "consciousness-raising and protest."

A few years earlier, a black critic in response to Washington's play *Oh, Oh Freedom*, in the L.A. Times (July 17, 1977) had lamented:

"...black theatre still is plodding along under its burden of trying to educate as well as elevate. No matter how delightfully done the product, black playwrights are still and most likely will be for decades to come, preoccupied with establishing us first as human beings..."

(Wanda Coleman)

The reader must now be left with "just these brief provocative words" from which varied arguments and conclusions can be drawn. One editorial comment — warning if you will, cannot be resisted. From my critical examination of the dramas (and their writers) that constitute this body of literature for black theatre, one tendency prevails. The better structured, more tightly written dramas come, as might be expected, from the large universities (read "traditionally white") with broad-based theatre departments where playwriting is taught as a specific concentration — Iowa, UCLA, Minnesota, Indiana. The plays more likely to reveal "real truths" of the black experience come from black colleges or where the playwrights sensibilities have been finely tuned by exposure to an abundance of black life experiences. What this body of literature needs most is a combination of the best instruction in playwriting with the most sensitivity for the black experience. If the Lorraine Hansberry Competition is to remain a source of vital black literature, a way must be found to bring these two essential elements together. In 1990 the winning script came from The University of Pittsburgh and in 1992 from The University of Missouri where the writers were guided by strong black theatre scholars. We may be moving toward this winning combination Let us hope so.

Obviously Lorraine's writing, philosophy, and spirit are pervasive and influential in the literature described here. We can all breathe a sigh of relief that her vision and wish in her prophetic words have not been in vain. We may be moving toward her final admonition to "perfect them!"

Winona Lee Fletcher
Professor Emeritus
Indiana University, 1996

The Plays

Bulldog And The Bear

by

Richard Gordon
and
Irvin S. Bauer

Bulldog And the Bear is the result of a collaboration between Richard Gordon and Irvin S. Bauer. The play *The Bulldog and The Bear* originally produced at California State University at Fullerton, won the 1983 American College Theater Festival's Michael Kanin and the McDonald's Lorraine Hansberry Playwriting awards. As a result of these awards the play was presented at the Kennedy Center in Washington D.C. In addition, the McDonald's Corp. in conjunction with the Lorraine Hansberry Playwriting Award, sponsored a workshop and public reading of the play in New York City, at New Dramatist. The non-performance workshop, conducted by Irvin S. Bauer, proved to be invaluable. The workshop and the subsequent reading proved very successful. However. at the end of the workshop, it was felt by the author that the play had not yet reached its full potential. Following the workshop it was agreed that the author Richard Gordon and the director, Irvin S. Bauer, would continue to work on the play. As the creative relationship grew, a slight revision grew into an extensive reworking of the play with major input by both parties. It truly blossomed into a beautiful collaborative effort.

List Of Characters

CHARLIE — 76 years old. Black and full of vitality.

GEORGE — 76 years old. White and in depression.

JIM — 47 years old. Son of George.

DORIS — 40 years old. Jim's wife.

ANGIE — 9 years old. Niece of Charlie.

ANGIE — Same niece at 36 years old.

ACT I

SCENE I

The lights come up on a small, cramped apartment that has had a very cursory renovation. It is as though a coat of paint was used long ago to hide the worn and tired space. It failed. The apartment lacks privacy. It is open-faced... that is there are no inner walls. The bedroom, up stage right, is really a small indentation just deep enough to accommodate two small beds and a small chest of drawers. There is a window just above the chest of drawers. Downstage right, extending across the stage, is the living room. It is furnished with an old sofa, a coffee table, an easy chair, all purchased from the Goodwill. The only place to really get away is the "escape hatch," the bathroom, just downstage right of the bedroom. It has a door one can actually close.

Down stage left is the kitchen furnished with a table, two chairs, a stove, sink and refrigerator. Stage left, between the living room and the bedroom, is the door to the apartment... and outside is the hallway. The hallway is not only a place where people come and go, but a place where, sometimes, magic happens.

CHARLIE, a 76-year-old Black gentleman, who looks, feels, and acts twenty years younger, is at the stove cooking. He wears ordinary clothing, and a special hat, old, worn and bent in a special Charlie way. He hums a tune, scats a little and does a wiggle and shake as he prepares his meal. He stops abruptly in the middle of his diddly, saddens and moves into the living room. He flops dejectedly onto the sofa, pulling his Charlie hat over his eyes.

CHARLIE
(*half prayer, half plea*) Find me, Baby. Find me.

> (*Lights dim on the apartment, and come up a "fantasy blue" in the "Hallway."* Seven-year-old ANGIE, crying softly, walks into the light. CHARLIE hears her.*)

Angie?

> (*He tilts the hat up, looks around... sees her. Smiling, he slowly gets up and shuffles his dance walk into her light... through the wall that isn't there.*)

Don't cry, Baby.

                              ANGIE

Uncle Charlie, why'd my daddy die?

                              CHARLIE

I don't know, Angie. I don't know.

                              ANGIE

I miss him, Uncle Charlie.

                              CHARLIE

So do we...

Angie, we don't always understand things like this. But baby...

> (He *assumes the attitude of a song-and-dance man... all gestures and smiles.*)

(*sings*) "Got a rainbow round my shoulder..."

> (*a funny little dance step*)

Ba da ba da...

> (*Finishes the refrain with a graceful gesture... hand out to her... head cocked to the side, or whatever wonderful bit of business the actor works out.*)

(*serious*) Baby, Uncle Charlie will be here. He'll be here long as you need him.

                              ANGIE

Ah, Uncle Charlie.

                              CHARLIE

I will ALWAYS be here...

> (*Lights begin to fade on* ANGIE, *as she backs away.* CHARLIE *watches her, then turns and takes a few steps into the living room. He looks back to where Angie was. The lights come up full on the apartment catching Charlie lost in time and space. He clinches his fist in anger.*)

Damn!

> (*Quiet. Shakes his head. Suddenly he remembers the pot cooking on the stove. He rushes to the stove and is relieved that his dinner is not burned. He tastes it.*)

They gotta have salt.

(CHARLIE *abruptly leaves the apartment. After a moment,* GEORGE, *a 76-year-old white gentleman, who looks and acts at least five years older drags down the hall. He is dressed in well-worn clothing, and displays a disposition to match... well worn. Shown in his attitude, even before he utters one word, is the fact that he is angry and disgruntled. He carries one suitcase, and a common paper bag that he handles as though it was something special. He stops, and knocks on the door. No answer. He notices the door is ajar. He pushes, sticks his head in. He checks the apartment number with the paper he's carrying and enters cautiously. He backs out once again and knocks on the opened door. Finally, with a "what the hell" shrug, he enters, but remains very tentative. He starts to leave but cannot follow through. His confusion is obvious.*

He slowly inspects the apartment, visibly disapproving of everything. He finds dust on the coffee table, a sock in the middle of the floor. He smells something cooking on the stove. He follows his nose and lifts the lid. He picks up a fork and starts to taste but quickly places the lid back. CHARLIE *enters, unnoticed by* GEORGE, *who walks toward the kitchen table.* GEORGE *stops and implores the heavens.*)

GEORGE

Judy, what have I done?

(CHARLIE *quietly goes back outside.* GEORGE *flips through a couple pages of a scrapbook on the table.* CHARLIE *makes a noisy entrance. He is carrying a box of salt.*)

CHARLIE

Hello.

(*George is startled.*)

You must be George. I'm Charlie.

(GEORGE *just stares in disbelief.*)

They told me you would be here today.

(CHARLIE *waits for George to say something.* GEORGE *doesn't.* CHARLIE *shows the box of salt.*)

CHARLIE

Salt. The doctor take you off salt?

(CHARLIE *moves to stove.*)

Took me off... But collards ain't greens without salt.

(GEORGE *wanders aimlessly past Charlie, into the bedroom.*)

I've been here two weeks now, and I wasn't looking forward to paying the whole rent myself.

(GEORGE, *in a daze, continues to look around at nothing in particular.*)

Kinda like the army, huh? I mean moving into a strange place... Not knowing anyone. You ever in the service?

(GEORGE *ignores question. He places the paper bag on the chest of drawers.*)

(*shrugs*)... I'm glad you're here.

(CHARLIE *returns to the stove and serves himself some greens.* GEORGE *closes the bedroom window.*)

You hungry? Ever had collards ?

(*He walks to George, with plate in hand. He places the plate just under George's nose.* GEORGE *looks, turns away.*)

They're good, man... Really good. I only wish I had some bacon in 'em. (*to himself*) Haven't had bacon since Porky was a piglet.

(CHARLIE *sits on sofa and begins to eat.* GEORGE *removes a crumpled bag from his coat pocket. He takes out crackers and cheese... his answer to collards.*)

You're welcome to join me.

(CHARLIE *gazing at the bagged bottle on the chest of drawers.*)

Say...? Is that... could that be... a gorgeous... genuine... bottle of Sherry?

(GEORGE *chomps on a cracker as he stares at Charlie.*)

Look. Long as we have to live together...

(CHARLIE *stops and decides to attack the "problem" head on.*)

You don't seem to like the arrangement.

(GEORGE *continues to ignore him.*)

(*Trying to be light.*) What is it? You don't like my "kind" or something? (*chuckles*)

(GEORGE *takes a deep, obvious breath... as if to say: "you said it, not me". He then sits on the edge of the bed, head down shoulders slumped, a picture of dejection. CHARLIE regards him a moment. He gets up and walks to the kitchen table, impatiently closes the scrapbook and places it under his arm. He fills the doorway carrying the scrapbook, walks toward GEORGE.)*

You come here to die?

Cause if you did, you can just leave. I can stand a little bitchin', a little selfishness, a little stupidity... Can even stand a little bigotry! But I won't stand for... wallowing self-pity.

(He OPENS *the bedroom window, leaves scrapbook on chest of drawers, and goes back to the kitchen table and his collards.*)

I just won't stand for it.

(GEORGE *reacts most to the opening of the window.*)

GEORGE

(*barks*) Everything dies!

CHARLIE (*startled*)

Not here. Not now!

(Anger *begins to bring GEORGE to life. He sits up erect, ready to do battle.*)

We don't have to beg it. It'll come in its own sweet time.

GEORGE

(Up in *the doorway pointing at Charlie.*)

Wait...

CHARLIE

Death's like... grammar.

(There *is a moment of unexplained communication, as they make eye contact.*)

Death ain't nothing but a period... Or an exclamation point. It all depends on how we attack life. (*laughs*)

GEORGE

Look...

CHARLIE (*still laughing*)

I guess in most lives though, death is a question mark. So you see, my friend... there ain't no place for...

GEORGE

(*erupts*) Now wait just a damn minute!

(*He punctuates his anger by throwing his bag of crackers and cheese into the trash.*)

Who put you in charge? I pay my way, just like you. I do what I want here. If... If I want to hang my head and die, I die. If I want to bellow, I bellow. If... if I want to be stingy with my wine, I'll be stingy... And if I don't wanna eat any goddamn soul food, I won't... And for your information... I HATE bacon!

(*GEORGE looking directly at Charlie as he moves.*)

And another thing... I want the window closed...

(*He goes and slams the window shut. He stands looking out the window.*)

CHARLIE (*startled, but pleased*)

Well! I can stand a little anger... a little fire.

(*He returns to his meal. He looks toward bedroom and decides to give it one more try.*)

Sure you won't have some? Beats the hell outta crackers.

(*GEORGE ignores the invitation.*)

Aw, come on, risk it.

(*GEORGE stands frozen. CHARLIE'S patience begins to wane as his irritation grows. He stops talking, places his fork down and walks into the bedroom. GEORGE becomes somewhat defensive as CHARLIE invades his space. CHARLIE begins to take off his pants. GEORGE retreats to the living room. CHARLIE just looks at the fleeing GEORGE in disgust. CHARLIE continues to undress with a flare.*)

Look Buddy! I didn't choose you either.

(*CHARLIE puts on a sweat pants, then removes his shirt. GEORGE tries to take no notice of Charlie, but he is forced to contemplate the fact that another person will be sharing his "space." He picks up the newspaper. CHARLIE begins to fool around, imitating the social worker that interviewed him. He is really speaking to George.*)

"Mr. Hampton, do you have any preference as to color, religion, sexual preference?" (*Answering.*) Mmm, I get to choose...that's nice... (*clowns*) Well, I'd like her about forty years old. mature. and with a large measure of (indicating breasts with his hands) class.

(*To George.*)

Kept trying to interrupt me... said he meant a MALE roommate...but I didn't hear him...

(*Addressing the interviewer.*)

Just don't make her a nag...can't stand a nag... an don't make her fat... and it'd be nice if she can cook... 'specially biscuits and country gravy... an... (*a dig*) collard greens... with bacon!

(*He glares at George.*)

Now the question is... are you ANY of those things?

(GEORGE *does not respond.*)

I didn't think so. So where'd you come from? No manners... No money... No sense...

(GEORGE *bolts up, anger swelling.*)

GEORGE
Who told you that!

(CHARLIE *stands in the doorway dumbfounded.*)

I said... who told you that?

CHARLIE
What'd I say?

GEORGE
Who said I didn't have any money?

CHARLIE
The office. They told me you...

GEORGE
They had no right!

CHARLIE

They only said...

GEORGE

That's MY business... They had no right to tell you that.

CHARLIE

They only said you would be getting some kinda check within a week or so... and if it would be all right if you moved in now. Sure. They didn't tell me the important part... that you was crazy!

> (CHARLIE *goes back to the bedroom*, OPENS *the window, puts on his hat and wraps a towel around his neck.* GEORGE *picks up his suitcase.*)

That's right... go on...leave.

> (GEORGE *glares at Charlie, as he grabs the paper bag off the chest of drawers.* CHARLIE, *immediately sorry, softens.*)

Look. we both know neither one of us would be here if we didn't have to be...

GEORGE

(*growling*) I don't have to be here!

CHARLIE

They just help put "old people" together, remember.

GEORGE

Maybe you have to be here, but...

CHARLIE

Look... all I'm saying... is... well... you can stay.

GEORGE

You LET me stay. What am I supposed to do, clap my hands like a trained seal? You let me stay...

CHARLIE

Come on, let's face it... sometime people need each other... ain't so bad.

GEORGE

I don't need you! I don't need this place. I got family!

CHARLIE

(*fed up*) Good for you! Maybe when I get back, you'll be... with "family"!

JIM

We do want you here, but...

GEORGE

(*angrily*) You say I can stay, now!

(He *mockingly, like a seal, claps his hands in Jim's face.*)

(*barks*) Auk! Auk!

No thanks. I choose to be gone from here.

JIM

You're an old man, Papa. And you're getting older fast. You used to be a real bear... storming loudly, hugging the world.   But for the past three years you've been in hibernation.   Winter is over, Papa. Wake up!

GEORGE

I'll make it.

JIM

Stubborn old fool! You've got nothing.

GEORGE

I'll get social security... What else does an "old fool" need, huh?

JIM

Don't expect any sympathy when you come crawling back!

GEORGE

I'll die first!

("I'll die first" *reverberates as lights fade on* JIM *and-*DORIS. GEORGE *moves back into the room as lights come up on the apartment.*)

I can take care of myself !

(He *stands in the agony of his dilemma. Finally, his shoulders heave forward, his head bows a bit.*)

Ah... Judy.

(He *surrenders.*)

Crazy, huh? Maybe so.

(He walks, with determination into the bedroom. He looks at the clutter for a moment, then takes several items of Charlie's off one bed and throws them onto the other. He removes items from the top drawer and stuffs them into the second drawer. He places the bottle on top of the chest of drawers. He sits. "Now what ?" He picks up Charlie's scrapbook and looks through it. His interest peaks... He looks close. He mumbles as he stares at a picture. He looks at a few more pages and flips back a couple of times to take a second look at a particular picture. The book holds a fascination for him. He forces himself to close the book, and with something akin to jealousy, tosses the book onto the other bed.)

Smart ass.

(CHARLIE enters... sees George but says nothing. He walks into the bedroom, starts to place his towel on the bed and notices the changes. Acknowledging the decision, he places the towel on his own bed.)

GEORGE
Go on... say it.

CHARLIE
Too tired...

(lets out a breath, and all the air goes out of him.)

You're here... Don't wanna be... but you are. That's okay.

Now, maybe I can finish my meal in peace.

(CHARLIE goes to the kitchen table. GEORGE once again picks up the scrapbook and after flipping through a few pages, he takes the book with him as he walks into the kitchen. He sits across from Charlie.)

GEORGE
In your book here?

CHARLIE
What?

GEORGE
You do all these things?

CHARLIE
Why else would they be there?

GEORGE

(*Almost an accusation.*) Joe Louis? Jesse Owens?

CHARLIE

(*mellowing*) Golden times.

GEORGE

(*not convinced*) Hmph... You don't look like a runner.

CHARLIE

(*referring to his outfit*) I don't?

> (CHARLIE, *on very safe ground, smiles and goes into his routine. He shakes his arms and legs, as if warming up. He acts it out as he speaks.*)

Listen... After Jesse won all those medals... And the cheering had died down... they had him doing all kinds of things... Once... even had him racing a horse...

Well, I was working through this town... I couldn't find a gig, so I hired on as a janitor for awhile. They had this promotion going and asked for runners. I wasn't 'bout to miss an opportunity to run against the "Hero of the Free World".

Now, in these races. they would give a twenty-five yard head start... but I wanted to make this a real race. I told 'em I was a runner and only needed ten yards. Ten!

Everyday for two whole weeks I trained...

> (He limbers up; *stretching, bending and sitting up. He gets into the classic starting position. Holds.*)

Bang!

> (He *darts out a few feet, then returns to the starting blocks.*)

A thousand times outta the blocks...

> (*again into the position*)

Bang!

> (*out again*)

Then a thousand more.

Finally that great day came...

> (He *creates the band and the crowd excitedly as he tells the story with growing joy.*)

The band was playing! The crowd was cheering! The sun was shining bright... And I was ready... to fly!

> (CHARLIE *again gets into the starting position... but this time for the real thing. Tense... nervous... expectant.*)

Into the blocks like I had a thousand times before... And the great Jesse Owens only ten yards behind... I felt 'em breathing down my back... His will to win was that strong! But I had my own need. My mouth was dry... my body tingled... I was ready.

BANG!

I was off! Running like the wind itself... I mean FLY. ..ING!

> (He *slowly crouches, shakes his head, puts his hands on his hips, and looks at George out of the corner of his eye.*)

(*slowly aiming it*) Jesse swooshed past me like I was a dead breeze... standing still...Swoosh! (*laughs*)

But I did... I did run against the great Jesse Owens.

> (GEORGE *just looks at him.*)

GEORGE
(*skeptical*) And Joe Louis?

> (CHARLIE *still in the memory.*)

CHARLIE
SW...OOSSHH! (*tilts his hat*) Yes sir I was humbled. (*laughs*) They lifted him high. I was right there liftin' him up too.

GEORGE
(*insisting*) And what about Joe Louis?

CHARLIE
What is this? All of a sudden you give me the third degree.

GEORGE
Just asking...

CHARLIE
Hey, I don't have to prove nothing to you... It don't matter what you believe!

GEORGE

(*taken aback... almost an apology*) Joe Louis... I saw him once. He was... all style. Took care of business... no messing around... He was beautiful.

(*quietly, cautiously*) You really fought him?

(CHARLIE, *allowing himself to come back to the telling, starts slowly.*)

CHARLIE

Style...? You know it...

He was at the downtown gym...

(*picturing it*)

...back around '43... They needed sparring partners, and me, at thirty-four, mind you... third on the list. They didn't know how old I was... but my legs knew... my arms knew. And when that first guy was knocked through the ropes. The next guy wouldn't get in the ring. Just ran away! Can you imagine that...! Giving up a chance to box with Joe Louis!

Well, as this chicken shit fled, all eyes turned to me.   (*whispers*) All I wanted to do was split, too. But... in my gut... in my gut I had this funny feeling that something special was 'bout to happen. Somehow... I climbed into that ring. The bell rang... the fight was on.

Before I could blink three jabs in my face. Ho ho... what a jab! Tried to cover up... couldn't. Tried to run backwards... didn't help. Bam. Bam, Bam! Three more on my nose. I covered up, grabbed him. The crowd didn't like that much. The crowd, Hell... I was running for my life... but I ran out of ring... then wham! Up side my head. I was spinning, reeling... stars whizzin' 'round...   pain in my side... my gut... my legs 'bout to buckle... and... and...(*slowly*) Joe grinned... backed off... had no reason to put me away yet.   The crowd loved it. "Kill him!" they shouted. Crowd... crowd was black... he Black, and so was I... didn't make no difference... The Brothers and the Sisters shouted: "Put the nigger away" "Kill 'em!" "Kill 'em!"

That was me they was yelling about... Me... whose blood they wanted. (*pausing for effect*) ...And then... it happened.

GEORGE

He knocked you out?

CHARLIE

BONG! ...Saved by the bell.

GEORGE

You lasted a whole round with Joe Louis?

CHARLIE

Sponged water down my head... Hands rubbing my hurt middle... wiping the blood from my nose... And, you know, through it all I was smiling. They musta thought I was nuts... But there I was... And there he was... across the ring ... the Brown Bomber himself!... And he was waiting for the same bell I was! I hurt... but somehow I felt like I was givin 'em something... felt special...Proud.... (*pausing for effect*) ...And then... that's when it happened.

Bong... I was out there again... Wasn't as scared... even a little cocky. (*chuckles*) I even threw a left... hit him on the shoulder. He seemed amused... We played a little... just kinda dancin' around... and then...(*baiting George*) it happened!

GEORGE

Now, he knocked you out.

CHARLIE

I ducked one of his play punches and caught him with a wild right hook to the mouth.

He went down! He sat on his seat! Oh, lucky, lucky, punch.

(*He's beaming, then the smile turns to fear.*)

He jumped up... his eyes a-blazin'. I backed up like saying I'm sorry. But he was a man possessed... He stalked me like I was Max Schmeling, himself. I ran... but like he said, "You can run but you can't hide"

He caught me with one of those six-inch jobs... And... Boom! (*grins... sings*) "And the lights went out all over the world."

(*pause, the pixie in him...*) But I laid him down, man!

GEORGE

(*impressed*) Oh wow...

(CHARLIE *shadow-boxes a moment as* GEORGE *excitedly.*)

What happened?

(CHARLIE *changes the subject.*)

CHARLIE
So... What kinda animal are you?

GEORGE
(*puzzled*) What?

CHARLIE
You know? That guy down at the office? (*imitating again*)

"Pick an animal most like you?"

GEORGE
Oh.   Yeah, he did.

> (He *looks at Charlie through new eyes.*)

You really knock 'em down?

> (CHARLIE *walks around George. looking him over.*)

CHARLIE
Let me guess. Now, I could be nice and guess all the animals with good public images... Like Fox... the clever fox? Or...? The king of the jungle...The mighty lion?

> (He *looks at George's receding hairline.*)

How 'bout... "bald" eagle...?

> (GEORGE *glares at Charlie.* CHARLIE *quickly explains.*)

The eagle who soars atop every American flag.

> (GEORGE *still glares.*)

Well, now... I could get ugly... eh... toad? Opossum? Skunk?   I could even-

GEORGE
Bear! I told him bear.

> (They *regard each other a moment.*)

CHARLIE
A bear? They shoot bears, man.

> (GEORGE *looks questioningly at Charlie.*)

Last week... Read it in the paper... Shot 'em dead.

GEORGE

What happened?

CHARLIE

Ate nothing but crackers and cheese for three days... went crazy.

> (CHARLIE *laughs.* GEORGE *is not amused.*)

(*seriously*) Ran from some zoo. He wandered down where he didn't belong. They say they tried to capture him alive, but they shot him dead.

> (CHARLIE *lets go of the moment. He bightens, starts to offer his hand but decides to give George a little space, waves instead.*)

Well, hello Bear, I'm Bulldog.

> (GEORGE *almost acknowledges the wave with a very slight raise of the hand.*)

GEORGE

Bulldog, huh...

> (CHARLIE *moves to the refrigerator.   Then nonchalantly…*)

CHARLIE

Who's Judy?

GEORGE

Who?

CHARLI E

Judy. Heard you talking to her.

GEORGE

You got big ears.

CHARLIE

Your wife?

> (GEORGE *glares at Charlie.*)

How long she been gone?

> (GEORGE *is surprised at Charlie's insight. There is an awkward moment of silence.*)

GEORGE

Three years.

CHARLIE

How long together?

GEORGE

Forty-nine.

CHARLIE

That's nice.

I know just how you feel. I had this dog once. Jenny.

(GEORGE *is angry until he sees the sincerity on Charlie's face.*)

I loved Jenny. Ten years. Then "poof"... gone. I know just how you feel.

GEORGE

A bulldog?

CHARLIE

(*reflecting*) Had Jenny with me one time when I was in Chicago. They said she would have to go. We both left... Hated back doors anyway.

GEORGE

(*loudly*) Was Jenny a bulldog?

CHARLIE

Eh. No. No, Jenny was a German Shepherd. But she WAS a BULL DOG, know what I mean? Took me a long time to get over it. I used to talk to her too. Still do sometime... Jenny...

(CHARLIE *slips into the fond memory.*)

GEORGE

What about your family?

(CHARLIE *ignores*)

CHARLIE

We used to run up...

GEORGE

What was your wife like ?

CHARLIE

Me and Jenny... We used to run up and down the beach... (laughs) one time...

(GEORGE *flips through scrapbook.*)

GEORGE

You got a picture of her here?

CHARLIE

(*exploding*) I thought we were talking about Jenny... My dog! Jenny!

(GEORGE *barely reacts. He continues looking through the book. CHARLIE goes to the window.*)

Sorry...

GEORGE

(*engrossed in book*) High school diploma, 1964?

CHARLIE (*trying to make up*)

You see...

GEORGE

64? You were over sixty years old.

CHARLIE (*flippant*)

So were you, my friend.

(CHARLIE OPENS *the window, then moves toward kitchen.*)

GEORGE

1969... graduated from Lemon Grove Community College.

What is this? Is that you? (*laughs*) You a singer? A song and dance man? (*impressed*) Boy... ran, boxed... song and...

(CHARLIE *somewhat uncomfortable, goes to the cupboard and takes down* TWO *plates.*)

(*still in book*) Blue? They called you, "Blue"?

CHARLIE

Not anymore.

GEORGE

"September 19, 1933. Charles 'Blue' Hampton sang and danced his way into the hearts of the delighted patrons of the Chicago Palace Club..."

CHARLIE

I'm not called that anymore.

GEORGE

(*enjoying*) Sounds like you were pretty good... Blue.

CHARLIE

I'm not called Blue anymore.

GEORGE

How 'bout a demonstration... Blue.

CHARLIE

(*angrily*) Can't you understand English... I don't do that anymore!

(CHARLIE *catches himself.*)

What about you? What's your claim to fame?

GEORGE

(*shrugs off question*) Eh... (*back to needling*) What kind of songs did you sing?

CHARLIE

What'd you mean, "eh"? What trips you been on?

GEORGE

Nowhere near as exciting as the Palace Club in Chicago. What was it like?

(CHARLIE *begins to serve greens onto the two plates.*)

Bet you had all the girls chasing you and...

CHARLIE

Where's YOUR scrapbook?

GEORGE

Don't have one.

CHARLIE

Yeah, you do. Everyone's got one...

(CHARLIE *brings the two plates to the table.*)

Maybe just in your head, but you got one...

(He *places one plate in front of George, then sits with his own plate.* GEORGE *looks at the plate then pushes it away.* CHARLIE *stares at George for a moment.*)

Old man? What you living for?

(GEORGE *looks at the plate and searches for a connection.*)

If you ain't living for tomorrow, it ain't for nothing.

GEORGE

Tomorrow ain't promised...

CHARLIE

Maybe not... But I live today knowing I'm gonna swing, jump, shout tomorrow... and if that don't work out...there's the next day.

GEORGE

Why you so fired up to have me eat these... greens?

Greens ain't got nothing to do with it! Eat 'em. Don't eat 'em…. Who cares!

GEORGE

Something new for your scrapbook...? Man dies... from "Soul-Food poisoning"?

(GEORGE *laughs and is a little shocked at the sound of his laughter.*)

You got Joe Louis and Jesse there... you don't need me.

CHARLIE

Bear! Humph... Ostrich.

(CHARLIE *turns away, shutting George out.* GEORGE *watches a moment. He starts to say something... can't get it out. He slowly gets up and goes to the bedroom. He retrieves the bag from trash. He walks to the table and offers Charlie some cheese.* CHARLIE, *surprised, takes a piece of cheese and a cracker. He eats.*)

CHARLIE

(*affected* French *accent*) Camembert?

GEORGE

(*affected* English *accent*) Cheddar.

>(*They almost laugh together. GEORGE reaches for the plate of greens.*)

Better 'n crackers , huh?

CHARLIE

Better 'n this cheese.

>(*GEORGE tastes a bit. CHARLIE eagerly awaits a reaction.*)

GEORGE

(*grudgingly*) Hot... food oughta be hot.

CHARLIE

(*delighted*) Wait'll you try 'em with bacon!

GEORGE

(*long suffering sigh*) I really DO hate bacon.

>(*They eat. The scene ends not on a bond of friendship, but on the first positive break. Slow fade to blackout.*)

ACT I

SCENE II

Tuesday, three days since last scene. GEORGE is asleep on the bed. He tosses uncomfortably, until he finally awakens, and gets up angrily. He examines his bed, and finds Charlie's "Afro" comb. Charlie is not in bed.

GEORGE

I found your damn comb!

        (He turns towards Charlie's bed.)

Where the hell are you...?

        (remembers)

Oh yeah... jogging. *(looks at clock)* Six o'clock in the morning. How perverted.

    (He looks at the comb, and with much curiosity, runs it through his hair. It does nothing. He tosses the comb onto Charlie's bed. He picks up a book near Charlie's bed... chuckle.)

Hamlet.

    (weighs the book in one hand and imaginary collard greens in the other.)

Shakespeare or collards...? What a combination... Which are you, Charlie...?

    (He tosses the book on the bed. Notices the OPEN window. He closes it with an exaggerated gesture of annoyance.)

Goddamn Charlie.

    (mutters to himself as he gets back into bed. He wraps the covers tightly around him with an exaggerated concern for warmth, and immediately falls asleep in the middle of his mutter.)

(Quiet)

(Charlie drags into the hallway from his morning jog. He is dressed in an old but flashy jogging suit. His "Charlie hat" is pushed back on his head. He is dripping wet with perspiration and breathes heavily. Wheezes. He finally... slowly musters enough strength to enter the apartment. He enters and leans against the door.)

CHARLIE

(a couple of deep breaths) You're in a rut George.

(glances in the direction of the bedroom)

A bear... huh!   "Hibernating"! You gotta strike out and meet the morning sun... *(talking self into it)* You gotta do something new everyday.

(not moving too fast to the kitchen)

You sleep, George... *(feeling better)* and the world will pass you by.

(gets a glass of water from the refrigerator and carries it into the bedroom)

Do you care, George?

(He shakes George, who does not respond.)

You'll probably live forever, you bum! Don't go for nothing, and probably live forever.

GEORGE

What are you rambling about?

CHARLIE *(his old self)*

(excitedly) George? What is it you've always wanted to do, but never did? Never did... for whatever dumb reason. What!

GEORGE

Sleep!

(CHARLIE ignores George's remark. He gets up and absent-mindedly walks back into the kitchen. GEORGE tries to go back to sleep.)

CHARLIE

How many times I've said: "I'm gonna. I'm gonna this... I'm gonna that..."

(He gets another glass of water.)

I should have done this, or that. How many times?

GEORGE
(*a complaint*) I found your comb!

CHARLIE
Hey! I've been looking all over for that...

GEORGE
In the bed!

CHARLIE
In your bed?

GEORGE
The bed, un-huh.

CHARLIE
(*matter-of-factly*) When you use my comb, George... I wish you'd put it back where you found it.

GEORGE
(*gets up*) I use your comb?

> (CHARLIE *pulls a long hair, one of George's, from the comb. He holds it between his fingers. GEORGE is embarrassed. CHARLIE, restless, walks to the kitchen, sits at the table.*)

CHARLIE
(*close to a primal scream*) Ugggah!

> (*he pounds the table*)

GEORGE
(*matter of factly*) Am I supposed to ask, what's wrong?

> (CHARLIE, *frustration spilling over, gets up, walks around flailing his arms.*)

CHARLIE
George, I gotta do something with my life.

> (CHARLIE *moves toward bedroom.*)

Where's your wine? It's time to pop that cork.

> (CHARLIE *picks up the bottle, which stands unbagged. GEORGE grabs for the bottle.*)

GEORGE

No way.

(*They struggle a moment over the bottle. GEORGE finally wrenches it away.*)

Too early for wine.

(CHARLIE, *angry, stares at George.*)

CHARLIE

I'm not your enemy!

(CHARLIE *storms into the bathroom, leaving George alone, holding the bottle. GEORGE suddenly feels alone and uncomfortable. He looks around, lost. He starts to say something to Charlie but cannot. He looks at the bottle of wine for a long moment, then slowly, in silence, he walks to the chest of drawers and carefully places the bottle back.*

GEORGE *moves aimlessly, to the kitchen as* CHARLIE *comes out of bathroom, goes into the living room and slumps into the easy chair. He is still anxious. He gets up muttering to himself. GEORGE silently watches.*)

The sand is running out of this old glass. (*reprimanding himself*)

No! No more of that.

(*Challenging George*)

Come on Bear! What is it YOU'VE always wanted to do?

GEORGE

(*shrugs*) Nothing...

CHARLIE

Come on, there must be something. Some hidden away deep down wish... a dream? A promise? Come on. Come on.

(GEORGE *goes to the cupboard looking for something to eat.*)

GEORGE

(shyly) Used to write a little.

CHARLIE

Good. What'd you write?

GEORGE

Not much... Little Poetry... Never did anything with them...

(He discovers there is no milk.)

No milk.

CHARLIE

There's a little powdered milk up in the cabinet.

GEORGE

No food, no money, no milk. (holding up box) I hate this stuff.

CHARLIE

You'll get used to it.

George? Why don't you do something with them now?

GEORGE

With what?

(GEORGE is now mixing milk... very poorly.)

CHARLIE

Your... poetry.

GEORGE

Gone... Like so many things in my life... lost..

CHARLIE

They're in your head, man. Your head.

GEORGE

(chuckles) If they're anywhere... they'd be in my shoe.

CHARLIE

Shoe...?

GEORGE

My business was quite personal. Personal enough for poems.

CHARLIE

(taking a new look at George)

You had a business? A real business!

GEORGE

(*nods*) Uh-huh.

CHARLIE

What'd you do?

(CHARLIE *looks around the room.*)

How'd you amass such a fortune ... Such a graceful retirement?

(GEORGE *gives up on breakfast, and moves toward bedroom.*)

GEORGE

(*proudly*) Shoes. Custom made.

CHARLIE

Well... a gen-u-wine cobbler...

GEORGE

(*musing... almost an embarrassed confession*)

Sometimes I'd write a poem for a pair of shoes I liked... Nothing big. light verse ..
but once in awhile... when it worked... When the magic was right. the words sang...

(*remembering*)

That's how... I got the wine. I gave a poem to this young couple because they... they
reminded me of what we had... Judy and me. They came back the next day and gave
me the wine. They said it was special like the poem.

CHARLIE

What happened? To the business?

GEORGE

Hand made shoes went out of fashion... Ya know... factories, imported shoes, (*making
a face*) plastic shoes.

CHARLIE

What'd you do?

GEORGE

Hung on for awhile... but the handwriting was on the wall... And I wasn't 'bout to
change... So I finally sold to some young buck. I guess by now he has a monster
chain of stores... "Buckaroo Shoes". Anyway, we had enough money to retire in
comfort. Travel... Do all the things we had talked about.

(GEORGE *becomes suddenly sad.*)

We never did.

CHARLIE

Why not?

GEORGE

Things happen. We just didn't.

CHARLIE

You "just didn't"!

(GEORGE *does not respond.*)

All those dreams, and the money to do them, and you "just didn't"?

(GEORGE *becomes more somber.*)

Only thing I see from those dreams is that wine and...

(CHARLIE *realizes this is painful for George.*)

You're right, sometime I talk too damn much.

GEORGE

(*a gesture of surrender*) Judy took sick. (*painful*) It took a long... time. Wiped out nearly everything.

(*the burden of it seems to cave his shoulders in*)

Lived on my own for awhile... flapped around that house like a fish...

(*George gets up, moves around the room as if moving would ease the pain.*)

Watched soap operas... "Family Fuss..."

(*imitates* M.C.)

"You have won a fabulous combination mini-max, washer-dryer, cement mixer.

(*squeezes his eyes shut... shakes his head, screeches*)

Yeah... (*makes a pfffth noise*) Liked the cartoons best... When I couldn't stand to watch that damn thing anymore... I'd walk...walk...walk... must have walked this city a hundred times.

(*he goes and sits, lost within himself*)

Can't live with myself... Can't live with anyone else... Grouchy... used up...(*gestures "what's the point*)... eh...

(CHARLIE *just nods in recognition.*)

(*George nods.*) Yeah...

(CHARLIE *continues to stare at George.*)

(*half joking*) Maybe... maybe I should have learned to run every day like you... I could have jogged my ass outta that... that...

(*an awkward quiet. GEORGE breaks it.*)

So... you got a sad story too?

CHARLIE

Hasn't everybody? When's your birthday?

GEORGE

What?

CHARLIE

(*almost singing*) When's your birthday?

GEORGE

Uh... July nineteenth.

CHARLIE

No, that's no good.

GEORGE

Wha...?

CHARLIE

(*Acts it out. Begins a soft shoe routine.*)

Tomorrow! Tomorrow's your birthday. I say? How old you wanna be?

(*He twirls... hand out as if to say, "You're on." George is dumbfounded.*)

Come on, George. How old you wanna be tomorrow?

GEORGE

Want to be? I'll be seventy-seven in...

CHARLIE

No!

(CHARLIE *tries to contain his excitement.*)

How old would you... or rather, how young would you like to be? If you could pick any age, what would it be?

GEORGE

Forty-three. I was solid at forty-three.

CHARLIE

Aw, come on... What about twenty-five, or thirty? You don't have to be conservative here.

GEORGE

Forty-three.

CHARLIE

(*doing his number... sings it, savors it*)

Forty three...   Forty...   Three...   For...ty.. threee... (*high stepping. Struts it.*) Forty three.

Okay. Tomorrow, Tuesday, March 13, is your birthday and you will be...(*doing a dance step*) forty-three.

GEORGE

Well, the the only gift I want is from the post office... and I have to be at least sixty to get that.

CHARLIE

Don't worry 'bout that. Your money'll be here when it gets here. In the meantime... eh...

(CHARLIE *suffers a sharp pain that moves on quickly.*)

GEORGE

What's wrong?

CHARLIE

Just another pain telling me to get a move on... to get it done.

GEORGE

Serious?

CHARLIE

You know how when we were young and we'd have a sudden pain here, or here, how we'd rush out to the doctor? But now when the pains come, we just let 'em pass and we move on to the next task.

What's the difference between now and then?

GEORGE

Beats me.

CHARLIE

The difference is, they just aren't a surprise anymore. And...

> (CHARLIE *gets up from the sofa and walks into the bedroom.*)

So... You got family, you say?

GEORGE

How long... this thing been bothering...

CHARLIE

(*insisting*) What kind of family?

> (GEORGE *starts to pursue further, then decides to respect Charlie's wish not to tread in that area.*)

GEORGE

Have I got family...?   How come kids grow into the worse kind of parents... to their parents?

CHARLIE

Punishment I'd guess...

GEORGE

Gettin' even... yeah, that's it. (*laughs*) I didn't tell them where I was moving, but I'm sure they've been to the office.

> (*Charlie is now seated on the bed, changing his shirt.*)

CHARLIE

If you don't want 'em to, why would they bother. You're grown.

GEORGE

Jimmie has some grand idea about rescuing me from the jaws of poverty... or from myself.

CHARLIE

Jimmie, huh?

GEORGE

Always Jimmie to me.

(*musing*) ...Never liked his name. Likes to be called, Jim. I call him Jimmie just to gall him. (*laughs*) He's very conscious about his age... jogs everyday. (*looks quizzically at Charlie, smiles*) Aw, he's a nice enough young man... Jimmie. I remember I took him to a baseball game. A big league game. Now, I don't know who was playing 'cause I hate baseball almost as much as I hate bacon. But I went because I had promised an eleven year old Jimmie that... Well. somehow I ended up catching a foul ball... Yeah, right in my cap. I was Jimmie's hero for months. Now he calls me an old fool. Jimmie!

Charlie... What is age anyway?

CHARLIE

Age? Some people think it's a number... like sixty-five, or seventy.

GEORGE

Some think once you turn seventy, you're a baby again... every need has to be taken care of...

CHARLIE

They think you forget how to work... or create...

GEORGE

How to think...

CHARLIE

Or feel.

GEORGE

They even think you forget... (*almost embarrassed*) ...how to screw.

CHARLI E

(*excitedly*) You think... you think we can get them at the office to provide us with a little physical therapy?

(*They laugh*)

Like riding a bike...

GEORGE

Yeah... but I don't remember the last time I rode a bike.

(*they laugh some more*)

CHARLIE

(*a new idea*) Hey. George... eh... be old.

GEORGE

What'd you mean?

CHARLIE

(*coaxing*) Come on... Let me see you be old.

GEORGE

(*not knowing what to do*) Eh... how old?

CHARLIE

Old... old...

(*he brightens with an idea*)

Old as that jerk at the office thinks sixty-five is.

GEORGE

(*Warming to the idea*) That old huh? Eh... what do I say?

CHARLIE

Anything.

(*getting excited*) No, no... I'll give you a line. Just walk across the room here and say: "If I want to bellow, I'll bellow."

(GEORGE *takes a deep breath and walks across the room delivering the line.*)

GEORGE

If I want to bellow, I'll bellow.

CHARLIE

No, no, George. Go back. You've got to show a little... eh... age... Try it again.

(GEORGE *goes back, and starts over. Before he can say the first word,* CHARLIE *stops him.*)

You're walking too tall.

(Bending over a little.)

GEORGE

If I want...

CHARLIE

That's it...

GEORGE

...want to bellow...

CHARLIE

Stoop over a little more.

(GEORGE complies.)

GEORGE

If I want to bellow...

CHARLIE

You got the whole world on your back, and you're trying to keep it from rolling off...

(CHARLIE demonstrates by swaying back and forth. GEORGE does the same.)

That's it.   That's it

(GEORGE is stooped over and swaying back and forth...)

GEORGE

If I want to bellow-

(GEORGE grabs his back and straightens up.)

Being old is hard...

CHARLIE

Yeah, I know. Now, do the same thing and shake a little. Wait.

(He has a brainstorm. He looks for something to use as a cane.)

Wait a minute. You gotta have a cane...Can't scare little kids without a cane...

(He finally takes the curtain rod from the bedroom window. He pulls it apart.)

There. Now shake a little.

(GEORGE *does a little.*)

GEORGE

If I want to...

CHARLIE

Shake a lot! And don't bend your knees when you walk... Like this... (*demonstrating*)
Just kinda shuffle, move like you walking on eggs without breaking 'em.

(CHARLIE *demonstrates, George tries.*)

GEORGE

If I want to bellow, I'll...

CHARLIE

It's coming... 'cept we gotta do something with your voice.

GEORGE

What's wrong with it?

CHARLIE

Too clear. Eh... Crack your voice a little.

GEORGE

How?

CHARLIE

How would I know? Just try it. Eh...eh... remember the old witch that gave Snow
White the poison apple?

GEORGE

I bellow...

CHARLIE

Good. Slow it down.

GEORGE

(*slowing it down and cracking his voice.*) If I want to bellow...

CHARLIE

That's it. That's it.

GEORGE

I'll bellow...

(GEORGE *is really enjoying himself as* CHARLIE *"conducts".*)

CHARLIE
Remember the world on your back... the eggs on the floor...

GEORGE
If... I... I... want... to...

CHARLIE
You're getting there. That's great.

GEORGE

(GEORGE *gets carried away as he repeats the line with a little extra oomph.*)

...B e l l o o o o ...If I want to Bellow, I'll Bellow... I'll... Bellow... (*doing a little old man dance*) If I wanna bellow I'll... Belllloooow...

(He *stops, exhausted, flops in a chair.*)

(*feigned excitement*) Well... Mr. Director, do I get the part?

CHARLIE
Ahhh... (*thinking it over*)

GEORGE
(*little old man's voice... cackling*) Do I get the part?

CHARLIE
I'm sorry. Sir. You are obviously much too young to be old.

(*They laugh*)

You're something else.

GEORGE
It was... eh... your great coaching.

CHARLIE
(*grinning, all modesty*) Yeah... I suppose so...

GEORGE (*thoughtful*)
You know... I'd really like to see your act.

CHARLIE
They tell me it was something to see... but no more...

GEORGE

singing and danc...

CHARLIE

(*avoiding*) Boy, if your Jimmie could see you now.

GEORGE

Unfortunately, I think that's the way he would play the part. That was kinda fun...

(*realizing that he's having fun*)

Well... that's one way to kill time....

(CHARLIE *becomes pensive and goes to the kitchen table.* GEORGE *is still wired.*)

(*like a little kid*) How 'bout some gin rummy?

(*He sits across from Charlie. fanning the cards.* CHARLIE *begins to slip into his inner despair.*)

CHARLIE

Damn... That feeling... can't seem to shake it. I hate that feeling... You know... of waste...? Like nothing... nothing at all.

GEORGE

(*shuffling the cards*) A little gin rummy'll settle the mind... Specially the way I'm gonna whip you.

CHARLIE

Too many missed beats.

GEORGE

Aw, come on... (*quoting Charlie*) "Won't stand for wallowing self pity".

(CHARLIE *glares at George.*)

You've done plenty... You've had a full life.

CHARLIE

It's not full yet! I'm still breathin'... So are you! Yeah. Think I'll get married or something. Write a book. Get a degree in art or law...

GEORGE

What for? What would you do with a degree? Five years from now you might be dead.

CHARLIE

Five minutes from now, so what?

What does death have to do with the time we have left?

GEORGE

Not much. (*offering Charlie the deck*) Come on, deal.

(CHARLIE *does not accept the deal.* GEORGE *takes the deck and shuffles.*)

CHARLIE

Not much, huh? You know... that would have been my answer too.

GEORGE

Cut.

CHARLIE (*He cuts*)

Then I started thinkin' on it... Death has EVERYTHING to do with the time that's left.

GEORGE

Pick up your hand.

CHARLIE (*unconsciously picking up hand*)

From the moment we're born... death is chasing us... pushing us.

GEORGE

Uh-huh... Your play.

CHARLIE

Death..makes LIVING serious business!

GEORGE

(*getting excited*) Discard.

CHARLIE

Write something about THAT, George. Without death, there'd be no hurry to do anything.

GEORGE

All this talk about death! Play!

CHARLIE

You're hearing the wrong part, George. Living! That's what it's all about. Death is... a... generator for life.

(CHARLIE *discards a card. GEORGE with much joy picks up the discard.*)

GEORGE

(*Laughing*) Gin!

(CHARLIE *barely acknowledges.* GEORGE *eagerly gathers up the cards.*)

Come on Charlie, two out of three.

(CHARLIE, *deep in thought does not respond.*)

Okay, okay... We'll play 'til you win.

(CHARLIE, *almost in a daze gets up. He appears lost and confused.*)

GEORGE

What is it Charlie...?

(*A sudden desperation comes over Charlie. There is a quiet urgency in his manner.*)

CHARLIE

George... George, if they come for you... you going?

GEORGE

(*not wanting to get serious*) Ah, come on...

CHARLIE

Damnit, George... If they come, are you leaving?

GEORGE

I... I just don't know. No money. No food. Maybe Jimmie's right... maybe I can't... (*anguish*) take care of myself... I don't know.

CHARLIE

It 's the choice between living and wasting... You do know.

(*Both men recede into a quiet reflection. When they speak, it's not to each other.*)

Sometime I wish I could really start over...

GEORGE

They say they want me there... 'specially Doris.

CHARLIE

Just start over. Never miss a beat...

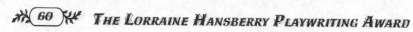

GEORGE

But they have a way of making you feel "in the way"...

CHARLIE

Make the right choices this time... Yeah... I'm starting over.

(CHARLIE *walks over to the coffee table, picks up the scrapbook and with increasing glee, he begins to tear pages from the book. GEORGE rushes to him.*)

GEORGE

Charlie! What are you doing!

(GEORGE *tries to take the book as CHARLIE continues to rip out pages. GEORGE finally gets his hands on the book and they struggle.*)

CHARLIE

(*shouting*) It's MY LIFE!

(GEORGE *realizes this truth and reluctantly surrenders.*)

GEORGE

You... You'll be sorry in the morning, that's all. (*passionately*) There's Joe... and Jesse in there... a lifetime!

CHARLIE

No... not a lifetime. Yesterday... Yesterday... Sweet yesterday.

(CHARLIE *drops the scrapbook, and engages a new energy.*)

Sweet all right... Sweet as Joe's short right... sweet.

(He *takes a fighting stance and begins to shadow box.*)

Come on, George... You be Louis...the Brown Bomber... I'll give you that rematch right now.

(GEORGE *is unwilling to join the game. He picks up pieces of the torn scrapbook.*)

Life's a prize fight, George.

(CHARLIE *continues dancing around. He jabs... sounding out each blow.*)

Tearing up a scrapbook... Bam! Bam! ...ain't nothing. But through life... Bam! ...ripping through life Bam! Bam! Bam! ...Now that's something! (*delivers knockout punch*) Pow!

> (CHARLIE *tires of-playing alone... pleads.*)

Come on, Bomber! Come on.

> (GEORGE *does not respond. He sits on the sofa with pieces of the scrapbook in his lap. CHARLIE, disappointed, drops his arms from the fighting stance and gives up on George.*)

You missing a beat, George... beat...Bet'ya Joe never missed a beat

> (He *drifts, slowly, into serious conversation with Joe Louis.*)

Did you, Joe?

On target every time...

> (He *drifts further.*)

What's the secret, Joe...? Huh? I gotta know, 'cause... somethin' real... is slippin' away.

Ever feel like you was nothin', Joe? Nothing...

(*Chuckles*) Not you... You were (*announcing it*) HEAVYWEIGHT CHAMPION OF THE WORLD!

> (He *smiles broadly and shakes his head as he bathes in the fond memory.*)

I stole some of your glory one time... Day after one of your fights... In the lobby of this hotel... Kid... eyes like moons looking right through me,... "Did he hurt you, Joe? I just... just like I was you... "No, kid." I gave him a playful sock on the jaw and walked away hoping I'd never see him again...

That kid.... Didn't wanna spoil his...

> (*unable to sell lie to himself, he confesses with vigor and joy*)

Hell, who am I kidding I did it for me!

Made me feel like a... a... Like the music... You were all ,music. Joe...

Before your fights we used to put on some Billie Holliday. Sit around outside in the thick night air...Billie kinda floating over us, soothing our nerves...And we'd talk and joke and try to guess what round you'd put him away...

And afterwards... after you did put him away... we'd just sit there and talk and laugh and fight the fight all over again... and then again... And then we'd wait... for the morning "sports extra" so we could see the pictures we painted with our minds...

You did us proud, Joe... Proud... You made life a good place to be... You made me feel like somebody...

Hot Damn! Champion of the world!

When did you first know, Joe...? That you had it...? I don't mean the crown or anything like that... I mean IT... the...the... Heart... the Stuff that makes you go on and on through all the mess and woe...

At a time when there was nothing but Church and sweat... when I was hanging out there with nothing but questions... You came along with one hell of an answer to the meaning of ME!... I wore you like a warm coat...

I needed you to win, Joe.   Every time you stepped into that ring... I was right there with you... In your corner.. Your waterboy cooling you down... Your manager... "Do it, Boy, Do it!'" "Hold that right up...hold it up... "Jab! Jab! Move... Jab! Jab! Jab!" Right there with you... Punches meant for you...

(The SOUNDS *of one of the Louis fights begins to float over the scene. It is barely audible but the volume is steadily increased until it equals the intensity of Charlie. Some of the words in his mind mingle with his own words.)*

I took! I took!

(He snaps his head back with each punch.)

Took 'em so they wouldn't hurt you... I needed you to win!

(He is now very elated and dancing around.)

And when you won, I shouted... and danced in the streets! Yeah...! And when everyone of 'em fell like dominoes, one...by. ..one...by...

(The announcer excitedly reports that the foe is down and begins to count just as CHARLIE says "one". CHARLIE picks up the count. We hear the roar of the crowd.)

...Two. Three... . ..eight nine... Ten!

(*we hear a loud cheer*)

I won... Don't you see, Joe!

(CHARLIE *throws his arms up in victory.*)

I won... won ... I won...

(*Slowly as his dream fades, his arms fall.*)

I... won. (*the sound of a man who knows he didn't*) I . . .won.

(*George just watches Charlie, his head bowed... grieving what might have been... as the lights fade.*)

End of Act One

ACT II

Scene I

Early the next morning. CHARLIE sits at the coffee table. He is dressed in his jogging suit, his "Charlie-hat" perched at a serious angle. He bends over the table working very intently and chortling to himself. GEORGE is at the stove preparing breakfast. CHARLIE picks up a piece of his handiwork... a pasted together page from the scrapbook. It is V...E...R...Y lopsided. He inspects it, shrugs and sighs "Oh well." He then looks closer at the page... remembering. The giggling of a young girl floats over his reverie. The lights dim to half on Charlie. George, in the kitchen is frozen in time. Fantasy lights come up in the hall way area. We again hear the sound of a little girl giggling... And Angie, now eleven years old appears. She is dressed somewhat "tomboyish" in sweatshirt and baseball cap.

ANGIE
...(*laughing*) Well flowers are pretty... butterflies too. But am I? Am I pretty Uncle Charlie?

(*insistent*) Uncle Charlie... listen to me... Do you think...?

> (CHARLIE *gets up, leaves the scrapbook and happily shuffles his way into her light... a song in his heart.*)

CHARLIE
Angie... Look at all the twinkling stars, will you.

ANGIE
Uncle Char...

CHARLIE
I just discovered what happens to the light between the twinkles.

ANGIE
The light between the twinkles?

CHARLIE

Yeah... I think... every time a child is born, a new star appears, and it becomes that child's star.

ANGIE

Really?

CHARLIE

Un huh... And I can tell you've found your star.

ANGIE

How?

CHARLIE

From the light between the twinkles.

(*He demonstrates with his hand as he explains.*)

Look... Here's a star twinkling. (*He opens and closes his fist, palm out, several times.*)

Now, Angie... Where does the light of this star go between the twinkles? When it's like this? (*Shows a closed fist.*)

ANGIE

I don't know.

CHARLIE

Well, my dear, the light from your star out there... the light between the twinkle...

(*He tosses the imaginary light into her eyes.*)

... goes right into your eyes. That's why they sparkle so.

(*He looks directly into her eyes.*)

Yeah, honey, you're pretty. Prettiest thing I know.

ANGIE

Uncle Charlie, I love you.

(*The lights begin to fade slowly as Angie gives him a big kiss and hug, then slowly starts to back away into the shadows of time. Charlie watches her, then sadly turns and goes back to the coffee table as the lights of time shift fully.*)

GEORGE

Breakfast is served!

(CHARLIE *does not immediately respond. He sits grinning in the reverie of his moment.*)

You Hoo...? You with us...? I said breakfast is served.

(CHARLIE slowly comes back to reality. He walks to the table, picks up the box of corn flakes and smiles. They sit down and begin eating. CHARLIE is still in somewhat of a dream state. GEORGE regards him.)

GEORGE
Charlie, 'bout last night...

CHARLIE
Yeah... I know... Stay... don't stay... Do what you gotta. It's your business... But I must admit there is something 'bout you.

GEORGE
And I have to admit there's something...

(*searches for the right word. Then innocently*)

... attractive about you, too.

CHARLIE
(*feigned concern*) Attractive? How do you mean that?

(*Looking askance at George.*)

How'd you answer that question 'bout sexual preference?

GEORGE
(*shocked*) Sexual preference?

CHARLIE
Standard question, remember?

GEORGE
No, I don't remember. What'd you say?

CHARLIE
I said... (*shaking his head gleefully*) Yes!

GEORGE
You would. What'd you really say?

CHARLIE

Well, now... This morning... (*chuckles, plays... sings*) "While jogging in the park one day..." (*He stops abruptly*) There was this sweet looking young thing sitting on the bench. Just watching. Now, she had to be there to see me. I mean, she's been there three mornings in a row... just watching.

I really jog good when I run by her. Straight and tall... Pull the tum in... No panting. Least not from the running. (*chuckles, still in the memory*) No... She let me know my preference loud and clear. I'll have to talk to her tomorrow. Don't want to miss that beat.

GEORGE

Charlie... What did happen to your wife?

CHARLIE

Never been married.

GEORGE

(*disbelief*) What?

CHARLIE

(*slightly irritated*) Just drop it, okay?

GEORGE

Well. Who's Angie?

(*At the mention of Angie, CHARLIE brightens.*)

CHARLIE

Angie. No wife, but there is Angie. No kids to call my own, but there's Angie. She's my heart. When she lost her... dad... George? Were your kids so desperate about their beauty? So unsure? "Am I pretty Uncle Charlie?"

GEORGE

Really close to her, huh?

CHARLIE

Nothing closer.

(*Both men look at each other... nod in understanding. There is a quiet moment. Both men fidget...awkward... GEORGE breaks it, looks at watch.*)

GEORGE

(*snaps*) Will you look at the time... I wanted to be there when the Post Office opened...

(CHARLIE *jumps up, almost knocking over the chair. He grabs his jacket, and runs for the door.*)

GEORGE (*startled*)
Wha... What's with you?

CHARLIE
(*out the door*) Forgot. Appointment with destiny. Places to go... Things needin' to be done... Later man.

(*He's gone, leaving George with his mouth open.*)

GEORGE
Hey...

(*He notices the "Charlie Hat" on the coffee-table. He grabs it and runs to the door. Shouts down the hallway.*)

Hey...! Hey, you forgot...

(*no use... He comes back into the room and closes the door. He looks down at the hat... spins it in his hands... Up in the air... catches it. Looks at it again. He laughs... and you can see the idea form in his head. He tentatively places the hat on his head. He feels it... tilts it "a la Charlie"... Grins like a kid... tries out the Charlie walk. He looks around as if somebody is watching him... More little boy charm comes out and he giggles to himself like he's getting away with something. He gets really cocky and struts around the living room. He stops as another idea grows.*)

Wait a minute Wait a minute wait a minute.

(*holds up his hand as if he had an audience*)

Just one minute... I'll be glad to...

(*He fixes the hat back on his head and assumes. with some difficulty. the stance of a runner in the starting position. He hurls himself forward, awkwardly.*)

SWWWW III SSSSHHHHHHHH... !

(*Bows his head*)

I was humbled... (*laughs*) Me... and JESSE OWENS...

(He savors it but a moment, then shifts personality by fixing the hat severe...
Serious stuff. He starts to bounce around... the fighter.)

B O N G...
> *(he dances, peppering the air with awkward rights and lefts. He reels back as if*
> *hit. Doubles up.)*

Bam... Bam.. Bam... Up beside my head.

> *(He reels again. Smiles.)*

Hey Joe... Rematch. This time, though... you watch yourself... Because, this time
I'm going to really hurt you.

> *(Shakes his head. Looks around. Snarls...)*

SHEEEET

> *(George's version of mean and nasty.)*

Lay you down for good man... Lay you dooowwwn, Motha... Motha... *(can't say it...)*
Mothagrubber!

> *(Throws his head back like a proud peacock. Shrugs. He fixes the hat again.*
> *Jaunty... rakish. He is now completely in a mood of his own making... He*
> *plays... and in his playing there is a silent tribute, mischievous, comic. A poignant*
> *and passionate salute to Charlie, and at the same time to blackness. He dances,*
> *prances, and mimes his dizzy impression. It comes bubbling out of him... a bit*
> *mad, giddy...hauntingly beautiful in its awkwardness.)*

I'm Blue... an I's gonna sing for you... *(sings)* Baby, Baby, Baby.

> *(He Stops singing, but continues expressing each word with his version of*
> *"Blackness".)*

Honey Chile... *(struts Black)* Hom...nee grits... black eye peas... Mammy... *(gettin' real*
down) Lay it on me Momma! *(arrogant)* If... I... wants ta... Bellow...

> *(He does the old man as he thinks Charlie might play it.)*

I'll... *(shaking it)* B e l l o w... baby!

> *(Back to strutting)*

Honey... Sweet thing a mine...

(*blurts out as if it was everything black he'd ever wanted to say, but was too timid to say.*)

BlackAssBlackAssBlackAss!

> (*beside himself with glee*)

OOOO... OO... WEEEEE!

> (*Stops. Stands erect. Declares a truth.*)

(*powerful*) COLLARDS AIN COLLARDS LESS THEY GOT BACON.

> (*The black Charlie pixie.*)

Ain had bacon since Porky was piglet!

> (*Stops in his tracks for a moment. We see an idea forming. Smiles. Cocks hat once more and High Steps into the living room.*)

(*steppin'*) Since porky was a piglet... a piglet.... a piglet... a boo boo be doo.

> (*He struts into the bedroom and picks up his coat. He prances to the door and opens it with a flare. He makes a grand exit, still wearing the hat. He struts down the hall... out of sight. Quiet. He struts back down the hall... Opens the door, sticks his head into the room and grins, and from the door, he tosses the hat onto the sofa...*)

(*ending the refrain*) YEAH!

> (*He struts down the hall and disappears as the lights come down on Scene One.*)

ACT II

Scene II

Later the same morning. CHARLIE is busy wrapping a large bow around an old portable typewriter. Against the bed is an old easel. As Charlie works, ANGIE, now 37 years old walks down the hallway toward the door. She is dressed in a modest skirt, blouse and sportcoat. She is also wearing a small fedora-like hat. Her hair is styled in such a way that the hat is barely noticeable. She has a slightly business look and manner. As she approaches the door, she stops and fixes her coat and hat, then nervously knocks on the door. CHARLIE only looks at the door. He makes no effort to answer it. ANGIE knocks again.

CHARLIE

(*as to a salesman*) What ever you selling, we ain't buying.

ANGIE

Uncle Charlie?

CHARLIE

(*quiet disbelief...*) Angie...?

> (He *stops abruptly as though caught.*)

Uh-oh...

ANGIE

Uncle Charlie, you in there?

> (CHARLIE *stands in agony, then scrambling, hides the scrapbook in the kitchen cupboard.*)

ANGIE

(*knocking*) Uncle Charlie!

CHARLIE

> (*Cocking his hat in his special way, he moves toward the door. He takes a deep breath, puts on a grin, and opens the door.*)

Angie!

ANGIE

(*somewhat cool*) Well... may I come in?

CHARLIE

Now... what kinda question is that... Come on in, girl.

(ANGIE *comes in, looks around. She is smiling perhaps a bit too much. She's trying to seem casual, covering her obvious anger.*)

ANGIE

Well now... How is good ole Uncle Charlie...?

CHARLIE

(*quietly*) Fine...

ANGIE

Fine? I bet you are just fine. Just shuckin' 'n jivin' and runnin' your game.

CHARLIE

Angie... I...

ANGIE

(mock concern) Ah, Uncle Charlie... you don't look so glad to see me... It's me... pretty little Angie, remember... You most favorite chile...

CHARLIE

I... I...

ANGIE

I surprised you... that it?

CHARLIE

Well...

ANGIE

(*drops the smile*) Don't even know why I came here.

Told myself... wasn't gonna look for you... didn't care if you went clear to... anyplace and never saw you again... told myself...

(*She suddenly stops.*)

You see... got me talkin to myself. You just a mean old man... don't care for nothing... nobody but yourself

CHARLIE

(*takes a deep breath*) Sorry ain't enough... but... (*can't finish*)

ANGIE

Robert said I better hurry up and find you cause I was driving him nuts... Been hard on the kids too... And... and... See what you do... (*sticking it to him*) U N C L E ... C H A R L I E...!

CHARLIE

Never meant to... I... (*turns away from her glare*)

ANGIE

Where you going...? You don't have to turn away... look me in the face... Explain something... anything to me.

(CHARLIE *doesn't move.*)

Ahaa... did I make you feel bad?   Oh... I know... Me 'n my big mouth... Want me to sing a little song...

(*she falls into old Charlie pose*)

...do a little dance?

(*She does a simple time step. She takes her hat off and tries to do a hat trick... spinning. flipping... rolling down her arm. It falls flat, as she can't control it in her agitated state.*)

And I practiced that... You don't know how long I practiced that...

(*she breaks... starts to cry*)

...to please you..

(CHARLIE *goes to comfort her.*)

CHARLIE

ANG...

ANGIE

(*pulls away angrily*) "The string has strung... Gotta run."

(*She stares holes in him. He retreats as if punched in the face.*)

"The string has strung... Gotta run...!" What is that... your exit line? Part of your "leave 'em laughing" routine?

(CHARLIE, *shaken, sinks deeper in frustration.*)

But I knew that line... Knew it... Couldn't get it outta my head... Where, oh where, had I heard... seen it before? (*slowly...*) "The string... is strung... Gotta run... (*snaps her fingers*) Your scrapbook!

(CHARLIE *in agony, can only sit.*)

Scrapbook. huh... self-satisfaction book...! Full of "I-in and "Me-in" (*pounds chest in mock exaggeration*) "woopee-in"...

(*quieter*) All the time I spent in that book... My favorite hiding place... There was this one space that used to fascinate me. Picture was gone but the note underneath still there... "The string has strung... Gotta run."

(CHARLIE *raises his hand to stop her.*)

Was a woman. Charlie. wasn't it...? A pretty dark skinned gal... long black hair... love in her eyes...

CHARLIE

Stop it. Angie...

ANGIE

That's the way I pictured her... Tall and slim.

Who was she. Charlie...? (*laughs*) I remember being kinda glad she wasn't 'round though... Wasn't ready to share you with nobody... (*painfully... softly*) Used to dream it was me in that picture... Just us. Me on your arm... Us in a horse drawn carriage... You my Black knight in shinning armour... Dancing under the stars in the moonlight, and just when I got it just about the way I wanted it... you'd walk out. (*fighting back the tears*) (*an admission*) Ne... never got that far in my dream... (*then vehemently*) But you would have...! You did!

CHARLIE

I... I... had to...

ANGIE

Bet you did. What ever happened to, "I'll always be there for you Angie...? How you gonna manage that...? Postcards?

CHARLIE

It... it was right for me to leave.

ANGIE

It was wrong the way you left.

CHARLIE

Ever since your father died... I... I've been hanging 'round. You a grown woman now... You don't need me anymore...

ANGIE

Don't tell me what I need, Uncle Charlie.

CHARLIE

You don't need me... Anyway, I not really your uncle... you know that.

ANGIE

So? I know that!

CHARLIE

(*snapping*) So, stop calling me Uncle!

(ANGIE *turns slowly to face him.*)

ANGIE

(*firmly*) You're Family... Nothing can change that.

(*They look deeply into one another for a moment. ANGIE breaks it.*)

And... and you're the one needing... You been to the doctor...?

CHARLIE

I'm okay. Fine.

(ANGIE *makes a move toward him, he retreats slightly.*)

Now you see what I'm talking about... You don't need my weight hanging 'round, dragging you down...

ANGIE

(*softens*) Did the doctor find something? Tell me...

CHARLIE

You gonna tip-toe around me the rest of my life...? I ain't been to no damn doctor.

ANGIE

Dr. Plummer called...

(CHARLIE *stops short. Silent for a moment.*)

CHARLIE

Doctor Plummer... Doctor Plummer... Never liked his name.. (*chuckles*) I bet, for hardening of the arteries... he prescribes Draino.

(ANGIE *stands unamused.*)

Look... I appreciate his concern... You can tell 'em that the next time you talk to 'em... but I don't want to end up in some hospital ward cooped up. plugged in and doped out. I... I will live every moment I can... I've got plans for tomorrow... next week and for the next decade.

When I left... I'm sorry... I thought... I really thought... I... (*can't finish*) Angie... I wouldn't hurt you... for anything.

(*He stands looking at her... his heart hanging out. She shakes her head... walks slowly to him... puts her arms around him. Hugs him.*)

ANGIE

(*softly*) Don't you ever disappear on me again. Do whatever you got to do... any way you want to... Just don't... Don't shut me out, Uncle Charlie.

CHARLIE

Never.

ANGIE

Deal...?

CHARLIE

Deal!

(ANGIE *looks around the room... notices the typewriter.*)

ANGIE

What's this... finally gonna start that novel?

CHARLIE

Not me... My roommate is, though... if he knows what's good for him.

(*He strokes the typewriter with pride.*)

Thriftstore special. His birthday present... He's forty three today. Having a little surprise party for him.

ANGIE

Forty three...?

CHARLIE

Uh huh... You'd like him. A shoemaker... He's gonna make me a pair of nice soft shoes for my dogs here.... He doesn't know that yet, either.

ANGIE

I'd like to meet this roommate person that you can actually live with. Am I invited to your party...?

CHARLIE

Well... It is a kinda special occasion... You see... George's been feeling kind of low... and... well...

ANGIE

Uncle Charlie... You scamming again...

(*The old Charlie. His face lights up. He takes his song and dance man pose. Sings.*)

CHARLIE

"Pick up all your cares and woe... here I go... swinging low..."

(ANGIE *joins, happily, they do "their" routine.*)

"Bye, bye, Blackbird"

(*They both laugh and enjoy their reunion. Angie hugs him again.*)

ANGIE

(*shaking her head...*) You're never gonna grow up.

CHARLIE

Tried it once... Blah!

(*salesman pitch*) Tell-ya-what-I'm-gonna-do... How 'bout you, Robert and the kids coming here for a real sit down dinner. Me and George, we'll cook it up proper.

ANGIE

We'd love that. When?

CHARLIE

Real soon... Real soon... (*half to himself*) Yeah... George's got this special bottle a wine I'd love to taste.

ANGIE

(*an apology*) Uncle Charlie... About the scrapbook... I loved that scrapbook. It gave me... hope. Kids love it too. Where is it?

CHARLIE

Well... I'm putting a new chapter in it... Get ready to be impressed.

ANGIE

(*surrendering*) Yeah... Uncle Charlie, I want that dinner real soon.

CHARLIE

Eh... Girl? How'd you like to spend some of your hard earned money on your dear old Uncle?

ANGIE

But Charlie, you just HATE charity.

CHARLIE

From you, I'll graciously accept.

ANGIE

What is it you need?

CHARLIE

Gotta have a cake... I saw the perfect one at the store just downstairs.

ANGIE

What kind?

CHARLIE

Chocolate, of course.

ANGIE

Of course...

(ANGIE *walks to the door, turns back to* CHARLIE. *They look into one another for a moment.*)

CHARLIE

...Eh... Angie... I miss the kids.

ANGIE

(*softly*) Yeah. They ask about you.

(CHARLIE *smiles, satisfied.* ANGIE *with a cryptic smile... full of mystery.*)

ANGIE

They all got it, you know.

CHARLIE

What's that?

ANGIE

Well, I better get that cake.

CHARLIE

They all got what?

(ANGIE *ignores the question and walks to the door.*)

ANGIE

Just down stairs, you said...?

(CHARLIE *a little hurt at being ignored, nods his head. ANGIE starts out the door, then returns to Charlie. She looks at him for a moment. She rushes over to him and gives him a kiss on the cheek.*)

You nut... They all got it!

(CHARLIE *looks blank*)

The light between the twinkle!

(CHARLIE *lights up in a smile. He can say nothing. Angie hugs him then slowly exits. CHARLIE takes a moment to recover, then remembers something. He rushes to the door in an effort to catch Angie.*)

CHARLIE

(*shouting*) And get me some baco...

(*He rushes out and bumps smack into JIM and DORIS, just arriving.*)

Oh. Sorry.

(CHARLIE *backs into the apartment.*)

Hello. Ah... You must be Jimmie and...

JIM

(*correcting him*) Jim. And Doris. We're here for George.

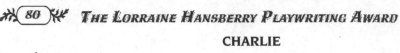

CHARLIE

Here for George?

JIM

Yes, the center said he was here.

CHARLIE

Ah... Yes. Come in. Come in. George is not here, he went to the post office.

Guess he didn't know you were coming?

(JIM *ignoring him, disdainfully*)

JIM

This is where you both live?

(CHARLIE *is peeved, and instantly into his scam.*)

CHARLIE

Yes. Eh... plus the girl that just left.

DORIS

She lives HERE?

CHARLIE

Oh, yes. That's George's girlfriend. She lives here, when she can. She just went to get me some bacon. (*smiling*) I make her call me "uncle".

DORIS

His girlfriend?

CHARLIE

Yes indeed. That's why he needs his check.

JIM

He won't get a check today. The papers weren't put in on time. (*softly*) Thank goodness.

CHARLIE

Aww. And it would have been such a neat birthday gift.

JIM

Birthday?

DORIS

Is it his birthday?

JIM

No... I don't think so.

CHARLIE (*innocently*)

Forty-three years old today.

JIM & DORIS

Forty-three?

CHARLIE

How time does fly.

DORIS

Are we talking about the same George?

CHARLIE (*playing it*)

Of course we are. Why else would you be here? (*excitedly*) Did you bring the stuff?

JIM

(*confused*) The stuff?

CHARLIE

Don't tell me you forgot. You were supposed to bring the incense and the water pipe.

  (JIM *and* DORIS *stand dumbfounded, as* ANGIE *rushes in, carrying a cake-box.*)

ANGIE

Take care, Uncle Charlie. Gotta run.

  (*places cake on kitchen table*)

I'll tell Robert what you said... Real soon, now... You hear.

  (*Jim and Doris look at each other in confusion.*)

CHARLIE

(*explaining*) A day here; a week there.

  (*Angie turns and sees Jim and Doris for the first time.*)

ANGIE

Oh... I didn't know...

CHARLIE

Eh.. Give your ole uncle a big hug... (*she does*) I'll tell George you said goodbye.

Oh. Excuse me... Where are my manners. George's older brother, Jimmy. and... and...

DORIS
Doris.

ANGIE
Nice meeting you. (*turns to Charlie*) Now Charlie... don't forget to call the...

(*he cuts her off and gently nudges her out the door*)

CHARLIE
Yes... I'll call the plummer tomorrow. Bye now... (*out the door behind her*) And don't forget where you live.

(He *gestures snatching a twinkle in his fist. He holds his fist up to her, almost a salute. Angie smiles and leaves. CHARLIE closes the door slowly... then turns quickly.*)

Now, let's see. You were supposed to...

JIM
Wait a minute, I think...

CHARLIE
Say! Your name's not Doris. Jimmie and.. and... Carolyn. Jimmie and Carolyn. Your name is Carolyn!

DORIS
My name is DORIS!

CHARLIE
Are you sure?

JIM
We're sure. We're also sure there's been a mistake.

CHARLIE
You ARE Jimmie, aren't you?

JIM
NO! Jim, not Jimmie. They must have gotten the papers mixed up at social services. They told us that (*tries to show Charlie a paper*) George Clark moved in here a few days ago.

CHARLIE

You mean George Patterson.

JIM

No! I mean George Clark... Seventy-six years old, and my father.

CHARLIE

(*laughing*) Your father? Forgive me for laughing, but your certainly older than George... He's only forty-three.

JIM

Not George Patterson! What's the use. Come on Doris, let's get outta here.

(*Doris and Jim make a quick exit. CHARLIE laughs, does a little dance step and flips his hat down his arm... He then places the hat roguishly over one eye, struts around the room. He, very pleased with himself, does a difficult jumping dance step, as the lights fade.*)

ACT II

Scene III

Same day, about four hours since last scene.   The apartment has been decorated with streamers and a couple balloons. CHARLIE snoozes on the sofa. There are two or three non-inflated balloons on his lap. GEORGE enters and goes directly to his room, hardly noticing the decorations. CHARLIE is awakened by the noise.

CHARLIE

(CHARLIE *jumps up, arms open in celebration.*)

Happy birthday.

(GEORGE *throws himself on the bed.*)

Where you been?

GEORGE (*doom*)

It's not my birthday.

CHARLIE

You're forty-three today, remember?

Here's your cake. And... here's your present. I mean it may be as old as both of us together... but like me, everything works.

(GEORGE *says nothing*)

I'm sorry there's only two balloons... Ever try to blow one of these suckers up... boy.

(Still *no response*)

What's wrong?

GEORGE

I'm not you, Charlie, let me be.

CHARLIE

So, your check wasn't there.

GEORGE

How'd you know that?

CHARLIE

Not hard to figure. It's all right.

GEORGE

It's not all right... Charity!

CHARLIE

I don't give charity. Your money'll be here.

GEORGE

But it wasn't today. I had things to do today. It's no use. When Jimmie comes, I'm leaving.

(CHARLIE *stares at him.*)

CHARLIE

Sun Village. Retirement with grace. You go there, you're dead. You know that.

(GEORGE *does not respond.*)

They were here, you know.

(CHARLIE *is immediately sorry for revealing the visit.*)

GEORGE

Who?

(CHARLIE *does not want to answer.*)

Who was here?

CHARLIE

(*trying to cover*) My Angie.

GEORGE

Oh. I thought you said, "they"?

CHARLIE

Meant Angie.

> (GEORGE *sits on the bed, studying a picture of* Judy. CHARLIE *drifts into thought about Angie.*)

I was dreaming of her, and she popped in.

> (*He shakes his head sadly.*)

Boy was I stupid!

GEORGE

You don't know what stupid is.

CHARLIE

(*still lost within himself*) Stupid. Really missed that beat.

Back when I was "Blue Hampton", I was a real player. Had all kinds of girls. Never a thought of getting married. I mean why should I? Had everything I wanted. Never a thought... Not until I met Eileen... Now, she was different. She had my nose wide open.

Mmn, I loved that gal... She lived in California and I was all over the country. I wanted her with me... and we did live together for awhile, but she couldn't handle being on the road all the time. I even tried to settle down in California, but I had the bug and couldn't handle everyday home life. We wanted each other, but our lives were so different.

Finally... she...

"Marry me now, Charlie, or let me go."

"Honey," I told her, "I'm forty years old and set in my ways."

"Marry me now!... or set me free."

"But..."

"Now, Charlie."

"I can't Baby, I can't..."

I ran back to being "Blue". But it didn't take me long to learn that I wanted her more than I wanted to be Blue...

So, I hurried back to L. A., with a wedding ring in my hand. It was so clear on what I wanted... what was right for us.

(*very joyful*) I hopped off that train and ran to her house.
(*to Eileen's mother*) "What'd you mean, she got married last week!"

(*He turns slightly and is now speaking to Eileen.*)

"Married? No, Baby, you can't be! You supposed to marry me. (*opens his hand*) See, I got the ring and everything."

She told me the baby she was carrying was mine.

"Why didn't you tell me?

(*He shakes his head, No.*)

"You wouldn't have trapped me. You should have told me!"

She made me promise... to never tell the child... Bill, became the father to my Angie.

I ran. I stayed away until I heard about Bill's accident. I thought about making a play for Eileen, then, but I couldn't. Something had died in us when I ran that first time... and... and I felt a kinda guilt... like I had "wished" Bill dead...

That guilt stayed in my way for over twenty years... Eileen died a couple a years ago.

(CHARLIE *almost in tears, continues.*)

I watched my own daughter grow up... knowing me only as... Uncle Charlie. (*grins a sad forlorned face*) So many times I've wanted to tell her... So many times.

GEORGE (*up and in the doorway*)

You should tell her. She needs to know.

CHARLIE

No. I can never tell her.

(CHARLIE *feels the full weight of his frustrations.* GEORGE *wants to comfort him but does not know how.*)

(*angrily*) Twenty years wasted!

GEORGE

(GEORGE *walks into the living room. He sits in front of the cake that Charlie had placed on the coffee table. Suddenly, he blurts...*)

I was arrested today.

(CHARLIE *does not immediately react.*)

CHARLIE

(*from far away, not in focus*) What'd you say?

GEORGE

I'd never been arrested in my life. But today...

CHARLIE

(*now clearer*) What'd you say?

GEORGE

It's true.

CHARLIE

(*understanding*) You were arrested?

(CHARLIE'S *attention is suddenly fully on George. Now* GEORGE *is the one uncomfortable.*)

What happened?

GEORGE

Nothing.

CHARLIE

Come on George... Arrested?

GEORGE

Why'd I bring this up. Look, I really don't wanna talk about it.

CHARLIE

And let my imagination go wild? You robbed First National Bank. Murder?

(*sudden insight*) Ah, I know. Indecent exposure.

(*George gives a look of disgust.* CHARLIE *interprets this as a maybe.*)

You didn't! You didn't let it all hang out... at your age. Shame... shame...

GEORGE

Shoplifting... It was shoplifting.

CHARLIE

You got caught shoplifting?

GEORGE

Yes. (*nods*)... I did.

(*referring to typewriter*) What's this for...?

CHARLIE

It's a typewriter... for writing. What were you stealing?

GEORGE

What am I going to do with a typewriter?

CHARLIE

George? What were you stealing?

GEORGE

I was released because I don't have a record.

CHARLIE

What was so important...?

GEORGE

Still might have to go to court. They'll let me know.

CHARLIE

Okay, George. You were caught stealing... and you may have to go to court. Now, what? What were you stealing?

(GEORGE, *pinned down, moves to the table.*)

GEORGE

...Eh... some... (*inaudible*) bacon.

CHARLIE

What?

GEORGE

(*soft, broken and still inaudible.*) Bacon...

CHARLIE

Come on George, don't mumble.

GEORGE

(*shouting*) Some bacon! BACON! I went to jail for stealing BACON!

(CHARLIE *slowly finds the irony in the situation and the laughter begins to build in him.*)

CHARLIE

Ba...Bacon?

GEORGE

They wanted Jimmie to come and get me. My little Jimmie... Can you imagine that... Kids... I would have spent twenty years in that hole before... (*laughing lightly*) Bacon!

(*their laughter builds*)

CHARLIE AND GEORGE

Bacon...

(*They roar, laughter bouncing from one to the other. They point at each other... Try to speak but laughing too much... can only get half the word "bac.." out... They double over laughing until the tears roll down.*)

GEORGE

(*squeaks it out through the laughter*) Bacon.

CHARLIE (*catching his breath*)

Boy this sure has been some night.

GEORGE

Yeah... Hey, let's go somewhere. Get outta this dump.

(CHARLIE *dismisses idea with silence.*)

Come on Charlie. Maybe we can do something... something to help us forget some of those stupid mistakes we've made...

CHARLIE

Stupid?

GEORGE

Yeah! A celebration to stupid. A celebration to all the stupid things we did... and do.

(CHARLIE *chuckles agreement.*)

How stupid it is to be dumb... how stupid to run from love... to steal.. especially bacon. How stupid it is to hate.

CHARLIE

Now, that's not always stupid.

GEORGE

How stupid it is to grow old.

CHARLIE

Now, that's stupid.

GEORGE

And all those stupid things we did in the name of youth...

CHARLIE

Yeah!

GEORGE

And it's stupid to be stupid.

(*They laugh*)

I'm ready to do something... even if it's stupid.

CHARLIE

What'd you have in mind?

GEORGE

(GEORGE'S *hand is resting on Charlie's hat. He rubs it unconsciously at first.*)

I don't know. Maybe...

(GEORGE *stops talking as he picks it up fondly.*)

(*chuckles*) Some hat. You left it here this morning.

(*Silently,* CHARLIE *places the hat on his head. And slowly tilts the back of his hat up with the heel of his hand so it slips rakishly over his eyes. He slides into his old routine. He points out toward imaginary audience. He "talk-sings" the song.*)

CHARLIE

...This song is about the Sandman...

(He begins a quiet, soft-shoe routine.)

Not that sleepy-time, dream-time dude...
But the other one...

(He stops. Thinks... Mouths the words. Nods his head.)

But the other one, (begins a slow shuffle)

That slow-walkin', finger-popin', (starts a rhythmic fingerpopping)
jive-talkin' danceman...
Sandman!

      (He stops again, but continues to pop his fingers as he tries to remember.)

...eh... eh... (remembers) ...yeah, yeah.

But before I do this number for you...

      (does a rather difficult dance step, awkwardly but with a flair... He smiles.)

You gonna have to come with me... to this special place...

      (He removes his hat and with exaggerated arm motion across his body, he extends
his arm to say "this way." He stands, arm extended for too long. It becomes
obvious that he is again lost.)

Now... ...eh ...eh (new start) ...to this special place... Now... Now... (got it) Now, this
place has a

      (outlines a big door)

great big Door

when you go in...

      (Outlines a V E R Y small door.)

And an iddity-bitty door when you go out.

      (He smiles in confidence. The words are all back now. He feels the joy of performing
returning.)

Now this means...

This means you can carry anything in that you wanna... But when you leave...
all "excess baggage"

like burdens and cares git left behind...

Dey just don't fit through the door!

This place...

This place is called...

"Saturday Night"

> (He *does a few fancy dance steps and whirls. He stops abruptly... realizing what he's doing.*)

GEORGE (*all aglow*)
That's it, Charlie! Yeah! You know that club down on ninth street? The Calendar Club, I think. I passed it the other day... Amateur Night every Tuesday... I think that's what the sign said. That's tonight.

CHARLIE
So?

GEORGE
So, you can do your act. No way.

CHARLIE
No way.

GEORGE
You can do what you just did... only all of it. You'll knock 'em dead!

> (*starts to imitate Charlie*)

"...Sandman... Sandman. finger poppin'...

CHARLIE
I told you I don't do that anymore.

GEORGE
Well, it sure does you...

CHARLIE
Besides... I'm no amateur.

GEORGE
They could care less about that. These places want entertainment... The better, the better. Come on, Blue.

CHARLIE

No.

GEORGE

Why not? It's you.

CHARLIE

"Blue Hampton" cost me my life. One of those stupid mistakes you were talking about?   No!

GEORGE

(*sighs, baiting*) All right. But I thought you... I mean... never miss a beat and all... Starting over.

I guess it's easy to tear up a scrap book... Harder to make it real.

CHARLIE

You've made your point.

GEORGE

Talk is an easy thing to do...

CHARLIE

George, you've made...

GEORGE

I don't know if you've got any beats left.

CHARLIE

Can it, George.

> (*They stop for a moment, only looking at each other. GEORGE asks straight out.*)

GEORGE

Come on, Blue. Do it for me?

CHARLIE (*hesitant, difficult*)

(*takes a deep breath*) You arrange it... I'll do it.

GEORGE

Now you talkin'!

> (*CHARLIE walks over to the cupboard, takes down a small tin can, and removes a twenty dollar bill.*)

CHARLIE

But it's stupid, you know. It's stupid to take your last twenty dollars and spend it on a lark... but I'll do it.

GEORGE

It's stupid to be poor.

(As Lights fade to black on apartment, we hear the sound of raunchy music and even more raunchy laughter. The sounds are all mixed together in the blackness, and form a nightclub cacophony. Some voices are distinguished through and over the din.)

VOICE

Bring on the dancing girls...

VOICE

I want the dancing girls!

VOICE

(drunk)... Enough of this shit...

VOICE

Give the guy a chance!

VOICE

Goddamnit, bring on the girls...

VOICE

Shut up...

VOICE

(announcement) The Calendar Club is proud to present Sweetwater Blue Hampton.

(We hear cheers, whistles, boos, and loud applause.)

CHARLIE (voice)

Eh.. Ladies... and... Gentlemen... ahh...

(Voice fades and blackness becomes still.)

ACT II

Scene IV

Lights come up slowly. Down the hall we hear bumping and scuffling before GEORGE and CHARLIE come into view. CHARLIE is supporting George who is bleeding from the nose. There is a lot of blood. GEORGE holds a very bloody handkerchief to his face and is also holding his side. In spite of his physical hurts, he is surprisingly chipper. He is singing "Sandman" as they come into view.

(*half laughing... giddy*) Wait a minute... Wait... I can walk...

> (CHARLIE *let him stand. He tries to walk... waivers badly... staggers slightly... a little unsteady but certainly not drunk. He laughs.*)

Whooo...

> (CHARLIE *again supports him. They stop in the hall resting against the wall...*)

CHARLIE
You need a doctor.

GEORGE
No, I'm fine. Really.

CHARLIE
Boy... what'd he do...? bust all the blood vessels in your face.

> (GEORGE *just laughs.*)

GEORGE
Boy... (*laughs*) Boy... they sure didn't know what to do with you... (*laughs*)

CHARLIE
No... guess they didn't...

GEORGE
I didn't know what he meant... (*laughs*) I sure know now...

CHARLIE

What...

GEORGE

(*really tickled... laughing*) Exotic...

CHARLIE

Yeah... Man, I've played some rough clubs, but that was the weirdest...

GEORGE

Weird and (*laughing more*) exotic...

CHARLIE

What you talking about...

GEORGE

When I called... he asked if your act was... exotic... (*laughing*) I... I told 'em you invented the word.

(CHARLIE *smiles lightly, not too amused.*)

CHARLIE

(*laughs*) Yeah...Come on... better get your exotic nose inside and clean it up.

(*They walk into the apartment. GEORGE, somewhat recovered, shuffles in to the tune of "Sandman". He goes to the easy chair, spins around and plops tiredly into the chair.*)

GEORGE

(*blows out*) Wheew...

(CHARLIE *takes the bloody rag from George, and goes into the bathroom. He comes out with a wet towel.*)

GEORGE

I haven't felt so good since... (*thinks... shrugs*) well, in a long, long time...

CHARLIE

(*handing George the towel*) All we had to do was leave.

GEORGE

Leave!

CHARLIE

Just go.

GEORGE

How could you think of leaving? The guy was an ass!

CHARLIE

A drunk ass!

GEORGE

He was insulting you. He was...

CHARLIE

He was drunk!

GEORGE

We COULDN'T "just leave"... ... He had it coming.

CHARLIE

Him...? The only blood on him is from you.

GEORGE

(*disgusted*) Leave!

CHARLIE

If you've entered as many back doors as I have, you'd know how to leave, too.

(CHARLIE *very tiredly goes to the refrigerator to get a glass of water for George.*)

GEORGE

Don't think that's anything I want to learn.

CHARLIE (Handing George the glass)

Well, YOU'RE only forty-three... I'm seventy-six.

GEORGE

Why'd you stand for it?

CHARLIE

Hump...

(CHARLIE *starts to answer directly, but thinks better of it.*)

You, man? What happened to you? You were a wild man!

(GEORGE *does not respond.*)

A real bear! Almost got the same thing, too... as that bear.

GEORGE

I just didn't like...He called you "coon."

CHARLIE

Been called that before.

GEORGE

I saw the look on your face.

CHARLIE

It wasn't that big a deal. Not worth all that... energy.

GEORGE

Just another one of those things I need to outgrow. (*laughs*) I did act like a teenager, didn't I?

CHARLIE

A forty-three year old.

GEORGE (*quietly*)

When those kids robbed me? I hurt one of them pretty bad. A boy really. When the police came... they had to pull me off of him. I still don't know what happened. I swore I would never get that mad again...It scares me...

(CHARLIE *Walks away... no dance in his step... no song in his heart.*)

CHARLIE

(*quietly*) Wish I'd had some of your fire...

GEORGE (*surprised*)

You... ?

CHARLIE

I was only jogging...

One cold night on the beach... Young hoodlums. Animals really.

(CHARLIE *goes deep into the memory, and begins to re-live the incident.*)

(*menacing tone*) "Hey Pops...? You got a dollar? We need some money."

I told them I didn't have any...

"You sure, Pops? It'd be a shame if we had to search you."

No. I don't...

(*they take Charlie's wallet*)

"you're right. No money here. Too bad... too bad old man."

Look, I'm just out jogging...

"You're old... You're Black... probably an Uncle Tom... and you got no money... Any reason we should let you live?"

I'm only...

"Well, old man... you're a runner aren't you? Let's see you run..."

I turned to run, and the next thing I remember was hearing voices over me. It was like I was there in the middle of the conversation, debating my own chances...
"Is he dead?"

"Not yet, but he's a gonner."

"He looks strong, he might make it."
I tried to open my eyes, and the only thing I was able to see was a sign on the wall that said, "HATE WISELY." I must have said hate or something because I heard someone say:

"Yeah. I hate the bastards, too."

I passed out with that sign on my brain... "Hate Wisely..."

I think that sign kept me alive.

(CHARLIE, *slowly comes back to reality.*)

So...

(*Quiet. Both men seem to unwind.*)

I'm tired. How 'bout some wine.

GEORGE (*guilty, but...*)

We... We don't have any wine.

CHARLIE (*rising to occasion*)

Fifteen years you've had that bottle... Come on, George... We've just had a glorious evening...

GEORGE

Sure. But... but... That bottle is for something... eh... (*grasps for the superlative*)... Special....

CHARLIE

Like what?

GEORGE

Like... like...

(CHARLIE *goes and gets the bottle.*)

CHARLIE

How many times have you said "not quite good enough"?

Well, you better write in your will that they pour it on your grave, 'cause the way you're going, that's the only way you gon taste it.

GEORGE

I'm not gonna open it.

CHARLIE

You know? You protect that bottle like a jealous father. Rockin' on your front porch. She remaining "pure" and locked in the house.

GEORGE

We're not going to open it!

CHARLIE

You've got a shotgun on your lap... a shotgun of... of chastity. And you are the last to know that you are simply infatuated.

GEORGE

Infatuated?

CHARLIE

Strung out! Nose wide open! In love with her yourself. (*pause*) You'll never find a moment "good enough" for the wine 'cause then you couldn't keep her. Maybe you should give her a name and sleep with her. How about Cherry? Yeah, I like that. (*Takes bottle in hand.*) Yeah, thirty years is long enough to be bottled up. (*He takes the bottle. He plays with the bottle as he charms it. He rubs his hand seductively along the sides. He becomes exaggeratedly passionate by the end of the speech.*) You are so firm and well shaped. You are the object of my every thought. I dream of you constantly. Your beauty and colore send me into ecstasy... Well, almost ecstacy, because to have you... to have you, would be the only true ecstacy. I want to pour you. I want to smell your exquisite bouquet. I want to feel you rush down my gullet, and warm my insides. I want to taste the vine from which you came.

I love you. I want you. I need you! Are you going to save yourself forever... forever, for the "perfect" one that'll never come? Are you... going to the grave... UNPOPPED!

(CHARLIE *laughs.* GEORGE *snatches bottle from Charlie.*)

GEORGE
Dirty ole man.

CHARLIE
Me? I saw that gleam in your eye at the Club.

GEORGE
You just don't understand. This wine was given us by a dear friend.

CHARLIE
A customer.

GEORGE
We agreed to-

CHARLIE
Who is we?

GEORGE
Judy and me.

CHARLIE
Judy?

GEORGE
Yes.

CHARLIE
When will the "we" share this wine?

GEORGE

This wine... (*having a hard time*) This is more than just wine! (*begging understanding*) Don't you understand? It... It is... It's all those things we never shared. All we missed. Wanted to, but never did. Never can now.

It's like a dream's corked up in this bottle. It's like if I let it out now, I don't know what will happen.

> (CHARLIE *suffers a sharp pain and grabs his side. He tries to hide it from George. GEORGE does not let it go unnoticed. Instead, he seizes the moment to change the topic of conversation.*)

Hey, come on... you would'a thought that bozo hit you instead of me.

CHARLIE (*recovering*)

It's nothing... I was taught to take a punch by the best... and I took 'em.

GEORGE

Yeah... I was the Brown Bomber tonight, wasn't I?... Bam! Bam! Bam!

Joe Louis! Charlie, you really must have been something... Tell me again, Charlie, how'd it feel... being in the ring with a real hero... Man!

CHARLIE

It never happened.

> (GEORGE *freezes*)

GEORGE

(*slowly*) Don't tell me that.

CHARLIE

Oh, I had my chance all right...(*hard confession*) But... I was the chicken shit who took off.

GEORGE

No... No... Don... Don't tell me that.

CHARLIE (*shrugs*)

It's time I told somebody. A dream... but it just ain't true.

> (GEORGE *looks at him for a long, quiet moment.*)

GEORGE

Truth! What the hell is truth anymore? We live. We dream and... and... we lie. We look at what we've done... closer at what we didn't do... So, so what... if in the end a little of our lie sticks to a little of our truth...

You know, Charlie... I think there's a statute of limitations on lies... If you hold on to 'em for over twenty years, they're yours...

Lies... truths too... dissolve... turn into dust... get blown away by the...

(*goes into his old man posture, but as Charlie would do it*)

bellowing of old fools.

(*He laughs lightly, looks at the bottle... then quietly...*)

I think... I think that's what I was trying to say about this wine... Maybe I'm afraid that... when it's gone... I'll be gone...

(GEORGE *takes a long look at the bottle in his hand, looks at* CHARLIE.)

(*nods his head*) Yeah...

(*He goes to the cupboard, gets two glasses and a corkscrew and returns to the table.*)

It's a good year, a good moment, and we are alive.

CHARLIE

We are alive...

GEORGE

We're together... and that's special.

(GEORGE *with much ceremony twist the corkscrew, then, with difficulty uncorks the bottle. He pours wine in the two glasses and hands to Charlie.*)

Let it breath, Charlie, let it breath.

(GEORGE *picks up his glass and starts a bad joke.*)

Well, Cherry, you...

CHARLIE

No! Forget that. This is special. A toast.

"A wine shared with dreams past... And with dreams yet to pass... To Judy!"

GEORGE

To Judy.

(*They taste and savor the first swallow for a long moment. They enjoy relax, and acknowledge their friendship. GEORGE starts to say something a few times. He laughs lightly, enjoying himself.*)

CHARLIE

What?

GEORGE

They are good...

(CHARLIE *starts to question, George cuts him off.*)

Say...eh...tell me... does all "soul food" taste as good as collards?

CHARLIE

No!

GEORGE

There's another thing, Charlie...? Well, I'm white, and you're black.

CHARLIE

(*surprise*) No?

GEORGE

Well, was being black, as rough as it seemed to me?

CHARLIE

Was?

GEORGE

All right, "is"? Like at the club tonight... That bastard.

CHARLIE

Who knows.

(CHARLIE, *grinning and nuzzling up close and chummy to George.*)

One thing I wanna know. (*jokingly*) Can I marry your sister?

(CHARLIE *laughs at his joke, but GEORGE is deadpan, serious and almost indignant.*)

GEORGE

Well, I don't know about that!

> (CHARLIE *stops laughing. He is hurt by George's reaction.* GEORGE *stares seriously at Charlie then...*)

Oh hell, go head!

> (GEORGE *burst into wild laughter, pointing a finger at Charlie, because his joke caught him.* CHARLIE *joins in the laughter as the lights fade.*)

ACT II

Scene V

Next morning. CHARLIE is busy setting up an easel. It is old and in need of repair. GEORGE is at the kitchen table. He is using the typewriter. Papers are all about indicating that he has been working for some time.

CHARLIE
(*completing task*) Now. All I need is a brush and canvas.

Hey, for someone who didn't know what it was for, you sure made a lot of noise with that typewriter last night... and this morning... and- Sure glad I didn't get you a drum.

What were you typing, anyway?

GEORGE
(*defensively*) Eh... just having fun... with something you said.

CHARLIE
Really? What?

GEORGE
About Joe Louis and Jesse Owens.

CHARLIE
What'd you write?

GEORGE
Just fun.

CHARLIE
Let me see?

GEORGE
Uh... no...

CHARLIE

Aw...come on... let me see.

GEORGE

Guess I did write it to show you.

(*He takes a pile of papers from the table and reads from the* TOP *page.*)

"Aah Yes...

Jesse did win the race that day... But everybody knows

it would have gone the other way,

Had not that very day...

Sweetwater Blue, faught...

And put...

Brown Bomber away!

(CHARLIE *is touched.*)

Just fun.

CHARLIE

Eh... What else you got there?

GEORGE

Oh... just more...

CHARLIE

Read it.

GEORGE

Not yet! It's not ripe. You know, I'm surprised Jimmie hasn't found me yet.

CHARLIE

Uh-oh. I guess I should have told you. They were here.

GEORGE

When?

CHARLIE

Yesterday, morning. Marched in ready to take you, period. No questions.

GEORGE

And...? Charlie...?

CHARLIE

They decided they made a mistake. Especially... (*laughing*) when they learned that the George that lived here, was forty-three years old and had a live-in mistress... You see Angie was just leaving... and...

GEORGE

Did you really?

CHARLIE

I did. I told them that the George here, was named George Patterson. I'm sure they'll be back with murder in their eyes.

You angry?

GEORGE

Maybe I'm supposed to be, but I'm not. (*intrigued*) A live-in mistress, huh?

(*They laugh some more*)

Nothing like the love of a good woman... (*Laughter ends. GEORGE becomes pensive.*)

CHARLIE

Tell me about her.

GEORGE

I miss her. The kids think I haven't cried, but I have. I used up most my tears before she died.

(*both men quiet*)

It's funny. I remember times when I didn't even like her. But now... (*sighs*)

It's worse at Christmas time.

(*CHARLIE suffers another pain.*)

CHARLIE

That damn gas again.

GEORGE

You better take care of that.

(*He gets the bottle of wine.*)

Here, have some more wine.

CHARLIE

No. No, you gotta save some for when you're alone with Judy.

GEORGE

Shhh. I know what I'm doing.

(*Pours a little wine in each glass.*)

Judy and I are sharing right now.

CHARLIE

That's what you were writing.

(*He tries to take paper from George.*)

GEORGE

(*laughing lightly*) I told you it's not about Judy. Like the wine, I'll share THIS in its proper time... when it's ripe.

CHARLIE

You laughed a lot today, George... that's good. I think there's magic in this wine.

GEORGE

I know it used to be fun... Charlie... Christmas... Christmas (*muses*)

(GEORGE *drifts into the memory of Judy.*)

Fun... like so many gone things

in my life...

It used to be fun...

I know...

But I can't seem to bring the Joy of it up.

It's like there never was a place inside me for it... 'cause I can't find a spot... soft enough to hold it.

But Christmas?

I've been there. But what did it all mean?

Tinsel? Lights? and the jingle jangle of change I hear now?

So many have come and gone...

only a moment

from Christmas to Christmas... And now the fluff is all I seem to grasp...

When Judy died, Charlie, her death was like a

gift to us because her suffering passed...

I spent forty-nine Christmases with her... and three...

Well, I don' t wanna spend another without her. Christmas... I remember the good times.

I remember one of my first Christmases... I understood all about Santa Clause, the Baby Jesus

and everything. I couldn't fall asleep and when I woke up, the sun was just coming up, and I flew into the living room and... opened ALL the gifts. Then I burst into Mama's and Daddy's room... Daddy had big eyes and told me to knock first next time... I handed Mama the gift I made for her. She hugged me and said she liked the picture of Daddy riding a buffalo... I felt real warm and loved inside.

Love has a way of showing itself at Christmas time.

I   remember when I was sixteen and in love.

I walked to the flower shop, and with all the money I'd saved, bought six beautiful roses... the only gift that could match, or show my love for... Hazel. I walked up to her front door... with "my nose wide open."

"Oh. Hello, Mrs. Cooper... is Hazel home?"

"Hello Hazel. I... I... I just wanted to wish you Merry Christmas."

(He *hands her the flowers.*)

She kissed me on the cheek... and said how sweet I was... and then from behind her pops up Joe Webster!

"Oh, hi Joe. Going together? That's nice. Yeah. Yeah, see you later...

All that money!

Money...

I remember one time when Daddy came and told us that times were hard and that it would be a lean Christmas.

We exchanged gifts that time; things we had made for each other... We gave from our souls.
I gave my little sister a letter in which I promised her I wouldn't hit her for a whole month.

God, that was hard.

We got close that Christmas.

Judy and me... We've had some special times.
We had a baby one Christmas... Remember the doctor said the baby would be here in early February... Something happened... Panic.

I prayed. It really looked bad. I prayed real hard… and …

And when the sun came up, I held a new son... Judy was fine and the baby was beautiful. And later, as I looked at my new son through that awful wired glass, someone walked by and wished me a merry Christmas. Not until then did I realize our son was born on Christmas morning... We almost named him Jesus, but didn't think that was quite right, so we named him Jimmie instead.

Oh, I do remember the good times with Judy. But Christmas is not so grand without you. Too lonely. There's no one I wanna be with, 'cept you... No one I wanna see... 'cept you.

George, George... look around and see all the blessings you've had. I look at the children and I see myself. I look at the sky, the clouds, the moon and the stars, and I see God. I look at a tree and I feel strong... I look into a rose and I see Love. I look into love and I see...

Merry Christmas. Judy!

> (GEORGE *slumps into a soft cry.* CHARLIE *lets him have his moment, then puts his arm around him.*)

CHARLIE

Thank you, George... She's beautiful... just beautiful.

GEORGE

Damn, Charlie, you're a friend.

CHARLIE

Yeah.

GEORGE

I really mean it. Not since Judy... eh... She was something special.

CHARLIE

I know.

GEORGE

You. Eh... Judy. I haven't had anyone I could... You know what I'm trying to say?

CHARLIE

I think so.

GEORGE

My feelings... sharing... eh...

CHARLIE

I know what you're saying.

GEORGE

Kinda funny it's you, though. Kinda like life coming 'round to set itself straight.

CHARLIE

Uh huh.

GEORGE

I saw myself in that drunk last night.

CHARLIE

I know.

(GEORGE *studies Charlie.*)

GEORGE

Yeah, you do, don't you?

Well, Charlie, I have to be clean with you.

CHARLIE

George... We'll never be "clean" with each other.

GEORGE

I...

CHARLIE

There things I've said... done... that I could never share with you. There's no need.

GEORGE

Maybe you're right there, but...

CHARLIE

No need. And life's too short to hold a grudge... Even against yourself.

GEORGE

Some things die hard.

CHARLIE

But they all do... die.

> (CHARLIE *reacts to a strange feeling in his body. Unnoticed by George.*)

GEORGE

Charlie... thanks... Thanks for doing your song tonight... Eh... I have a song for you too.

CHARLIE

A song?

GEORGE

Well, maybe a song. The words, anyway. Maybe you can put the music to it.

CHARLIE

You rascal! Where is it...?

GEORGE

When I finish it.

CHARLIE

Eh, George? You were right... Blue needed to get out.

(CHARLIE *suffers something different than what he's experienced before. No pain, but he is wobbly. It really scares him.*)

GEORGE
What's wrong?

CHARLIE
I don't know. For a moment I felt tired and alone... except for Jenny. I saw Jenny.

(*quickly*) George, promise me something. Let's stick it out here. We can make it. We both have things to do. I gotta paint those pictures...

(CHARLIE *grabs George by the arm.*)

We both have things to do, Right?

GEORGE
Right. So you just take care of yourself. See a doctor and get that... that pain or whatever it is... fixed.

CHARLIE
(*suddenly upbeat*) Yeah, I will. I will.

We can fix this place up... make it a real home. You can make curtains.

GEORGE
Why me?

CHARLIE
'Cause... 'cause... I thought of 'em.

GEORGE
(*laughs*) Well... Well you can crochet little doilies for the table there.

CHARLIE
Deal.

(CHARLIE *walks slowly from the kitchen table toward the bedroom. He stops in the living room and continues in a tone much too serious.*)

I only know I want you to stay. Don't go away... I need a Bear around.

GEORGE
(*touched*) Come on now, let's not get... Hell. Don't you go either... I... I need you too... ya ole Bulldog.

CHARLIE

I'm not about to go anywhere... 'cept lie down a bit... (CHARLIE *lies on the bed. George begins to put away groceries he bought.*)

GEORGE

You sleep, Charlie, and the world will pass you by!

You bum! You'll probably live forever. Didn't think I heard that, did you?

(CHARLIE *does not respond.*)

Maybe you need a birthday and a new age too. How old YOU wanna be.

Judging from the way you were chasing that filly around this morning, I'd say you'd like to be about twenty. Boy did you strut.

Were you really trying to pick her up?

CHARLIE

Would have too... If you hadn't come along with your bag of groceries, and talking about..."It's time for breakfast, Dearie..." When'd you become such a joker?

GEORGE

Who me?

(He *excitedly goes to the bag.*)

Hey! Hey, I bought bacon... two pounds.

CHARLIE

Well, you're getting close. But George, some things beat even bacon.

(GEORGE puts the bacon in the refrigerator.   CHARLIE suffers a pain.)

GEORGE

'Sides, I was only protecting you. That young thing just mighta done you in...

CHARLIE

(*to heavens*) No.

GEORGE

She couldn't be any older than the wine...

CHARLIE

Not now! I gotta fight...

(GEORGE *is still in the kitchen, not really seeing Charlie, but sensing something wrong.*)

GEORGE

No older than Cherry...

CHARLIE

Let me finish one painting... (*shouting*) Eileen!

(GEORGE *can no longer avoid. He runs into the bedroom as CHARLIE struggles off the bed.*)

GEORGE

One painting... you got dozen...

CHARLIE

Not now! Louis... Wait Joe. Joe... I'll fight you! Come on Joe...

(*He throws a left and a right and begins to shadow box clumsily. He falls and GEORGE catches him. He continues to fight as George places him on the bed.*)

GEORGE

Damn it Charlie, wait!

(GEORGE *runs to the table and pick up his papers. He rushes back to Charlie.*)

CHARLIE! WAIT! It's ready. Charlie... This is you. This is for you...

(CHARLIE *is dead*)

Don't you want to hear... hear.

Damn Charlie... Just when I was... You ole son of a bitch... You dirty ole... Bulldog...

(*Knock on the door*)

(*angrily*) Go away!

JIM

Hey Dad, It's us.

(GEORGE *falters a moment, gathers himself, then goes to the door.*)

DORIS

Hello, Papa, how you doing?

GEORGE

Hi kids. Come on in. Eh…Charlie's asleep. We can talk in the kitchen.

DORIS

Come on Papa, we've come to take you home.

JIM

Everything is set. You'll like Sun Village.

DORIS

What he means Papa, is you can come home… if not home, at least we can take you out of this... Papa, just come home.

GEORGE

I don't know why you bothered to come. You don't belong here. It's best you leave.

JIM

Dad, we're not leaving without you.

GEORGE

I don't know who you've come to bury…but my name is George Patterson, I'm forty-three years old, and I'm a bear.

JIM

Dad. Enough of this nonsense.

GEORGE

(*emphatically*) JIM!

(JIM *reacts to George calling him "Jim". He listens.*)
(*softly, lovingly*) Jim…I'm all right. For the first time in a long time, I'm all right. I do choose to stay here. I'm not in hibernation. Winter is over!

(JIM *and* DORIS *see the empty bottle of wine on the table.*)

JIM

Dad? We are here if you need us.

GEORGE

I know and thank you. Now please, I would like to be alone.

(JIM *arid* DORIS *exit.* GEORGE *walks toward the bedroom.*)

Sweetwater Blue Hampton… Sandshiftin Sandman… Shakespeare…Bulldog… You know Charlie… It's stupid to die.

(He sits on the bed across from Charlie. He still has his papers in his hand.)

Well, this is for you, Charlie my friend... No, this is of you.

(He starts to read... but stops, stands and OPENS the window. He sits back down and reads.)

My youth's not spent
it's in my heart like a gift.
Each morning
I untie my heartstrings,
Place the precious twinkle of youth in my eyes,
and challenge the day as a spendthrift.

I celebrate today
for what I'll do tomorrow
And I don't dwell
On the days I've spent,
But on the gift of today alone.

So,
If I never untie another bow,
or hear another child laugh, and
if I never stroke another canvas,
Don't mourn too much for me, cause
I will have spent my life to the
moment...

(George looks at Charlie. He picks up the Charlie Hat from the floor and holds it fondly...pats it. He finally places it over Charlie's eyes the way he sometimes wore it when he snoozed. He stands for a moment looking at his friend, not knowing what to do.)

Charlie ... Charlie ... Oh Charlie ...

(does an awkward "Charlie" like soft shoe... a last heart broken gesture of farewell. He shakes his head... then slowly from the depths of his grief...)

If... I... I want to bellow... (lifts his head defiantly) I'll bellow... I'll bellow... (almost a howl) I'll B E L . . L . . L . . O . . . W . . . W . . . W . .

I'll bellow ... bellow ...

Bellow...

(*George muttering, "bellow" brokenly, almost inaudibly, near tears, head bowed, chin in chest, swaying back and forth. Charlie's head slowly turns one finger slowly tilts hat up one eye opens.*)

CHARLIE

If I knew you were going to make such a ding dong… I'd a checked out weeks ago.

GEORGE

(*incredulous*) Why you… Charlie you… (*sputtering*) wha wha whaaaaaa… (*then his face lights up in a big smile, his body relaxes as it sinks in*) C H A R L I E… (CHARLIE *cocks his head, fixes his hat jaunty - shrugs - grinning from ear to ear.*) Char…

(*and the two friends speak their affirmation of life and love to one another with all the inarticulate beauty and eloquence of the human pantomime as the lights fade on a very happy pair of guys.*)

The End

Second Doctor Lady

A play in one act

by

Endesha Ida Mae Holland

CAST

PHELIA .... The Narrator

AINT BABY .... Middle age midwife

MAN SON MATTHEWS .... A young boy

NURSE .... White hospital attendant

MRS. NATHANSON .... White woman in hospital

DR. FEINBERG .... Elderly General Practitioner

EULA .... Neighbor woman

RUBY LEE .... Neighbor woman

MAGNOLIA .... Woman in labor

JESSIE LEE .... Magnolia's son

BABY BROTHER .... Magnolia's son

MR. JOHNSON .... Magnolia's husband

BUDDY BOY .... Cab driver

TIME: The recent past

PLACE: A small town in the Mississippi Delta

SETTING: On the front porch of Aint Baby's House and other specific areas from Phelia's memories.

PHELIA: Aint Baby and me were sitting on the porch together. She was taking the hem put of my choir robe. And, I had to sit there watching because I was learning how to sew. (*They both wave and call to people passing on the street.*)

AINT BABY: Ahm doin' tolaber well, Puddin—with de Lawd's help.

PHELIA: Hey, hey dere, Puddin. I'll see you later. I'd rather been at the Walthall Picture Show, watching Shirley Temple, and keeping cool in the air conditioned theatre. We sat on the side nearest Miss Sug's house to escape the bright hot glare of "Ole Hannah," as Aint Baby called the Sun. (*Stands and looks up the street.*) Dere go Bro Pastor, Aint Baby.

AINT BABY: (*Waves and calls to Bro Pastor.*) Bro Pastor! Bro Pastor! Doncha fergit to go by and see Suster Morehead.

PHELIA: "Ole Hannah" was some terrible that day. She was bearing down so hard, you could see the heat waves. In fact, it was so hot the flies wouldn't fly. Since Aint Baby didn't have no 'lectric fan, we would sit on the porch trying to catch any breeze that was blowing. We didn't talk much, cause talking just made us hotter.

MAN SON MATTHEWS: (*Excited and frightened.*) Ain't Baby! Ain't Baby! Sweetney call you!

PHELIA: Hollored Man Son Matthews as he came running to beat the band out of Dixie Lane Alley. (*Explain to audience.*) Man Son was dusty from head to foot. He must've come through the sand pile out of Mr. Will Huggins' house, at least that was the quickest way to out house from the Buckete where Man Son's family lived, his six brothers and sisters and him and his mama, Sweetney.

MAN SON MATTHEWS: (*Enters*) Oh, Aint Baby, Sweetney need you real quick. She's crying! Her stomach hurt real bad!

PHELIA: Aint Baby opened her arms to catch the stumbling boy. Man Son laid his cockerburrell head in Aint Baby's bosom and cried and cried, tears meeting under his chin.

AINT BABY: Whoa boy, whoa. Hold it for a minute. Come on it chile, come on in. Phelia you git up and git dis here boy a drink of wader, and one of dem tee cakes. Now boy you set rat here on dis garry and take holt o yoself. Hurry up Phelia, quit slow poking round. (*Phelia enters house.*) Set down son, set down rat here, ever thangs alright now.

MAN SON MATTHEWS: Aint Baby, we better git on back to de house, cause Sweetney is sum sick. She told me to come rat on back, as soon as I tell you to come mere.

PHELIA: I came back on the porch with Man Son's glass of water and tea cake. The boy drained the glass and started nibbling on his teas cake. He had delivered his important message, and now he was satisfied that help was coming. Aint Baby was going to see about Miss Sweetney. Although, I had heard her tell Miss Nollie Bee, Miss Dossie Ree, Miss Susier Morgan and Miss Willie Lee that she wasn't gone wait on Miss Sweetney Matthews no more, cause Miss Sweetney hadn't paid her granny bill from the last baby. I knew Aint Baby's steady voice would soon put Miss Sweetney at ease; her strong arms would encircle her body; her quick fingers would gently pull and push; while her iron eyes would plead with Miss Sweetney to "bear down."

AINT BABY: Ya run on back now boy, and tell yo mama ahm gone be dere in a hour o so. She be alright til I git dere. Tell her dat I be dere soon as I ketch up with Buddy Boy; and den I got to stop long de way to see bout Lillie Mae, cause she is kinda sick too. Run on now boy. (*Man Son leaves through Dixie Lane Alley. Aint Baby enters house.*)

PHELIA: I just knew she was going; she always did. Somehow she managed to catch up with Buddy Boy, the cab driver. When nobody else could find Buddy Boy, Aint Baby could. Buddy Boy would waddle out of his own Chrysler—the one he paid cash for, after he got his pension—he weighted near bout four-hundred pounds. He would catch Aint Baby under one arm, take her "doctor's bag" in the other hand, and lead her to his old trap, and off they would go. Anybody seeing them riding together would know that Aint Baby was on another case. Aint Baby delivered a lot of Black babies in our county. She was even called in to the country hospital to "assist" the doctor with the White women, when they couldn't birth their babies.

(*Lights up on Hospital room. White woman has just had her baby after a long strenuous labor. She is assisted by a white nurse. Doctor Feinberg and Aint Baby. Aint Baby stands at the foot of the bed.*)

DR. FEINBERG: Well, now, Mrs. Nathanson, you are going to be just fine. Isn't she, Aint Baby?

AINT BABY: Yassur, Docdur Feinberg, she showly is! (*To woman in bed.*) Ya gwine be alright now, Miss Nateson, Lawd's willing.

MRS. NATHANSON: Thank you Aintie.

AINT BABY: Hit wusn't me—hit wus de Lawd. (*Lights down.*)

PHELIA: Ever since the time Miss Sweet Chile Brown died trying to have her baby, Ain't Baby hadn't wanted to go to the county hospital to wait on the White women anymore.

(*Lights up on two women hurrying towards Goodson's alley.*)

EULA: You mean dey wouldn't let her in.

RUBY LEE: Gurl, she ain't turned White yet, is she?

EULA: Couldn't dey see she was dying? (*They pass into alley. Lights down.*)

PHELIA: Miss Sweet Chile Brown had bled to death, in the back of Mr. Sonny Love's ambulance, before dey could get her back into her house. When Aint Baby heard about Miss Sweet Chile's death, silent tears had rolled down her black cheeks, until the front of her smock was soaking wet.

AINT BABY: (*From inside the house.*) 'F Dockdur Feinberg hada been at de horsepital, dey da tooken pore ole Sweet Chile in;stead o sending her back home.

PHELIA: Aint Baby would say that for the next year. She had a lot of confidence in Doctor Feinberg. He had talked Aint Baby into becoming a midwife.

(*Lights up on Doctor Feinberg coming along the street. He stops in front of Aint Baby's house. Stands with foot propped on steps. He calls into the house.*)

DR. FEINBERG: Aint Baby…Aint Baby… you in there?

AINT BABY: (*Comes onto porch, looks wary.*) Yassur! Here I is, Docdur Feinberg.

DR. FEINBERG: I swear, Aint Baby, your petunias get prettier and prettier every year…

AINT BABY: (*Uneasy*) Thank ya sur. I tries.

DR. FEINBERG: Aint Baby…Ya'll need somebody to take over looking after the women and all. Since Mama Condy died, there ain't been nobody special.

AINT BABY: Naw Sur, dere ain't…

DR. FEINBERG: Well, I told them down at ththat you're real good with the women.

AINT BABY: I does my best, Sur.

DR. FEINBERG: So, we want you to come down to the Health Department, in the morning, to be certified to be a midwife.

AINT BABY: A midwife! I'll cum down dere, Docdur, but I ain't got no book learning o nothang.

DR. FEINBERG: Now, Aint Baby, that's all right. You'll do just fine—everybody says so.

AINT BABY: Yassur, I does whut I kin. Ahm gwine be dere.

DR. FEINBERG: I know you will, Aint Baby. (*Moves up the street.*)
One day I want you to teach me your secret—on how to grow flowers.,

AINT BABY: Yassur. But ya been saying dat fer de last twenty-odd years. (*Dr. Feinberg exits. Aint Baby enters house. Lights down.*)

PHELIA: Not long after that, Doctor Feinberg had stopped calling Aint Baby a midwife and started saying she was a Second Doctor Lady. She could reach inside a woman's body and do all sorts of things with her hands, things even Doctor Feinberg couldn't do. (*Sits*) I remember one time Aint Baby had a case way out on Duck Hill; and she took me with her. She told me to stay in the yard with the rest of the children. I tried to, honestly. But, my curiosity got the best of me, so I led the line of peeping children to the window, and that's how I got the chance to see Aint Baby do her Second Doctor Lady work.

Miss Magnolia Johnson had thirteen children, already. Doctor Feinberg had told Miss Mag if she had anymore babies she was going to die. But Miss Mag didn't pay him no mind. Her and Mr. Johnson said when the Lawd got ready for her, she would go and not before. So they kept right on, until Miss Mag got in the family way again. And, that's why Aint baby and me were there. (*Phelia moves to the window. Jessie Lee and Baby Brother enter and join her.*)

(*Lights up on the interior of the Johnson's house. Magnolia in bed, legs spread wide apart in readiness for delivery. Aint Baby is seated in straight-back chair, near the bed. Bottle of RC cola sets on nearby table. Magnolia is in labor. She moans softly. Exterior lights on Phelia, Jessie Lee and Baby Brother. They are watching through the window.*)

Well, anyway, we children were peeking through the window when Miss Mag screamed real loud, and almost jumped out of bed. Aint Baby didn't say anything; she just moved her chair and RC closer to the bed. Then she made strange sounds deep down in her throat; and her iron eyes closed for a moment or two. (*Magnolia's labor pains intensify. Aint Baby busies herself wiping and cleaning Magnolia.*)

AINT BABY: Bear down, Mag—not too hard now. (*Magnolia moans repeatedly.*)

PHELIA: Miss Mag was moaning and screaming now. The bed was full of blood and do-do. The more Aint Baby cleaned, the more Miss Mag do-doed. Mr. Johnson heard Miss Mag hollering way down at the Oil Mill. So he stopped work and came home.

(*Mr. Johnson enters the house. He is weary and frightened. With a look of defeat.*)

MR. JOHNSON: How is she, Aint Baby?

AINT BABY: (*Approaches him.*) Take you pantces off, Johnson. (*He looks surprised.*) So dat I can lay dem on Mag's bed. (*He takes pants off, hands to Aint Baby. She zips and buttons them. Places on bed with legs hanging over the side.*) Dis here'll ease Meg's pains, some.

PHELIA: Ease the pain! Frankly, I couldn't see how Mr. Johnson's old greasy, smelly pants could do much good. But I guess Aint Baby knew what she was doing.

MR. JOHNSON: (*Approaches bed. Holds Magnolia's hand.*) Hit's okay, Maggie. De Lawd'll make a way.

AINT BABY: (*To Mr. Johnson.*) Ketch her up round do sholdurs dere, Johnson; so dat we kin turn her head to de Nawth.

MR. JOHNSON: Alright, Aint Baby. (*He gently turn Magnolia. Her head is faced away from the audience.*) Is dis here right, Aint Baby?

AINT BABY: Dat's hit, Johnson. Heist her back up, and let me slide his here ironing board under her. (*She carefully places the ironing board under Magnolia.*) Now dere— dat'll help her a-lot. (*To Magnolia.*) Breather easy, Mag—take shorter breaths. (*Magnolia moans.*)

PHELIA: Miss Mag was moaning now and white stuff was coming out of her mouth. You could see right then that Mr. Johnson was scared. And so were we children peeking through the window.

MAGNOLIA: Lawdy, Lawdy, Lawdy, help me Savior. Ya knows I needs ya Lawd! Help me Jesus, help me.

(*Aint Baby pulls chair to bed. She sits very still. Mr. Johnson stands at foot of bed.*)

PHELIA: By that time, I saw a tiny black foot pop out of Miss Mag's bloody slit. Mr. Johnson's eyes were as big as a saucer. But Aint Baby acted like she was in a trance, cause she just sat there and turned here ageless face to the tarpaper ceiling. Miss Mag was hollering some kind'a pitiful. She kept trying to get up. But Aint baby took her by the shoulders and laid her back on the pillow. Then Aint Baby's iron eyes began to glow. And the muscle right over her left eye started jumping real fast. And then her eyes flowed into her as she knelt between Miss Mag's open legs.

I saw Aint Baby take the tiny black foot and gently push. She pushed until the small foot was back into Miss Mag's stomach. And then, she took both her hands and folded them like she do when she's praying. And then she put her hands way up into Miss Mag. Miss Magnolia moaned so sad the walls were shaking, and I thought the house would fall down. Then Miss Mag passed out. By this time all the children were hollering and crying. Old Baby Brother looked like he was going to faint. Big old Jessie Lee's short was full of throw-up. But I refused to take my eyes from the window.

(Mr. Johnson sits in the chair to the side of the bed.)

Aint Baby had both of her arms in Miss Mag and she was twisting and prodding and talking in a low strong voice. But things didn't look no better. Miss Mag was hardly breathing now, and Mr. Johnson was no good at all. He had pulled the chair up to the side of the bed and he had his hands over his face. But, I could see that he was crying. Aint Baby nodded her head to Mr. Johnson and he got up and stood by the door with just his shorts on cause his pants was still on Miss Mag's bed. (Mr. Johnson rises and stands by the door.) Then Aint Baby took her hands out of Miss Mag's stomach and they were some kind of bloody. The front of her smock was soaked red with blood. She backed into the corner closest to the window, and let me tell you; she started speaking a language I had never heard before. I was scared then, I just knew Miss Mag was dead. Now, the thing that happened next was really what scared me. Aint Baby walked slowly back to the bed, and without touching Miss Mag at all, she began to talk in this strange language again. I thought Aint Baby had gone crazy. But Lawd, have mercy, I saw a black ball appear between Miss Magnolia's legs, the slit was now round. Aint Baby kept making these sounds and moving her arms like Mr. Monroe, the choir director. Miss Mag was still passed out, and Mr. Johnson just stood and looked like he didn't believe what was happening. Then the round black ball just slid out a little, and I could see it was the head of the baby. Aint Baby turned the baby round in Miss Mag's stomach!

(Jessie Lee and Baby Brother begin laughing and hugging each other.)

Mr. Johnson sprang to life. He ran toward the bed and fell on his knees and turned his head toward the tarpaper ceiling. Then he looked at Aint Baby for a long time with tears rolling freely over his worn face. Aint Baby slapped the baby's bloody booty and his cry filled the house. Aint Baby then spit into Miss Mag's navel and added something out of the nature sack she wore round her neck. And then, she took her dog finger and stirred in Miss Mag's navel.

(Phelia, Jessie Lee and Baby Brother enter house. Aint Baby gives Phelia a drink of RC Phelia drinks and then passes the RC to the other children.)

I swear, Miss Mag opened her eyes and reached for her baby. She sat up in the bed and started smiling. All of us children were crowded round the bed trying to get a look at the new baby boy. (Phelia exits house. Lights down on happy interior. Phelia sits on steps.) And shortly after that Doctor Feinberg and the other folks started calling Aint Baby the Second Doctor Lady.

AINT BABY: (Calls from the house.) Phelia! Uh Phelia!

PHELIA: (STARTLED) Mam?

AINT BABY: Ya git up and come go wit me!

PHELIA: Yas'm, I'm coming. Aint Baby stopped my reminiscing. (*Aint Baby enters porch.*) She came out the front door wearing her white uniform, stocking, shoes, and cap. She held her black "doctor's bag" in one hand, and her RC under one arm, then she felt round her neck for the string that her nature sack hung on. Feeling it there, she smiled.

(*Sound of car pulling to the curb. Buddy Boy enters from the street.*)

Buddy Boy's car slid up to the curb; he got out and came up to the steps.
(*Buddy Boy takes Aint Baby's "Doctor's bag" and escorts her to his car. They exit.*)

Aint Baby was going to see bout Lillie Mae and then on to bring Miss Sweetney's little boy on in to the world....

BUDDY BOY: (*Coming back up the street.*) Phelia! Gurl, Aint Baby say ya better come on here; and quit slow pokin round.

PHELIA: (*Moves toward car, stops and tells audience.*) When I have a baby, I'm not gone have no midwife. I'm gone send for the Second Doctor Lady.

CURTAIN

Silent Octaves

by

Brenda Faye Collie

Characters

Benny Williams: A black ex-musician, mid forties

Leella Williams: Benny's wife, black, mid forties

BJ: Benny's son, early twenties, black

Pete Bailey: Leella's brother, late forties, black

Smokey Joe: A black ex-musician, mid sixties

Pigmeat: A black ex-musician, late thirties

Alton Smith: Pete's business associate, black, early fifties

Scenes

Act 1

Scene 1:   Benny's home. Early that morning.

Scene 2:   Smokey Joe's Club. That evening.

Scene 3:   Benny's home. Later that same night.

Act 2

Scene 1:   Benny's home. The next morning.

Scene 2:   Benny's home. Later that night.

Scene 3:   Smokey Joe's Club. Later that same night.

Act 1

Scene 1

The scene opens to a railroad flat basement apartment. Stage right is the kitchen area. Stage center of the kitchen area is a table with three chairs. All three chairs have newspaper in the seats. Up stage center is a refrigerator and a cabinet which divide the kitchen from the living room area. Sitting on the cabinet is a toaster. Stage right is a door which leads into the street and near this door is a suggested window, stove, sink and other kitchen furnishings.

The living room acting area is stage left. Stage center of this acting area is a sofa. Behind the sofa is a small pathway leading to other parts of the apartment. Up stage left is the door which leads into the street. A small arm chair which is located a little down stage left is a bit ragged. Down stage is a suggested window. The characters move freely from the living room to the kitchen during the apartment scenes.

As the lights rise LEELLA, who walks with a slight limp is quickly preparing breakfast. She moves rhythmatically, softly humming to distorted electronic music coming from the radio. She goes to the cabinet, takes out two plates and places them on to the table. She looks at the table, smiling to herself as she goes and pulls another plate from the cabinet, placing it on to the table. She goes over to the pan full of frying bacon. BENNY enters wearing pajamas walks over and flicks off the radio.

LEELLA
Benny, I was listening to that.

BENNY
How can you? Noise is all it is. Wires-plugs. If a permanent power failure would come-they would all be lost. Some fools thinks that's good music. Huh-there're no sockets in the soul.
(LEELLA PLACES A SAUCER OF BURNT TOASTER ON TO THE TABLE. BENNY PICKS UP A SLICE AND STARES AT IT. LEELLA GOES TO POUR ORANGE JUICE)

BENNY
You have to be at work early this morning, huh?

(BENNY LETS TOASTER DROP TO THE SAUCER)

LEELLA
Yep. I find out how I did on my test today.

BENNY
I hope a lot better than on this toast.

(LEELLA BEGINS TO SCRAPE THE TOAST WITH A KNIFE)

LEELLA
You can put some jelly on it. And stop being so grouchy 'cause you didn't want to get up this morning.

(BENNY LOOKS INTO THE REFRIGERATOR)

BENNY
Where's the strawberry jelly?

LEELLA
You know BJ likes that kind too. He finished it off yesterday morning.

BENNY
Looks like everything else in here too. I'll just have bacon and coffee. I'll skip the toast.

(LEELLA BRINGS OVER A PLATE OF BACON)

LEELLA
It's that darn toaster.

(BENNY BEGINS TO EAT THE BACON)

LEELLA
Save some of that bacon for BJ.

BENNY
I saved some for him yesterday. I found it in the box when I came in. Hell, I thought he stop eating bacon.

LEELLA
He might have eaten it, if you would of given him the chance. Asking him twenty million questions. He wasn't in the house long enough to get a good night sleep from the bus ride.

BENNY
It don't take a good nights sleep for him to say where he's been and what he's been doing.

LEELLA
Maybe if you would of came straight home from work, you would of gotten answers.

BENNY
You were home. Where has the boy been?

LEELLA
Chicago. Working.

BENNY
Doing what?

LEELLA
(HESITATING) In a gas station.

BENNY
(CHOKING ON HIS COFFEE) Pumping gas?

LEELLA
(QUICKLY) He fixed refrigerators for a while.

BENNY
If I would of known he was...

LEELLA
Maybe that's why he hasn't written, because you would be pestering him to.

BENNY
Don't blame me because he was too lazy to pick up a pencil in two years. Too cheap and selfish to send even a Christmas card-and had you around here moping and crying Mother's Day 'cause you didn't have a card to put on the table.

LEELLA
I suppose you didn't miss the Jade East Cologne. You haven't touched the bottle since he left.

BENNY
I don't wear that kind anymore.

LEELLA
No, you just stand-staring at it on the dresser holidays.

BENNY
(DISGUSTED) Pumping gas. Christ.

LEELLA
He may go right back, if you keep acting like that. He's home Benny. Finally home. Let him enjoy it. Maybe he can help you and Pete down at the office. He said he worked as a DJ in a small disco-tek. They even let him manage the place the nights they took off. They really liked him he said.

BENNY
(DISGUSTED) Disca-tek. Other people's music. He should of been out there—

LEELLA
Benny, please don't start with that.

(BENNY WALKS OVER TO THE KITCHEN WINDOW)

BENNY
Well it shows. Can't you see it. He can't stay away from music. It's in him.

LEELLA
He quit after a few months.

BENNY
'Course. Playing other people's music and managing a place like that is not him. He always does things ass backwards. But he's home now and I'm going to...

(BENNY POINTS TO THE WINDOW)

Look at that! They're throwing garbage out of the window again. You lazy good for nothings. You want to know why you live in garbage and filth?!

LEELLA
Benny, come away from there yelling, before someone hears you.

BENNY
No wonder the trees are bald. Look at that one-a can of pork 'n beans sprouting from the branch. Have you ever notice that all the trees in New York are bent over?

LEELLA
Benny get dressed it's seven-thirty. You know Pete will be here soon.

BENNY
Hell, even the smallest.

LEELLA
You wouldn't have to see it, if we lived someplace else.

BENNY
We will Lee and when we look out of the back window, we wont see pink napkins covering the ground. As soon as things pick up. I promise.

(BENNY TAKES THE BROOM AND GOES QUICKLY OUT OF THE DOOR)

BENNY
For many moons you've been—Benny come back in here before someone sees you with no clothes on. That can is too high up there and—

(BENNY ENTERS WITH A PORK 'N BEAN CAN IN HIS HAND AND IS PULLING PINK NAPKINS FROM THE BROOM STRAW)

BENNY
We need a rake.

LEELLA
I've just given up trying to keep back there clean and you're still trying. You always want to do the impossible.

(SOUND OF GARBAGE FALLING)

BENNY
(YELLING OUT THE DOOR) God damnit! What do you think garbage cans are for?

(TO LEELLA)

Do you know how much money Pete and I spent on garbage cans last year and the beginning of this one for the buildings? Guess?

LEELLA
I don't want to guess. Pete will be here in a few minutes.

BENNY
Nearly two hundred dollars. And that's not counting for the chains. Some fool steals them-the kids opens the bottom, ties them to the fire escapes and use them for basketball hoops or take the lids and stick their feet in them to make snow shoes. The bums and junkies build fire in them to warm their hands and cook over them. Along with Pete's wasting money, that's one of the reasons we can't move away from here.

(BJ ENTERS)

BJ
What's all the shouting about?

LEELLA
Your father is fussing at the people upstairs for throwing garbage in the back. Remember, how we use to clean up the back area in the building I was the super of.

BJ
Yeh. The time I got a nail in my foot and you were scared to death I would get lockjaw. (MOCKING) "Doctor, Doctor will my baby be alright." (LAUGHING) Telling me, "I'm going to fix you a big plate of french fries with ketchup."

LEELLA
(WARM HEARTEDLY) Go on sit down.

BENNY
(SITTING NEAR BJ) I don't remember that.

BJ
You were on the road Pop. I think in Los Angeles with the Edward Allen Quartet. By the time you came home, I was up bouncing around.

BENNY
There wasn't anything that could keep you down long back then. I guess it feels good to be sleeping in your own bed?

(LEELLA LOOKS FROM BENNY TO BJ AS SHE PLACES TWO SLICES OF TOAST IN THE TOASTER)

BJ
Yeh.

BENNY
Your mother ain't moved a thing, since you've been gone. Notice?

BJ
Yeh. Like I left it.

BENNY
Well she uh... changed the curtains a few times. I... uh painted it the same color last year. We had paint left over from painting time on our buildings. But-uh mostly, mostly everything is the same.

(BENNY SOFTLY TAPS HIS FINGERS ON THE TABLE)

BJ
(FEELING AS IF HE HAS TO SAY SOMETHING) I see y'all replaced the cracked glass in the window I broke.

BENNY
Yeh. Yeh.

LEELLA
Bacon is right in front of you BJ. Your father has finished and he's getting ready to go and get dressed.

BENNY
Wait a minute. I have time. So uh...your mother said you were in Chicago. Couldn't you find any places to play out there?

BJ
I didn't look Pop.

BENNY
You didn't look. Well how do you?...

LEELLA
(PURPOSELY INTERRUPTING) How many eggs do you want BJ?

BJ
None. I'll just make a sandwich when the toast is ready.

LEELLA
What kind of breakfast is that this morning?

BENNY
Probably all he's use to hopping from job to job.

BJ
(ATTEMPTING TO JOKE) Sometimes less than that.

LEELLA
Well you're home now. I'm going to make sure you have some neckbones and ham hocks to stick to those thin ribs of yours. Skin and bones.

BENNY
So, what are you going to do while you're home, besides stuff yourself with neckbones and ham hocks.

LEELLA
Let the boy eat first Benny.

BENNY
What-you're the only one able to ask questions? He can eat and talk this morning.

BJ
I haven't exactly decided what yet.

Benny
Then why don't you come on down to Smokey Joe's with me tonight, when I get off of work. It will be just you and me, and a few old musician friends of mine, who's been stopping down there since they're on their way through town. They're interested in young musicians. You...

(BJ GOES OVER TO THE REFRIGERATOR)

BJ
I'll be busy Pop.

BENNY
Doing what? Look at me when I'm talking to you. You ain't going to starve. You ain't going to lay up around here all day like you use to either. Now...

LEELLA
Don't badger him Benny. He just got back...

BENNY
Badger?!

LEELLA
It means to...

BENNY
Damn it. I know what it means. I went to school. I appreciated what my family tried to do.

BJ
Didn't you tell him?

BENNY
Tell me what?

BJ
I have a High School Equivalency diploma, like Moma's working on.

BENNY
High School of Music and Art would of recommended you to a music conservatory with a scholarship. Didn't they say he was conservatory material? Didn't they? You

have to admit that Lee. What was so important you had to do, you couldn't take advantage of that opportunity beats the hell out of me. Why couldn't—

BJ
No more questions alright Pop.

BENNY
Questions only bothers a man when he has nothing to say. That's it, isn't it? You've been doing nothing but throwing your life away. Your mother has been telling me some of the things you've been doing.

(BJ WALKS AWAY FROM BENNY. BENNY CATCHES HIM BY HIS ARM)

What the hell is it? All of this pretending to be so tired yesterday morning—can't answer simple questions this morning. Too ashamed to tell me yourself.

BJ
Ashamed?! Damnit, you listen Pop—

(BENNY WALKS TOWARD BJ)

BENNY
Who in the hell do you think you're talking to like that?!

(LEELLA GOES AND STANDS BETWEEN THEM)

LEELA
He didn't mean it Benny.

BENNY
Boy, you aint been away that long, that you can cuss at me.

(BJ WALKS AWAY FROM BENNY)

BJ
I haven't been away long enough!

(BENNY ADVANCES TOWARD BJ)

LEELLA
Stop it! Both of you. Bickering like cats and dogs. No one would ever think you were father and son.

(LEELLA SCRAPES HER LEG AGAINST A NAIL STICKING FROM THE CABINET)

Uh...Benny you said you were going to fix that thing.

(BENNY AND BJ MOVE OVER TOWARD LEELLA)

BENNY
Let me see.

LEELLA
It's alright.

(THE TOASTER BEGINS TO SMOKE. LEELLA SEES IT FIRST) Damnit.

(BENNY QUICKLY GOES OVER TO THE CABINET WITH A FORK. HE IS ABOUT TO STICK THE FORK INTO THE TOASTER WHEN BJ RUNS OVER TO HIM, TAKES AWAY THE FORK)

BJ
Pop, are you crazy? That's the first thing I learnt in basic electricity class. Never put a metal object into anything plugged in.

(LEELLA NURSE HER LEG)

LEELLA
You've been saying for two days that you're going to fix that. The toaster is acting up.

(LEELLA PUSHED NEWSPAPERS FROM ONE OF THE KITCHEN CHAIRS)

The screws in the chairs stick into your behind. I'm sick of...

BJ
I'll look at the toaster later and see what I can do.

(BJ EXITS, BENNY REACHES DOWN TO LEELLA'S LEG AS SHE RIPS OPEN HER PANTY HOSE)

BENNY
Did it pierce the skin?

(LEELLA MOVES HER LEG OUT OF HIS REACH)

LEELA
Just a scratch. They can't get infected anymore than they already have been. I'll put on another pair.

(BENNY REACHES OUT AGAIN TO TOUCH HER GENTLY)

BENNY
Let me see how bad it is?

LEELLA
I said it was alright. (SLIGHT LAUGH) Did I tell you what they call me down at the job? Rainbow Legs. (SOFTER TONE) You didn't smell any liquor on his breath, did you? I didn't smell any when he came home last night.

BENNY
No, I didn't smell anything.

LEELLA
You had to start needling him.

BENNY
I didn't needle...

LEELLA
After you promised.

BENNY
Alright, if that's what you want to call it. Lee, sometimes I want to pick up something and knock him up 'side his head. Knock some sense into him. The boy is twenty and all he does is pussy foot around. At twenty – hell at seventeen, me and my horn was out there trying to make waves. BJ just wonders around like a chicken with his head chopped off. What hasn't he wanted to do. No direction.

LEELLA
Can you blame him? A child needs that when they're young. You were out making waves.

BENNY
Not all the time. But you would be happy filling him up with neckbones all of his life. He'd be a jack-of-all trades – a master at none.

LEELLA
At least the day is here, I can give him more than a mayonnaise sandwich when he is hungry.

BENNY
It wasn't all bad Leella. Remember...

LEELLA
For who Benny?

(THERE IS A KNOCK AT THE DOOR)

LEELLA
Get your clothes on.

(PETE ENTERS WITH TWO BOTTLES OF CHAMPAGNE)

PETE
Hey, good morning. (TO BENNY) Man, aint you dressed yet?

LEELLA
He's been up. Just too lazy to put something on.

PETE (TO BENNY)
Well get a move on.

(BENNY TAKES FROM PETE THE TWO BOTTLES OF CHAMPAGNE)

BENNY
For me? Thanks. But I'd rather get my back salary. (POINTING TO ONE OF THE KITCHEN CHAIRS)

Remove the newspapers and sit down while I dress.

(LEELLA TAKES THE BOTTLES FROM BENNY)

LEELLA
Benny stop it. You know these are for me. The two birthday presents he's forgotten.

PETE
That's business champagne.

(PETE PULLS A SLIP OF PAPER FROM THE BAG, HANDS IT TO BENNY)

Take this. Mark it down in your books as business expenses.

BENNY
Three dollars. It matches our profits for the last few months.

PETE
Our past business profits. I've invited over a new associate. Uh, Alton Smith and he's gonna help put us on our feet.

BENNY
Who is he?

PETE
Get dressed and you'll find out.

BENNY
If this is one of your cock-eyed...

PETE
It's the best one I've ever had. Go on. He'll be here soon.

(BENNY EXITS)

LEELLA
Why didn't you call to let me know, that you were inviting someone by?

(LEELLA QUICKLY BEGINS TO TIDY UP THE KITCHEN TABLE AND GOES QUICKLY INTO THE LIVING ROOM TO TIDY UP)

PETE
My phones off. Relax Lee. We're going to be talking about big money. Not what kind of finisher polish you use.

(PETE WATCHES LEELLA AS SHE STRAIGHTENS UP)

Do you need money for some stockings. I know you're not going to work in those raggedy things.

LEELLA
Of course not. I ripped them on a nail, when Benny and BJ were arguing.

(PETE SITS IN THE ARM CHAIR)

PETE
About what?

LEELLA
What don't they argue about.

PETE
Hey, hey don't let that upset you too much. Things are going to be better for everybody after today.

LEELLA
I hope to hell you're right. It use to take a crowbar to part those two. It's Benny mostly. You've notice how he's finding it harder and harder to go to the office. He's restless with the buildings not making much profit. He's not coming home nights Pete.

PETE
Maybe he's...

LEELLA
He came in five this morning. Five-thirty yesterday morning. He thinks I'm asleep when he comes tipping in. I got up this morning and cracked the door open. Do you know what he was doing? Standing at BJ's door staring at him. Like he use to do when he came home off the road.

PETE
He's probably stopping and having a few drinks, a few laughs. The same thing I've been doing more of lately. Me and Alton. Lee, we were out talking 'til four this morning and it sounds good Lee. (SHORT PAUSES) How would you like to walk into an office with leather chairs standing on crome legs, silver ash trays where all you have to do is push a button and the ashes would fall to the bottom. Carpet that makes you think, you're going to sink right into the floor.

LEELLA
It is really that good?

PETE
Bright walls. And we'll let you pick the colors.

LEELLA
Yellow or white.

PETE
L-shaped desks.

LEELLA
And real palms in big pots.

PETE
Sun shining through big picture windows. You can pick the drapes. And when you walk out of the elevator, you can walk right up to the executive secretary and say, "I want to speak to my brother or my husband." And she'll push the button on the intercom.

LEELLA
And we can kiss this place good-by!

PETE
Hell, I might even start smoking cigars. (MAKING A GRAND MOTION WITH HIS HAND) Bailey and Williams Real Estate. This is going to do it for us Lee. The world may be falling apart, but somebody in our family is finally going to make it big.

(BJ ENTERS)

Hey, BJ!

BJ
Uncle Pete. I thought I heard you out here.

PETE
You're looking good. You were asleep when I came by yesterday. Yeh, you look fine.

LEELLA
He just needs a little fattening up.

(BJ OPENS THE REFRIGERATOR AND TAKES OUT A CONTAINER OF ORANGE JUICE)

BJ
What's with the bubbles?

PETE
Business. Hey, you don't—I mean—not as much as you use to.

BJ
No. Even if I did, I couldn't down this stuff.

PETE
A lot better than sitting on a park bench downing Sneaky Pete, 'til your brains are scrambled.

LEELLA
Pete.

PETE
I'm only giving him some sound advise. If you're going to be a drunk, be a high class drunk.

LEELLA
He's not drinking. He's got a high school diploma. He's even completed a course in uh...

(LEELLA HUNCHES BJ TO SPEAK)

BJ
Basic electronics.

PETE
Good. If you ever need anything. You come see Uncle Pete like always. I'll fix you up.

(PETE PULLS A ROLL OF BILLS FROM HIS POCKET. HE GIVES A BILL TO LEELLA)

I was just telling your mama she needs some new stockings.

(PETE SHOVES A BILL IN BJ'S POCKET)

I know you can find something to do with that.

BJ
Thanks. But it's just a loan, 'til I get myself straight.

LEELLA
BJ, why don't you sit in on the meeting with Pete and your father?

PETE
Uh, that's not a good idea. (PAUSE) I'm uh—sure BJ has a lot of things to do, just getting back into the city. Friends to visit.

LEELLA
He can take time to find out what you two are doing. After all it just might be his business later on. (TO BJ) This way you and Benny can—

BJ
Moma, stop trying to play matchmaker between me and Pop.

LEELLA
So you like it this way?

BJ
No, I don't like it this way, but he's hard to talk to.

LEELLA
Try harder.

BJ
You mean, get down on my knees. (KNEELING) Clasps my hands. (CLASPS HIS HANDS) And say, "Oh Pop, forgive me for not living up to your expectations."

LEELLA (COLDLY)
Why don't you try talking with a little love in your voice and less sarcasm?

(LEELLA MOVES AWAY FROM BJ)

BJ
Okay, I'll stay.

PETE
Listen uh, you and Benny can bridge your gap some other time. This meeting means big money and I promised Alton it would be private.

LEELLA
What's private between family? Like I said before BJ may be running—

PETE
But not today.

LEELLA
That's nonsense. I don't see why—

PETE
Just the three of us Lee. (TO BJ) Hey, did you get any wheels while you were away?

BJ
Are you kidding?

PETE
Well, come on out and check out my set, before the agent comes and picks it up. I have to keep it parked in the shade.

(LAUGHING, BJ AND PETE EXIT OUT OF THE KITCHEN DOOR)

BENNY (ENTERING)
Now, what kind of business do we have with this—where's Pete?

LEELLA
Out showing BJ his car. This sounds big Benny. Important.

BENNY
What is it?

LEELLA
He didn't tell me exactly, but when Pete gets like this, he really has a hold on something.

BENNY
I would like it if he would just stop taking over in here. Inviting this guy here without asking me, like he pays the rent.

LEELLA
He has paid our rent a many of times. Let you become his partner.

BENNY
It don't make him head of this house.

LEELLA
I'm going to try not to be late tonight. I'll bring home some Chinese food. We'll treat ourselves with BJ home. You know like we use to. Come home early. It will be just the three of us.

BENNY
Alright.

LEELLA
And Benny, if you're home and BJ is here. Don't be so hard on him. Be pleasant.

BENNY
Alright.

LEELLA
Benny—

BENNY
I'll be pleasant.

LEELLA
What I meant to say was try to show more interest in the business. The only money I—we ever had has gone into it.

BENNY
I've been working on some guidelines Pete and I will have to follow, if we're ever going to get our head above water.

LEELLA
Benny—

BENNY
Yeah Lee.

(BENNY PICKS UP THE FIVE DOLLAR BILL FROM THE TABLE)

Where did this five dollars come from?

LEELLA
Pete gave it to me to buy panty hose.

BENNY
I *can buy you panty hose*! You don't *need* to get money from him for panty hose.

LEELLA (TAKING THE MONEY)
Alright Benny. Alright. I'll see you tonight.

(PETE AND ALTON ARE HEARD OFF STAGE. LEELLA KISSES BENNY ON THE FOREHEAD)

I don't want to be late. I have to change these.

(PETE AND ALTON ENTER THROUGH THE KITCHEN DOOR AS LEELLA EXITS)

PETE
You can see from out here why I jumped at your offer. The two buildings we own are worst than this one.

ALTON
I can see why you don't live in your own.

PETE
Hey Benny...Alton, the other half of Bailey and Williams.

ALTON
Which half?

PETE (LAUGHING)
Funny uh Benny?

BENNY
I see you have been admiring the view.

ALTON
Pig sty is more like it. But most of the buildings down this way are or on the verge of becoming so.

(BENNY POINTS TO THE ARM CHAIR)

BENNY
Sit down, state your business.

PETE
Didn't I tell you he was business all the way. I struck gold when I let him come into partnership with me.

ALTON (LIGHTING A CIGAR)
Then why isn't your business doing so well?

PETE
Sometimes he thinks he's managing bands.

BENNY
The truth of the matter is, Pete here too often mistakes the number of zeroes on a dollar bill. Spends more 0's than he has.

ALTON
We all do that sometime.

PETE
This is what me and Alton has been talking about Benny. Giving us more 0's to spend. The building on 139th Street—

BENNY
Yeh, what about it?

PETE
We've been paying high insurance premiums, right?

BENNY
Yeh. That's another reason we can't move.

PETE
With maintenance and everything else.

BENNY (TO ALTON)
You want to take it off our hands?

ALTON
Buy that decaying pile of bricks.

PETE
You see Benny—

BENNY
Look Pete, I've been doing some figuring and if we cut down, get repairs done—

PETE
Alton don't want to come into business with us on the buildings Benny.

BENNY
Who does?

PETE
Nobody.

BENNY
Then what in the hell are we talking about?

(LEELLA QUICKLY ENTERS WEARING A DIFFERENT PAIR OF LIVELY PANTY HOSE)

LEELLA (ENTERING)

Benny, remember to—

(LEELLA SEES ALTON)

Excuse me.

(ALTON TENSE, LOOKS AWAY FROM LEELLA AS HE PUTS OUT HIS CIGAR)

BENNY
Lee, this is—

PETE
(QUICKLY TO ALTON) This is Benny's wife. My sister.

ALTON
(NOT ENTHUSED) Nice to meet you.

PETE
(QUICKLY TO LEELLA) Aren't you late?

(LEELLA WALKS OVER TO MEET ALTON)

LEELLA
Almost. Nice to meet you mister—

(PETE QUICKLY BLOCKS HER PATH)

PETE
Well get a move on. (PULLS MONEY FROM HIS POCKET) Take a cab.

(LEELLA STARES AT BENNY WHO DOES NOT LOOK PLEASED WITH PETE GIVING LEELLA MONEY. LEELLA PUSHES THE MONEY BACK INTO PETE'S HAND AS SHE STARES AT BENNY)

LEELLA
I have the tokens the school gives me. (EXITING) Benny remember to come home early.

(LEELLA EXITS)

PETE
(TURNS QUICKLY TO ALTON) I didn't know she was still here. (TO BENNY) Why didn't you tell me she was still here?

BENNY
She lives here. (VOICE TRAILING OFF) Not like some people.

(ALTON GATHERS HIS WALKING STICK AND HAT)

PETE
She's alright. Family. She's on this Ceta program, where she is working on getting her high school diploma thing, while she goes to secretarial classes twice a week. They place her on a job while she learns and trains.

ALTON
So.

PETE
Hey, she's alright.

ALTON
You said *nobody* would be here but us three.

PETE
That's all that's here now. Right Benny?

(BENNY GIVES NO RESPONSE)

Sit down. Relax.

(ALTON THINKS FOR A SECOND, THEN SITS IN A KITCHEN CHAIR)

BENNY
Let's get on with it. (HOLDING UP A FOLDER) Now we bought that building for—

PETE
Damn it Benny! Alton don't buy buildings like ours.

BENNY
Then what in the hell does Alton do?

ALTON
I'm renovating a few apartment buildings downtown. I can use a partner for the project.

BENNY
Hold it.

(BENNY PULLS PETE OVER TO THE SIDE)

We can't afford a project as big as that. We're making it now by the skin of our teeth.

PETE
Will you shut up and listen. That's the building you helped purchase after Lee's accident. So you have to be with this all the way.

BENNY
What?

ALTON
We're going to burn it down.

BENNY
You're going to do what?

PETE
(QUICKLY) That way we'll get back all of the high insurance premiums 'cause we're in a high risk neighborhood. Get it Benny. We pay plenty on that insurance. Now, we're going to cash it in.

BENNY
I get that you are both talking like a bunch of fools.

ALTON
There's nothing new to this. It's done all the time Benny.

BENNY (PETE)
Have you forgotten we collect rent from that building. People are living—

ALTON
People live in this one—but the only way the landlord is ever going to make a profit is to set a match to it.

BENNY
Where did you dig this character up?

ALTON
Your business is going right to the bottom.

PETE
He's right Benny. Think. Soon there will be no hope for us.

ALTON
Soon those rat traps will be condemned.

PETE
You'll lose them both—go bankrupt.

ALTON
Rent control won't help you, with a lot of welfare leaches in them.

PETE
We'll lose everything all together. Man, that's what we're facing.

BENNY
Look man, we don't need this. Maybe we can make it. I've developed this plan here that—

PETE
This is instant! Guaranteed! *Now!* I told Alton the name of the insurance we do business with. He knows for a fact from the cases he's been involved with that they pay immediately.

BENNY
How do you know it's guaranteed?!

ALTON
How do you know anything until you try it? You look like a man who—

BENNY
You stay out of this. What do you know about me? *Nothing* at all and I don't know you from Adam. (TO PETE) And I think you know him less.

PETE
Benny, come on man. (TO ALTON) Hey, Alton I'm sorry about this man, but sometimes—

ALTON
It's cool. Sometimes little fish are frightened of the big ocean.

BENNY
And I suppose you are a great big whale, sitting there so smug.

ALTON
And that bothers you don't it? Don't envy it man. Jump in.

BENNY
Envy!

PETE
Come on. Hey. Hey. Cool off. Benny sit down.

(BENNY EXITS, PETE LOOKS BACK AT ALTON)

Yeh. Yeh. Go on in there and cool off some. (FALSE SMILE) He'll come around. It's new to him. Sometimes he gets all worked up, then puff, he comes right to his senses.

(PETE PULLS OUT A BOTTLE OF THE CHAMPAGNE FROM THE REFRIGERATOR)

This will calm us down.

(ALTON GLANCES INTO THE REFRIGERATOR FROM WHERE HE IS STANDING)

ALTON
I'll pass on the champagne. But I'll take some of that Tropicana orange juice. Made with one hundred percent—and that's how I do business when I'm involved Pete. I think you follow my drift.

PETE TAKING OUT ORANGE JUICE)

He'll come around.

(BENNY ENTERS WITH PICTURES, AN ALBUM AND A METAL BOX WHICH CONTAINS AN UNSIGNED CONTRACT)

BENNY (TO ALTON)
You see this?

PETE
Benny, what are you bringing that stuff out for?

BENNY
Shut up.

(BENNY HANDS ALTON THE ALBUM)

Look at this?

(ALTON STARES AT THE ALBUM)

ALTON
An album. So what?

PETE
He cut it with a group he was with.

BENNY
Yeh. That's right. (PUSHES A 8X10 PICTURE IN FRONT OF ALTON) The Albert Holmes Quartet. (POINTING TO PICTURE) That's me with the sax.

ALTON
I've heard of him. He's good.

BENNY
And you had to be good to play with him.

(BENNY PUSHES ANOTHER PICTURE BEFORE ALTON)

BENNY
I know you know who this is? I was to go to Europe with them right before they made the big time. (opening the metal box) Here's the contract right here.

ALTON (NOT INTERESTED)
It's unsigned.

PETE
He didn't go. My sister was in the hospital.

ALTON
Too bad. Thanks for the trip down memory lane. I like to know something about the men I work with, but what does this have to do with the price of tea in China. These souvenirs of your youth.

BENNY
Souvenirs of my youth?! They ain't souvenirs man. That's the second phase of the plan I've been working out Pete. A few musician buddies of mine are in town—and they asked me to come on tour with them. I haven't told Lee yet. I was hoping you would be with me, to hlep her see how good it would be if I was making money on the road while you were back here and—

PETE
Benny, stop talking like a fool—tours. Christ.

ALTON
(STANDING) Well you don't need me.

PETE
Hey, Alton man he's just talking? (TO BENNY) Tell him you're jiving man.

(BENNY GIVES NO REPLY)

ALTON
Show me to the front door.

BENNY (WALKING TO KITCHEN DOOR)

Why don't you go out this way? Youll feel right at home.

ALTON
One of the most saddest things there is, is a man who thinks he can swim, refuses help, as he is going down for the third time.

PETE
Come on. This way. Let's talk. (AS THEY EXIT) Benny sometimes is a little—

(BENNY STANDS AT THE KITCHEN TABLE WITH THE PICTURES, ALBUM AND METAL BOX. HE STARES AT THE CONTRACT AND GENTLY PLACES IT BACK INTO THE METAL BOX. HE STARES AT THE PICTURES AND A SMILE COMES TO HIS FACE. THEN HE PICKS OUT THE ALBUM AND RUBS HIS HAND GENTLY ACROSS IT. HE BEGINS WHISTLING A JAZZ TUNE TO HIMSELF AS HE TURNS TO TAKE THE ITEMS INTO THE BEDROOM. PETES'S ENTRANCE STOPS HIM)

PETE
Are you crazy?! He's an important man. I talked like hell to get him here. What do you want to do? Keep us crawling on our bellies for the rest of our lives. Going on a tour.

BENNY
It's the truth. Man they asked me Pete. They may even give BJ a tryout. I've been sitting in with them some nights and man it feels good.

PETE
And that's all you'll ever get is a good feeling. But Benny this is something that can—

BENNY (HOLDING UP THE FOLDER)
This is the way Pete. Like I told you. This and me out there playing again.

PETE
And how long will that take? FOREVER! (TAKES THE FOLDER AND RIPS IT IN HALF) Forget it! We go *this* way. I got Alton to give me the names of two guys to do it. One may be out of town because of some trouble, but Alton says the other guy can get someone to help him. Thanks to you, I had to pay him just now for this information. He's pondering over if he should even take us on as his partners. Hell, we do this—we can take or leave him.

BENNY
Pete, I don't like this man. Look, all we have to do—

PETE
Remember the promise you made to Lee, when she was laying up in that hospital burnt after the accident.

BENNY
Yeah man but—

PETE
This is the only way that is going to put you into a position to make it up to her.

BENNY
So you won't talk to Lee about—

PETE
Christ! Call them and tell them you have other commitments. And I won't mention anything at all to Lee, you've said here about some band. I have the last of our money here. Alton says it will be enough.

(BENNY WALKS AWAY FROM PETE)

Alton says the first thing we should do is—

BENNY
I don't want to know the details.

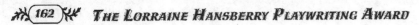

PETE
Now, look Benny we are in this thing togeth—

BENNY
Do it okay! Do it! I'll pull my weight when it's done. I don't want to hear how Alton does business.

BLACKOUT

ACT 1

SCENE 2

As the lights rise BENNY and SMOKEY JOE are sitting at a table. This table is in the back room of SMOKEY JOE'S club, which is in the basement of a building. SMOKEY JOE is playing solitaire. BENNY is drinking a beer.

SMOKEY JOE
So, what did they say?

BENNY
They'll see me the next time they blow through town. Damn, I was hoping they would be here tonight. They have a gig in Chicago—a replacement. Can you dig that Smokey? They were called to replace somebody else. They are really doing good. I sounded good with them, didn't I?

SMOKEY JOE
A little rusty.

(BENNY STARTS TO REPLY)

But good.

BENNY
My lips are out of practice—muscles weak. I don't breathe like I used to. It was kind of hard sometimes holding those long notes, but I was doing it just the same.

(BENNY LAUGHS)

The place is going to be kind of dead since they won't be here tonight.

SMOKEY JOE
Yeah. Those boys really brought back the days of the a Hot Cha's. Ooooowweeee, back in the twenties—thirties—forties this place use to be jump'n. Man, that's when Harlem did the Sciddy-doe-doe. During the wee hours, when the big names would finish doing their thing downtown (LAUGHING) boy you should of seen them making it on uptown. They'd have competition among each other—to blow each

other down with the horns—drum each other out—and slide fingers across keyboards that sung their names.

BENNY
Sure. Sure Smokey.

SMOKEY JOE
You think I'm jive'n?

BENNY
You must be jive'n. As many of those places I use to hang around as a kid. Man, it hurts my heart to see so many of those places gone—boarded up. Shoot, play your card game old man and start talk'n like a fool

SMOKEY JOE
(LAUGHING) They didn't call me Smoke'n Joe for nothing. I could smoke up some Ivory. (VOICE TRAILING OFF) Yeh. Them boys come'n around here, took me back.

BENNY
You ain't the only one. Looks like we all ain't got to go to Europe to make it now.

SMOKEY JOE
Damn, I lost. (YELLING) Hey, Pigmeat come shuffle for me!

BENNY
Now all this place harbors are—

(PIGMEAT ENTERS)

SMOKEY JOE
Leave my man here along.

PIGMEAT
Heey Bennny, the lonng winndedd. You got a case quarter for the machineee mannn.

BENNY (TURNING AWAY)
No.

(SMOKEY JOE TOSSES PIGMEAT A QUARTER WHICH FALLS TO THE FLOOR AS PIGMEAT TRIES TO CATCH IT WITH SHAKING HAND. PIGMEAT GOES TO HIS KNEES CRAWLING TO GET THE QUARTER)

Christ.

(PIGMEAT STANDS AND COMES OVER TO THE TABLE AND BEGINS TO SHUFFLE THE CARDS)

SMOKEY JOE
After this, straighten up and set a couple of traps around.

PIGMEAT (BOUNCING)
Sure. Sure Smokey. (TO BENNY) Heey, I heard you playying the other night Bennny mann. (BEATING ON THE TABLE) Bop... Bop... Bop. You were grrooovve'nn. They—they didn't even recognize me man.

BENNY

Can you blame them? Willy "Pigmeat" Johnson, the man with the beat. Begging for quarters—shuffling cards. What a damn waste. Man get away from me. You were at the top. Really up there.

PIGMEAT
Nahh. Mann nahh. I was beating mann—beating and my hands wanted to do their own thing. I tried to stop them. I tried. I'd—I'd drink every now and then you understand. But after a while. I-I needed something to calm my nerves. Things happen slow you down.

(PIGMEAT GOES INTO A SLIGHT METHODONE KNOD)

Bop...Bop...b

(BENNY HOLDS UP A GLASS)

BENNY
This happened to you. God knows what else is running through your body.

PIGMEAT
Nahh mann. I'm—I'm going to play again man. Make—

BENNY
Sure Pigmeat. Pounding your empties into trash cans.

PIGMEAT
Nahh mann nahh.

SMOKEY JOE
Stop riding him Benny. You turnt those boys offer down today.

PIGMEAT
They—they asked you to play with them?

BENNY
Get lost.

PIGMEAT
They asked you man? If—if I was given that chance—

BENNY
I said—

PIGMEAT
Why?

(BENNY TOSSES A QUARTER TO THE FLOOR. PIGMEAT QUICKLY PICKS IT UP AND EXITS)

SMOKEY JOE
He'll probably sleep well tonight. Benny you have the natural talent of making a man feel small.

BENNY
(DRINKING) Just sit there and play your card game, Old Man.

SMOKEY JOE
You're brother-in-law again.

BENNY
(POINTING TO THE TABLE) Here. Four of hearts. Place it over that five of clubs.

SMOKEY JOE
You shouldn't let him get to you.

(BENNY PLACES THE CARD DOWN, SEARCHES FOR ANOTHER PLAY)

BENNY
Here. Right there. Put that ten of diamonds over that Jack of Spade.

SMOKEY JOE
You aint never gonna get anywhere with him.

BENNY
Nobody asked you. I didn't come in here—

SMOKEY JOE
Alright. Alright. Get another drink.

(SMOKEY JOE THROWS DOWN THE CARDS)

BENNY
I'ma settle my tab soon. Soon Smokey.

SMOKEY JOE
Tab? Bring the bottle in. (LAUGHING) It ain't gonna do nothing but collect dust anyway. (PUSHED CARDS ACROSS THE TABLE) Hey, Benny shuffle for me?

BENNY
Get your slave to do it. Lost playing against yourself.

SMOKEY JOE
Go ahead. Probably can't find Pigmeat right now any way. I'll show you how to play, if you want to.

(BENNY STANDS AT THE TABLE SHUFFLING THE CARDS)

BENNY

Watching you is enough for me.

SMOKEY JOE
But you ain't never sit down and got the full hang of it. It will give you something to do while you sit in your office twiddling your thumbs.

(SMOKEY JOE TAKES THE CARDS AND BEGINS TO LAY THEM DOWN QUICKLY WITH ONE HAND)

You lay your cards down on the table.

BENNY
Smokey, I really ain't interested—

SMOKEY JOE
Wait a minute. Now, from the deck you go one...two...three. Listen up. You'll appreciate this one day.

(BENNY LAUGHS, KNODDING HIS HEAD TO HUMOR SMOKEY JOE, HE HELPS SMOKEY JOE WITH THE CARDS)

Alright. Now, can you place the eight of hearts over this nine of diamonds?

BENNY
Sure.

SMOKEY JOE
I thought you've been watching me play. You can't do that.

BENNY
Yeah you can. Hearts and diamonds goes together. Name a woman that won't give you her heart, if you give her a diamond—and a club if you try and take it back, saying you're just another spade. You ain't too old to forget that.

(SMOKEY JOE LAUGHS)

SMOKEY JOE
Tell—tell Pigmeat to come in here. I got to tell him that one.

(BJ ENTERS)

BENNY
Hey BJ. Smokey this is my boy. You know, the one I was telling you about. He would of given those boys back then a run for their money.

(SMOKEY JOE AND BJ SHAKES HANDS)

Sit down son. Sit down. He's uh...visiting his mother and me.

BENNY
Didn't I tell you?

SMOKEY JOE
So, how did you like Europe?

(BJ STARES AT BENNY. BEFORE BJ CAN REPLY BENNY SPEAKS)

BENNY
He liked it fine.

SMOKEY JOE
I remember back in nineteen forty—

BENNY
Smokey, don't start on any of your old stories. Bring us something. (TO BJ) You drink beer don't you?

BJ
Yeah Pop.

BENNY
Well move old man. Put it on my tab.

(SMOKEY STARES AT BENNY. BENNY GIVES SMOKEY A KNOD. SMOKEY UNDERSTANDING, SMILES AND STARTS TOWARD THE DOOR)

SMOKEY JOE
You see how your old man bosses me around in my own place.

BENNY
If I didn't come in here every once in a while, you'd start talk'n to these cards.

(SMOKEY JOE EXITS)

BJ
Pop, why did you tell him I was in Europe?

BENNY
What was I surpose to tell him, you were pumping gas in Chicago?

BJ
That's what I was doing.

BENNY
Well no more. I've been checking around. There're plenty bands looking for horn players.

BJ
I came to get the key Pop, so I can get into the house. Moma's not home yet. I saw Uncle Pete's car near the house, but not him.

BENNY
Wait. Listen to me. Now one of these fellows I talked to is young—just like you. He's doing small things, but you never know.

BJ
Pop, didn't you hear me this morning. Look, why don't you play with this fellow yourself. (SHORT PAUSE) You're not and neither am I. So, let's just stop—

BENNY
Then what are going to do?!

(SMOKEY JOE ENTERS WITH A BEER AND A BOTTLE OF LIQUOR, FEELING THE TENSION HE LEAVES)

I gave you a gift. When you were little all you wanted to do was play. I couldn't tear you away from that dime store sax. Don't you remember what you use to say to me, "I want to do what you do Daddy." Remember that—you wanted your own horn to play in the Junior High School band. You didn't want theirs. "If I'm going to be good. I need the best." What happened to all that good sense BJ?

BJ
Pop, I want to do other things.

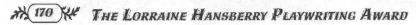

BENNY
What haven't you done. Tried and failed at. What is next on your mind that will hold your interest for ten minutes. You always end up right back here fighting the gift I gave you. What is it? You think I'm going to interfere. I'll stay out. Let you do things your way, but do something for Christ sakes.

BJ
Maybe you're right. I failed at everything. Even being a drunk, but Pop—

BENNY
Thank God, you had sense enough to leave that mess alone. Those fools, sitting on park benches—the great basketball pros to be. Winning community trophies when they're not too high or drunk to show up for a game. Now all they have is a cheap bottle of wine in their back pocket or the ribbon, "Rest in Peace" across their chest. But you still have a chance. I always dreamed you—

(BJ STANDS)

BJ
And that's your dream. Not mine. Not mine! Tell me something Pop, when will the day come that you will say to me, "Fine BJ. Good."

BENNY (STANDING)
When you do something worth it. So far all you've done—

BJ
Pop, you are really—(BARELY ABLE TO SPEAK) I told Moma—one day Pop—ahh, what's the use?

(BJ EXITS. BENNY RUNS HIS HAND IN HIS POCKET, PULLS OUT KEYS, STARES AT THEM, TAKES A FEW STEPS TOWARD THE DOOR, STOPS REALIZING BJ HAS LEFT THE BAR BY NOW. SMOKEY AND PIGMEAT ENTER AS BENNY IS POURING A DRINK)

SMOKEY JOE
Hey, everything alright between you and your boy?

BENNY
Man, what happens to kids when they grow up? They get lost—stupid.

SMOKEY JOE
(TO PIGMEAT) Shuffle. (TO BENNY TRYING TO JOKE) The same thing that happens to many grown folks. (SLIGHT LAUGH) But tired bones and gray hair just makes them more distinguised.

BENNY
Let's go back Smokey.

SMOKEY JOE
Where?

BENNY
To the days when this place was jump'n. We can play again. Fix the place up a little.
You, me, even Pigmeat.

SMOKEY JOE
Who'd want to hear a couple of old has beens like us.

(SMOKEY JOE LOOKS AT HIS FAKE HAND)

Especially me.

PIGMEAT
I want in Benny.

BENNY
(TO SMOKEY JOE) You can sit in some nights.

PIGMEAT
Yeh. Yeh Smokey. (HEARING MUSIC IN HIS HEAD) Bop...Bop...Bop. I—I cann get
my skins from my brother mann.. He's-he's keeping them safe for me.

BENNY
What do you say, Old Man? Right here! In your own place playing again.

(SMOKEY REMOVES HIS FAKE HAND FROM HIS SLEEVE, PULLS OFF THE SOCK
AND STARES AT IT)

SMOKEY JOE
Man, if this could operate by batteries, I stick one in every finger—to hell if finger
nails grew or not. Yeh. Yeh. (WIGGLING THE FINGERS ON HIS GOOD HAND) But
this one—this one can still play a mean melody—

PIGMEAT
(HEARING MUSIC) YEH.

SMOKEY JOE
For my grand daughter. "Play it again grand daddy." She always says to me. And I
play Mary Had a Little Lamb or Three Blind Mice, like I'm on a Jazz mobile riding
through the streets. Man, her giggles are like bravos.

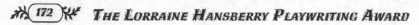

BENNY
Let's stop talk'n about it and make plans to do it.

SMOKEY JOE
Alright. Alright! Maybe they'll start calling me five finger Joe. But, if these fingers could move. I'd dance them up and down a keyboard and turn them all black—crisp—and blow them all away like dust.

BENNY
We don't have to dream about it.

PIGMEAT
I can get Snow Job and his bass.

BENNY
Is he clean of that—

PIGMEAT
Yeh mann. He's on methodone like me. He's clean I swear.

SMOKEY JOE
We're gonna take it back. Yeh, our own musicians club on weekends. We'll change the name to Weekend Forty. Yeh. Yeh.

(BENNY BOUNCES THE KEYS IN HIS HAND)

BENNY
We'll be doing our own God damn dream.

BLACKOUT

ACT 1

SCENE 3

The scene opens in Benny's apartment. PETE is in the living room area speaking on the telephone. He is pacing as he smokes a cigarette. A bottle of champagne sits on the coffee table.

PETE
Two hundred, like I told you...Look I left a message for you hours ago...Why haven't you found somebody to help you?...What do you need an extra guy for anyway? Alright. Alright to look out...That's right. I want it done tonight. Alton Smith, man...Yeh. He gave me your name and number. You're Bill right?...Okay, he said I was to leave a message...What's with the third degree?

(THERE IS A KNOCK AT THE DOOR)

Yeh! (INTO THE TELEPHONE) There's someone at the door... I'm straight. No funny business. Look, you're not being set up. I'm at my sister's place...Yeh, Al the Man. So you know I'm okay...Will you do it for that price?

(THERE IS A KNOCK AT THE DOOR)

Yeh. I hear you! (INTO THE TELEPHONE) Hold the phone. I'll get rid of...Wait a minute...Alright. Alright. Call back in ten minutes. Ten minutes. Not ten hours.

(PETE HANGS UP THE TELEPHONE AND GOES TO THE FRONT DOOR)

Alright! Alright!

(PETE OPENS THE DOOR. BJ ENTERS)

BJ, uh—I almost forgot you live here now.

BJ
Do I?

PETE
Uh—nobody's here and I'm waiting for this call.

BJ
A chick or business?

PETE
(WINKING) What do you think? You know how it is? They can cut off my phone, but nothing changes.

BJ
It damn sure don't.

(BJ SITS ON THE SOFA. PETE LOOKS AT HIS WATCH, PULLS A PACK OF CIGARETTES FROM HIS POCKET, BEGINS TO LIGHT ONE)

BJ
Can I have one of those?

(PETE QUICKLY HANDS HIM THE LIT CIGARETTE)

PETE
Here, take this one.

BJ
What is it, Uncle Pete?

(BJ RESTS HIS HEAD ON THE BACK OF THE SOFA)

PETE
(LOOKING AT HIS WATCH) What is what?

BJ
You go away. Come back. Thinking things will be different. Surrender to that urge to come home.

PETE
You and Benny?

BJ
Yeh. Me and Pop. I tried to talk to him tonight when I went to him for the key. On both points I came out empty.

PETE
Well, maybe in a while you and Benny will eventually patch things up. (PULLING A COUPLE OF BILLS FROM HIS POCKET) Hey, you don't want to sit around here. Go on out and—

BJ
When will that happen? In the afterlife? Listen to me Uncle Pete. I don't want to play the horn. That's not why I came home.

PETE
Then why don't you go back to where Benny is and tell him. Look, uh—BJ right now I really don't have the time—this is an important call and—

(BJ STANDS QUICKLY WALKS TOWARD THE FRONT DOOR)

BJ
Sure. Sure Uncle Pete. I understand. You have too many important things to do. Everybody is doing something important buy BJ. BJ is doing nothing.

PETE
Wait a minute. Sit down.

(BJ SITS ON THE SOFA. PETE POURS HIM A CUP OF CHAMPAGNE)

This shouldn't hurt you.

BJ
I don't feel what he feels anymore. I don't think I really ever did.

(PETE PLACES THE CUP INTO BJ'S HAND. BJ RUBS THE CUP BETWEEN HIS HAND AS HE STARES AT IT)

I just wanted to be with him the times I could. The sweat pouring down his face— his eyes shut tight—swinging that sax in the air—his rocking—bouncing—fingers weaving up and down. It made me feel good sitting on the edge of the stage. "That's my Daddy," I'd think to myself, staring out at the audiences who'd be clapping, whistling. He was someone special, which made me someone special—'cause I was his son. But I was a kid then. I don't want to imitate him anymore.

(BJ PLACES THE UNDRUNK CHAMPAGNE ON THE COFFEE TABLE. PETE PICKS IT UP)

PETE
(DRINKING) Understandable.

BJ
Oh yeh. (SHORT PAUSE) To Pop, I'm still that damn kid with a dime store sax, sitting on the edge of the stage.

PETE
A stage he's not on anymore himself. He's doing other things.

BJ
Damn that old bastard! Nothing changes uncle Pete. Not a God damn thing.

(PETE PICKS UP THE BOTTLE OF CHAMPAGNE, POURS HIMSELF MORE)

PETE
(LOOKING AT HIS WATCH) What are you going to do now?

BJ
I don't know. Get a job. A room. I shoudn't of come back to this house. Get some cash. Then go back West or maybe down south. Florida or Something.

PETE
Running away like you did before. You ain't going to do like you did before, are you? Not giving your mother a word. You're her only boy.

BJ
I'm not a boy anymore.

PETE
Alright. Alright. Her only child. Offspring. (SHORT PAUSE, SLIGHT LAUGH) My old man use to say to me, "You're the only boy." But talk is cheap BJ. (TURNS TO BJ) You can prove Benny wrong. Hell, your grandfather was just as bad with his bad mouthing. (SHORT PAUSE) I wish he was here today. Right now! (DRINKS) No. Tomorrow. Tomorrow is when I wish he would just rise himself out of the grave and *stand* right here before me. I'd look that old man straight in the eye and say, "Look at me. Look at me!"

BJ
Yeh. Tell him that Uncle Pete.

PETE
That old man use to whip my tail so bad, my butt looked like it had ridges. I use to stand on the bathroom sink and look at it in the bathroom mirror. Red welt looking like a painter had later taken a brush and touched them up with deep purple. Tiny beads of blood would stain my underclothes for days, as I would sit on my knees with my friends, trying to pretend my body wasn't sore. Hell, I didn't see anything wrong with hanging on the corner—not going to school. What did hard work ever do for him? Not a damn thing. He got tired of whipping my tail after awhile and said to me one day, as he was about to lay that extension cord on my back, "You ain't nothing. You ain't never going to be nothing. So be the best." (SLIGHT LAUGH) You should of seen his face when I bought the first building from the City for a dollar to renovate it and make it work. He told everybody's grandmother that someone in our family going to own something. (MOCKING HIS FATHER) "It's good to see you moving further than me. That's how it's suppose to be." He died with a damn smile on his face and I've been living in hell ever since. (DRAINING THE

BOTTLE) Yeh, I wish he was here tomorrow. I'd take him down and buy him a new suit—some bad ass shoes and march him right back to the grave—twist his arm—pull the bone from the sleeve if I had to and tell him, "Admit I'm something. No matter how I got there. Admit I'm something, 'cause I ain't never going to be buried in borrowed clothes."

(PETE THROWS THE CHAMPAGNE BOTTLE IN THE TRASH. SHORT PAUSE.)

BJ
(SOFTLY) Uncle Pete?

PETE
(TURNS TO BJ) You have to do things. Things like me and Benny are doing. But we need help.

BJ
Pop didn't say anything to me about y'all needing help.

PETE
Don't worry about it. You just get your job and run off. Me and Benny will see that things get done. See that your Moma don't have to keep working when her legs pain her. We'll take care of it.

BJ
If there's something I can do I'll—

PETE
Forget it alright. Just forget it. There is nothing you can do. So go on in the backroom or outside someplace. I don't want you around when I get this call.

(BJ WALKS TOWARD THE DOOR, STOPS, TURNS)

BJ
It has something to do with tomorrow don't it? What is it?

PETE
I said—

BJ
Don't treat me like Pop, Uncle Pete!

PETE
Tell me something boy? Have you ever done something that would put you in jail? I don't mean stealing bubble gum from the candy store man. Hell, we've all done that. I mean something big.

BJ
Like what?

PETE
Arson for insurance money.

BJ
What are you going to do that for?

PETE
For money, fool. I just told you. That's what that fellow Alton was doing here this morning. Me and Benny are going to burn down one of the buildings.

BJ
Do people still live in it?

PETE
Yeh. Do you want to go along with this guy Bill or do we ave to bring in an outsider?

BJ
Uncle Pete, I don't know. Pop is involved with this?

PETE
Forget it. I think you see now why he didn't tell you about it.

BJ
Wait a minute.

PETE
I don't have a minute. He'll be calling in a minute. Now either you're in and we keep this a family thing or you can run off to Florida or where ever. But don't come complaining to me the next time you come home, 'cause Benny still sees you as a kid sitting on the edge of the stage. He's on this stage now! Now do you want to show him you're worth something? He don't even have to know you're involved.

BJ
(THINKING) Not—not until I want to hell him.

PETE
And then, if you want to go to Florida, you can go.

(PETE HOLDS ENVELOPE FULL OF MONEY BEFORE BJ)

This is how much we're paying the buy Bill. You'll get the same. Even a bonus. It will start you off right.

BJ
I might just stay here. The City has some good training schools.

PETE
You can take your pick.

(THE TELEPHONE RINGS TWICE)

Answer the phone.

(BJ A LITTLE HESITANT STANDS STARING AT THE PHONE)

If you study long, you study wrong. Pick up the phone boy.

(BJ QUICKLY PICKS UP THE TELEPHONE)

BJ
(SPEAKING INTO THE TELEPHONE) Yeh...he's standing right here.

PETE
Yeh...You don't have to worry. I have somebody. Family.

LIGHTS FADE

ACT 2

SCENE 1

The scene opens in BENNY'S apartment. LEELLA is sitting at the breakfast table. BENNY enters whistling. He is wearing pajamas. LEELLA stares at him curiously, pretending not to be paying much attention. BENNY goes straight to the refrigerator.

BENNY
Morning.

LEELLA
What was that you brought home last night, in that package?

BENNY
BJ drink up all of the orange juice?

LEELLA
And it looks like all of the liquor he could find. What did you say to him last night, when he went to that place to see you?

BENNY
Nothing. Nothing at all. I was just as you wanted me to be—pleasant.

LEELLA
Pleasant don't look the way he did, when he came in here last night.

(BENNY CONTINUES TO WHISTLE)

Benny, do you hear me? He came in here, looking like something the cat dragged in. Like he was fighting—his hand was bandaged and he was filthy.

BENNY
I tell you Lee, I was pleasant. We got to talk'n. He even forgot to take the key. Now, fix me a couple of eggs.

LEELLA
Eat egg rolls.

(BENNY LOOKS IN THE REFRIGERATOR, PULLS OUT A BOX OF CHINESE FOOD)

BENNY
Look Lee, I'm sorry I didn't—

LEELLA
What I want to know is—is it for me?

BENNY
What?

LEELLA
The package. Is it something for me, since you didn't come home last night, after promising me you would?

BENNY
I'm sorry Babe. I couldn't get away.

LEELLA
I see. You were to busy to come home. Had more important things to do, than be home like I asked you to. Out with your friends. You didn't even ask me how things went for me yesterday. I've just been sitting here waiting for—

BENNY
How did things go?

LEELLA
Fine. I only made six errors on my typing test. I typed sixty-nine words per minute. They are sure I'll be able to be placed somewhere typing fifty words a minute.

BENNY
Good Lee.

LEELLA
What's in the package you brought in here then—if it's not for me?

BENNY
I picked up a sax last night—cheap at a pawn shop. A friend of mine, Smokey Joe, down on Lenox, knows the guy.

LEELLA
You talked BJ into—

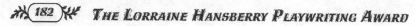

BENNY
It ain't for BJ, Babe.

(LEELLA QUICKLY GATHERS HER STENOGRAPH BOOK FROM THE SOFA)

LEELLA
I don't want to be late this—

BENNY
Lee, it's just a few guys. A hand full of us playing every now and then.

LEELLA
And then more and more.

BENNY
No Babe.

LEELLA
Until you have a gig here and then one there. I don't want to hear it Benny. Just take it back.

BENNY
It's a club of ex-musicians.

LEELLA
Who's gonna want to become active again. And you'll be right there leading the pack.

BENNY
I'm telling you, it ain't like that.

LEELA
Me? You're telling me? This is me you're talking to. I kow you Benny.

BENNY
Then you know how much this means to me.

LEELLA
I'm leaving for work. Work. That's how people live in this world. They don't leave something like that business deal between you, Pete and that fellow that was here yesterday. Something that Pete says will really pull us forward.

BENNY
Who said anything about I was going to stop working with Pete?

LEELLA
We've been through this before. I listened to you when you wanted to go back—
(MOCKING). "Play again just one more time." God knows where you would of been
in that job.

BENNY
Some big job. Twenty desk crammed in a room. Men breathing down my neck as I
tried to sell those ads. Saying exactly what was on those cards. Word for word into
that phone. Christ.

LEELLA
They put your name on the blackboard—we were doing good, 'til some old musician
friends started talking to you about playing again.

BENNY
That was a whole lot different from this Lee. Besides that job wasn't me anyway. By
the time I could sit back, see my name on the blackboard, somebody else's name
was up there.

LEELLA
And by the time the group you was with started to make some progress, another
musician was in your place.

BENNY
We just couldn't get along. But I could of done well with Edward's group in Europe.

LEELLA
Sure! You liked it when I was mopping piss out of hallways. Shoveling coal into
exploding boilers. You didn't care that I—

BENNY
Stop it, Lee.

LEELLA
How many—how many gigs did you play when you were blowing, "You Made me
Love You," in front of Macy's? Who gave you work?

BENNY
Those were slow times.

LEELLA
Riding up and down subway cars with a sign around your neck, "I am blind. Give
what you can. God Bless You." Shaking your tin cup for nickles and dimes. I ain't
young no more Benny, to sit and wonder will you bring enough money home to pay
bills. In the hospital—

BENNY
Damn it, I haven't forgotten—

LEELLA
And I ain't forgotten how you put that damn horn before me.

BENNY
I tried that night Lee. I tried—

LEELLA
You said you tried.

BENNY
No Lee—

(LEELLA WALKS AWAY FROM BENNY)

LEELLA
You tried alright. When it was too late.

BENNY
Listen to me Lee—

LEELLA
I don't want to be late.

BENNY
We use to be able to talk Lee.

LEELLA
I don't have time.

BENNY
Take time. Sit down Babe. People need time for themselves. Slow down. You look tired Lee.

LEELLA
I guess I should stop pushing so much. I just know if I try, I can get up to seventy- maybe seventy-five words per minute.

BENNY
Sure you will Lee.

LEELLA
Those young girls in my class type like lightening. Fingers justa going. (LOOKING AT HER HANDS) My fingers do get stiff sometimes.

(BENNY TOUCHES HER FINGERS)

BENNY
I bet you're right up there with them

LEELLA
(MOVING HER HAND AWAY) Oh I try now. They don't leave me too far in the dust. (SHORT LAUGH) But my back do ache sometimes, when I don't sit just so.

BENNY
(WARMLY, A FALSENESS) But you hang right in there. Lee, you know, sometimes you could come down to the club—hear me play—

(DOESN'T GIVE LEELLA TIME TO REPLY)

You can—you can bring the girls from your job some nights. (SLIGHT LAUGH) Remember, how jealous your friends were the night I met you in that club?

LEELLA
I don't know why. All you was doing was showing off during your solo.

BENNY
I was playing just to you, even though a few of them were winking.

LEELLA
You were looking good coming over to me with that reed hanging out of your mouth—with that thing strapped to your neck.

BENNY
The stage lights really made that baby sparkle.

(LEELLA STANDS)

LEELLA
Yeh. You looked ten feet tall, (THINKS) then.

BENNY
Wait a minute Lee. Sit down. (SLIGHT LAUGH) Remember, when you'd tell me, "I don't want no other woman's face reflecting on this sax." And you'd wipe it off 'til it glittered. Now, Lee these fellows—

LEELLA
It don't glitter for me no more, Benny. I ain't the giggling girl in that club you serenaded—

BENNY
What happen to her, damn it?

LEELLA
She's married to an ex-musician.

(SHORT PAUSE)

Get dressed for work Benny. I have to get—

(BJ ENTERS WITH A NEWSPAPER UNDERNEATH HIS ARM)

BENNY
What happened to your hand?

BJ
Oh this? I've been out playing basketball, Pop. Winning trophies to show you. (HOLDING UP HIS HAND) Isn't this pretty. (IN PAIN) Damn.

LEELLA
Come sit down. Will you tell me now how—

BJ
I don't want to sit down. Is that alright Pop? Can I stand? Permission to stand Pop?

BENNY
What the hell is wrong with you? (REACHING FOR BJ'S HAND)

BJ
I think you'll want to see this first. (BJ HANDS BENNY THE NEWSPAPER) Puff—up in flames.

(BENNY READS, THEN SLOWLY LOWERS THE NEWSPAPER. HE SLOWLY WALKS OVER TO THE LIVINGROOM AREA WINDOW.)

LEELLA
What is it? (PICKS UP THE NEWSPAPER) Good God. "TWO DIE IN HARLEM BLAZE." Don't you think you or Pete should go down and see—

BENNY
Let me think Lee.

LEELLA
I can imagine how the parents of those children are feeling now.

BJ
Pretty bad I suppose.

LEELLA
They ought to set the ones responsible to flame. They know it's some arsonist. We put all the money we have into that building and to lose it—

BJ
(LIGHTING A CIGARETTE) It's insured isn't it, Pop?

(BENNY GIVES NO REPLY)

LEELLA
Thank God for that. Still those children—

BENNY
Shut up, will you Lee.

BJ
Don't you even care, how the parents feels, Pop? To know that their children's flesh was burning—bones giving off a glow like charcoal at a bar-b-que.

LEELLA
BJ—

BJ
Or maybe you want to just think about their pain as their nerve endings shot it through their bodies. Their crying, their sleeping, clothes burning like a torch eating away at their hair, crackling. How it smelt when they found them in the closet.

BENNY
That's enough. What are you drunk, is that it? Or have you been out there smoking that dope shit? Now, either you sit down or lay down.

BJ
I thought you would like to hear. You're never around when things like this happen. Is he mama?

BENNY
Alright. You made your point. I would of been there with your mother when she had her accident. I would of done anything to prevent what happened.

BJ
Accidents are prevented by never happening at all!

BENNY
That is, isn't it? That's what you hold against me, because I wasn't there. (TURNS TO LEELLA) And you never told him.

LEELLA
There was never anything to tell.

BENNY
That's it. (TO BJ) Admit that's what it is? That's what you hold against me. My not being there.

BJ
I don't hold a damn thing against you, Pop. You're not worth that much thought.

(BENNY MOVES TOWARD BJ. LEELLA STEPS IN BETWEEN THEM)

LEELLA
(SOFTLY) Just go and get dressed, Benny.

(BENNY LOOKS HARD AT BJ, THEN EXITS. BJ BEGINS TO UNWRAP THE PAPER FROM THE SAX)

BJ
What's this?

LEELLA
Get it out of here.

(LEELLA PUSHES THE SAX ACROSS THE TABLE)

BJ
He never stops.

LEELLA
He wants to play again. Start a club of all things. BJ talk to him and—

BJ
Moma. I'm tired of talking to him and I've talked enough for him.

LEELLA
Has so much—

BJ
Look moma—

LEELLA
Have you grown to hate him so much, you won't even talk to him to make him see the mis—

(BJ WALKS TOWARD THE KITCHEN DOOR)

BJ!

(BJ STOPS)

BJ
What in the hell do you want from me?

LEELLA
To help me!

BJ
BEAT IT WITH A HAMMER, LIKE YOU DID THE LAST ONE MOMA! Just leave me alone!

(THERE IS A KNOCK AT THE FRONT DOOR. LEELLA GOES TO THE DOOR, PETE ENTERS)

PETE
Hey BJ, I want to talk—

(LEELLA STEPS IN FRONT OF PETE)

LEELLA
Pete I have to talk to you—

(BJ EXITS OUT THE KITCHEN DOOR)

PETE
Later baby.

LEELLA
I know about the fire, but first (WHISPERS) Benny, he's—

PETE
Everything is going to be fine. Hey, ain't you late for work?

(BECOMING ANGRY LEELLA GATHERS HER STENOGRAPHY BOOK AND POCKETBOOK)

LEELLA
Yeah. Yeah. (VOICE TRAILING OFF) Don't want to be late.

(LEELLA SLAMS OUT THE FRONT DOOR, PETE RUSHES TO THE KITCHEN DOOR, SIGNALS BJ TO COME)

PETE
Come here man!

(BENNY ENTERS)

BENNY
PETE! (FLINGS NEWSPAPER AT HIM) You said nobody would get hurt.

PETE
What do you think, I wanted it this way?

(PETE NEAR KITCHEN DOOR SIGNALS BJ TO WAIT)

BENNY
"Everything will be fine." Like hell they're fine. Getting some damn fools that didn't know what they were doing.

PETE
Alright. Alright, some mistakes were made.

BENNY
Some people are dead!

PETE
Pull yourself together. What do you think, I don't care? I, I'm sorry. Okay, sorry. But I can't let that get to me and neither can you. Benny, this is it! We are on our way. Now, our next step is to go down to the office—business as usual.

BENNY
Sure, we'll collect the rent and answer the phone to the complaints. And to all those living—we've put out into the street—Merry Christmas, you running—choking—procession salvaging fools. Just thought we would save you the trouble of paying your rent next month.

PETE
Look, what's done is done. I'm not going to let you ruin everything. We own that building together, remember. Which means we're in this together. You carry your weight.

BENNY
Twenty-five families. What in the hell I could have been thinking of to go along with—

PETE
Forget that will you and go and get dressed, so we can get those papers filled out and be there early when they trace us as the owners. Hell, they're probably better

off. The city will put them into a fancy hotel for Christmas, the Red Cross will give them food, the Salvation Army will see to it they have presents. By New Years they'll be in the City Projects filling out housing complaints against them. Things will keep moving and we have to do the same.

BENNY
Man, you are really—

PETE
I want to be at the office by eight-thirty this morning Benny.

(BENNY EXITS. PETE WALKS TO THE KITCHEN DOOR, STEPS OUT, IS DRAGGING BJ IN)

BJ
You lied.

PETE
Shut up. You stupid—

(BJ PULLS AWAY FROM HIM)

What went wrong? You didn't go did you?

BJ
I went. I swear it. I found the guy Bill. He was waiting right where he said he would be. But something went wrong—

PETE
I know that fool. What?

BJ
We were running and he fell—before we could get to the other roof. Then the smoke—

PETE
Where is he?

BJ
I left him. I had to. His leg was busted. I couldn't jump with him. We didn't think it caught the first time. We went back. Poured the gasoline—and—and the flames. He tripped over loose bricks. His leg went through the roof. I dragged him out, but I had to leave him. His leg was bubbling—the smell—his screaming. A fire ladder was coming along the edge. I saw it coming through—through the smoke. I said, "Let me go man, they're coming." The roof was getting hot—sticky. My feet was getting hot. So, I hit him! Hit him! 'til he let me go. Made it over to the other side. That building was going up so fast.

PETE
Why didn't you meet me like I told you to?

BJ
I—I wasn't thinking. I went to the drug store and got something for my hand—then I just tried to get the smoke out of my lungs—I started to think, maybe Pop would be there.

PETE
The next time I give you a plan, you follow it. He wasn't there.

BJ
Uncle Pete, I have to get away from here.

PETE
Sit down.

BJ
The money—money you promised me.

PETE
Yeah, what about it?

BJ
Where is it? Man, I got to get away from here.

PETE
You and your old man are just alike. When things get a little rough, you want to run and hide. There is no money to give you—

BJ
You said two hundred and fifty.

PETE
And you said you could help do the job right. But things change, like plans change. Are you sure Bill is dead?

BJ
I don't know with all of that smoke.

PETE
It's important that you know BJ. If you would of used your head, you would have money. Bill was laying on that roof, right in front of you. What the hell you think was in that envelope, I told you to give him? Matches?

BJ
I wasn't thinking.

PETE
Then you wait, like the rest of us.

(PETE PULLS A BILL OUT OF HIS POCKET, GIVES IT TO BJ)

BJ
Ten. Look, I almost got killed out there and all you're giving me is a—

PETE
Enough to keep you in sheet music. You pretend to be interested in music for a while. Try to get along with Benny, for your mother's sake. And pray Bill is dead. And if he is, I'll pay you—when I get it. But if he's not, what are you going to do with the money anyway? How far will it take you, when they track you down like the rest of us? I learnt something a long time ago. There's just so far you can make it in this world, if you allow yourself to become frightened too fast. You take things easy. Easy. Or you're dead before you start.

(PETE TAKES A FEW STEPS TOWARD THE FRONT DOOR)

Hey, Benny get a move on, it's eight-thirty!

(TURNS TO BJ)

We're in this together. Remember that.

BLACKOUT

ACT 2

SCENE 2

The scene opens in BENNY'S apartment. LEELLA is in the kitchen area hammering a nail into the kitchen cabinet. The toaster lies in pieces on top of the cabinet. One of the kitchen chairs is on the floor turnt over. BJ is asleep on the sofa in the living room acting area. BENNY enters through the kitchen door, carrying the saxaphone case. The case has a small silver lock on it. He has been drinking a bit.

BENNY
Don't say nothing to me Lee.

(LEELLA BEGINS TO HAMMER LOUDER. BENNY TURNS THE CHAIR RIGHT SIDE UP)

You didn't have to fix the chair.

LEELLA
Things have to get done.

(LEELLA BEGINS TO DIG INTO THE TOOL BOX AND TAKES OUT A SCREW DRIVER AND A LARGE SCREW)

BENNY
I just had a couple.

LEELLA
You and BJ both. He just stumbled in a while ago. You wanted him like you. Look at him over there on the couch.

(BENNY WALKS OVER TO THE REFRIGERATOR, OPENS IT, PULLS OUT A BOX OF CHINESE FOOD)

BENNY
Chinese food taste good the second day.

(LEELLA STRUGGLES WITH THE SCREW)

LEELLA
Ain't nothing good when it's old. Cooking it over don't make it better.

BENNY
Me and Pete filt out the insurance papers. Talked to the investigator. Everything is fine. (SOFTLY) Fine.

(BENNY SITS PLAYING IN THE CHINESE FOOD)

LEELLA
When will the check come through?

BENNY
The check will be in the mailbox soon, he said. Real soon. Arson. It's not our fault. (VOICE TRAILING OFF) Not our fault. (STARING AT LEELLA) That screw is too big.

(LEELLA DIGS IN THE TOOLBOX AND TAKES OUT A NAIL AND BEGINS TO HAMMER. BJ TURNS ON THE COUCH)

Wait a minute. Wait a minute Lee.

(BENNY KNEELS DOWN BESIDE HER)

LEELLA
I just want it fixed. As long as it stays up I don't care.

BENNY
It's just going to come apart again.

LEELLA
Like everything else in this place. I gave BJ some hot sauce to make him throw up. It made him feel better. Do you want some?

BENNY
No. Get up from there Lee. I'll fix it later.

LEELLA
When? When will you have the time with the job—and playing with your club? When do you ever have the time to do some of the things I want—need for you to do?

BENNY
With BJ home now—

LEELLA
(STANDING) BJ?—Why isn't he going on the road soon? That's the gibberish he telling me. He was drunk (HOLDING UP THE TOASTER) he made the toaster worse than it was. He had pieces all over the table, after he disected it. Saying, "I'm good at this Moma." I asked him to put it back together later when his hands were more steady. But he kept right on, "I'm really good at this Moma, you'll see." Then he got mad and threw it to the floor. He was trying too hard.

BENNY
I'll get you another one.

LEELLA
I'll get it myself.

BENNY
When are you going to start letting me do things for you, Lee?

LEELLA
When have I ever prevented it. Here.

(LEELLA HANDS BENNY THE HAMMER AND PLACES THE TOOL BOX NEAR THE KITCHEN TABLE)

BENNY
I don't mean hammering nails.

LEELLA
Then what? It sure as hell can't be getting us out of here. Having better things. Chairs to sit on. Showing some initutive—

BENNY
You never needed me for that. You had Pete, with his dumb schemes.

LEELLA
Pete makes things happen. You're jealous of Pete because you could never do that. He tries to do things while all you do is try to become something you'll never be.

BENNY
Not jealous, but sick. Sick of his influence over you—and BJ, as a matter of fact. (POINTING TO HER PANTY HOSE) And his handouts.

LEELLA
He was in our corner when we had no where to turn. My brother brother—

BENNY
And sick of that being rubbed in my face.

LEELLA
Benny, you've been drinking and you're talking like a fool.

BENNY
(MOCKING) "Benny, you've been drinking and you're talking like a fool." There's always something wrong with Benny. Well let me tell you something that brother of yours is not all peaches and cream.

(BJ TOSSES ON THE COUCH)

LEELLA
I don't want to talk about this anymore. You're drunk. Go lay down like your precious son over there. Both of you are alike in more ways than I like to think of. Turning into drunks. That's your family line—not mine. We don't have those kind of people in my family. All of my family are hard working people that drink to be sociable. They ain't—

BENNY
My father—

LEELLA
Drunk himself to death and killed your mother. Drove her to an early grave. But I made up my mind when I joined this program, (HOLDING UP STENOGRAPHY BOOK) I aint going to let you do that to me. I aint going to allow myself to be dragged down any further with your foolishness.

BENNY
What the hell do you know?! You didn't know my old man. All you saw was what other people saw and thought the worst. You never heard them laughing together. He could tell some stories that old fool. And the times he did get work, he'd bring all of us a cookie and a penny Mary Jane without fail and a package of BC for Mama. Mama would always have a headache when she came home from working at the Fish 'n Chip joint. He'd place the Coke and BC right on the kitchen table. I can remember asking him once, "Daddy, why do you drink that stuff all the time 'til it makes your eyes droopy? He'd say, "You don't need your eyes open to see a large floor in a movie house. And you ain't got to be sober to stick a mop into a pail of water." Once he hurt his leg real bad when he fell between a row of chairs. Mama took on another job 'til he was better to look for another one. He use to have us laughing—cracking up—Mama too. "You ever notice that those movie stars like Lana Turner and the like sleep in make-up and them long eyelashes and nobody goes to the bathroom or to work? The only problems they have are love problems or catching the bad guy." He use to say,"Why don't you do that Eloise? Paint your toes and nails and put some of those lashes that looks like spider legs. And I'll be the hero that conquers the palace like Errol Flynn and let somebody else sweep up the popcorn, Chocolate Malted Balls and Bon Bon boxes." He use to say—

LEELLA
I have a test tomorrow. I don't want to hear anymore old men's dreams.

BENNY
We use to be able to talk Lee. I want to talk to you. Come here.

LEELLA
For what? More old stories—more lies.

BENNY
I never lied to you Lee.

(LEELLA WALKS OVER TO THE SAXAPHONE CASE BRINGS IT OVER AND SLAMS IT ON THE TABLE)

LEELLA
Then what in the hell is this?

BENNY
Alright. Alright.

LEELLA
The same old thing again.

BENNY
It's not the same, I'm not moving backwards Lee. We're moving forward.

LEELLA
Never with this. (LEELLA PICKS UP THE HAMMER) I got rid of it once—

(BENNY TAKES THE HAMMER AWAY)

BENNY
I tried to hock it that night of your accident Lee, but I couldn't. When the man asked me how much I wanted, I turnt away. He offered a good price and I wanted to bring money home to you and BJ. Do you think I liked not bringing nothing home? But, but Edward was working on this deal for Europe. And I thought maybe just one more day—hold on to it just one more day. So I didn't come home. I thought I'll wait—I'll wait 'til I have that contract in my hand to show you.

LEELLA
And you still want to hold on to it, even now when there are no more days?

BENNY
I still have the nights Lee.

LEELLA
And what does that leave me? (EXITING) I have studying to do.

(BENNY REMOVES A SILVER KEY FROM HIS POCKET AND UNLOCKS THE CASE. HE TAKES OUT THE SAXAPHONE AND ASSSEMBLES IT, PLACES THE REED INTO HIS MOUTH, TAKES A NAPKIN FROM THE TABLE AND WIPES DOWN THE SAXAPHONE GENTLY. ALL HIS LOVE FOR THE SAXAPHONE IS VISABLE. THIS SHOULD BE DONE SLOW AND WITH CARE. AFTER A FEW SECONDS THE BUSINESS RECORD IS HEARD)

RECORD
Mr. Alexander R. Johnson
1156 Ocean Drive, Glendale Ohio, 65710
Dear Mr. Johnson: An appointment   (BENNY PLAYS SAX)
has been scheduled for you in the
department of Ophthalmology. General
Clinic on—

(BUSINESS RECORDS STOPS)

LEELLA (OFF STAGE)
Benny, stop blowing that thing.   (BJ TURNS ON COUCH)
(I'm practicing for my test tomorrow.

RECORD (LOUDER)
Mr. Alexander R. Johnson
1156 Ocean Drive, Glendale Ohio, 65710
Dear Mr. Johnson—

LEELLA (OFF STAGE)
Benny, will you stop blowing that thing!

BENNY
Somebody is going to listen to me.

RECORD   (BJ EXITS OUT KITCHEN DOOR,
Genera Clinic on September 11, 1977.   PLAYS THE SAX)
Upon your arrival at the hospital,
please proceed to the hospital parking   (BJ EXITS TOSSES AND TURNS.
ramp #1 adjacent to the main entrance.   HE BEGINS TO SHAKE)
If ramp #1 is full, hospital parking ramp
is available to patients and visitors.   BJ
For your convenience, you may wish to   Let go of my leg Bill.
use the patient unloading area under
the Main Entrance Canopy before   (BJ GAGS AND CHOKES, KICKS)
parking your vehicle. After parking—

We got to go back man. It didn't catch.

LEELLA
Benny, do you hear me?

(LEELLA ENTERS THE LIVING
ROOM AREA)

God damn it Benny! I told
YOU I HAVE A TEST—

(LEELLA SCREAMS)

BJ!

BJ
Stop the screaming!

(LEELLA BACKS AWAY AND RUNS OUT THE KITCHEN DOOR)

LEELLA
Benny!

(BJ ROLLS TO THE FLOOR, SHAKES)

BJ
We got to go back man, it
didn't catch.

(BJ IS POUNDING HIS HEAD ON
THE FLOOR)

(BJ SLOWLY GETS UP FROM THE FLOOR, WALKS TO THE KITCHEN AREA TAKES
A TOWEL AND BEGINS TO WIPE HIS FACE)

Benny, BJ, he's beating his head on the floor.

(THE SOUND OF BENNY PLAYING STOPS ABRUPTLY. BENNY AND LEELLA ENTER
THE KITCHEN)

BJ
I'm alright, Moma. Just a little taken back. I heard my name being called. (TENSE)
It was you wasn't it Moma? Pop?

BENNY
Why were you hitting your head on the floor? What's the matter with you son?
Why—

BJ
Nothing. Moma came in as I was getting up. I slipped. My head snapped back.

LEELLA
BJ you were hitting—

BJ
My head snapped back, Moma.

(THE TELEPHONE RINGS. BENNY ANSWERS IT. DISGUSTED, LEELLA EXITS)

BENNY
Yeh. What is it Pete?…When did he?…Yeah…Okay. I'll wait 'til you call back.

(BENNY HANGS UP THE TELEPHONE SLOWLY)

BJ
What Was that about?

BENNY
Nothing that concerns you—business.

BJ
It was Uncle Pete, wasn't it?

(BENNY DOESN'T REPLY)

Pop?

BENNY
What?

BJ
It was Uncle Pete wasn't it? Where is he? Is he home?

BENNY
No. Now, go in your room and lay down.

(BENNY IS PLACING SAXAPHONE IN THE CASE)

BJ
I'm not a kid you can order to bed anymore, Pop. If Bill is conscious, I have a right—

BENNY
Bill? What do you know about a Bill?

BJ
Nothing. Forget it. (STARTING TO EXIT) I'm tired.

(BENNY GRABS BJ BY THE ARM)

BENNY
Tired hell. What do you know about a Bill, god damn it?

(BENNY SWINGS BJ AROUND)

Answer me.

BJ
I heard Uncle Pete mention his name.

BENNY
When?

BJ
When he let me in after I left you at that run down club, alright.

BENNY
What did you hear?

BJ
Enough.

(BENNY MOVES AWAY FROM BJ)

BENNY (DREADING THE ANSWER)
Like what?

BJ
You two needed another guy to go along with Bill, didn't you?

(BENNY A BIT CONFUSED GETTING THE ANSWER HE WAS NOT PREPARED FOR)

BENNY
No. You went? Pete sent you and *you went*. (ANGRY) You idiot. Why?

BJ
To please you. To do something—something once that would please you.

BENNY
To please me! You stupid—

(BENNY ENRAGED GRABS THE TOASTER CORD FROM THE TABLE AND VIOLENTLY SWINGS AT BJ, HE MISSES)

You ass backward—

(BENNY SWINGS AGAIN AND MISSES BJ. LEELLA ENTERS)

LEELLA
Benny!

(LEELLA RUNS OVER TO BENNY AS HE IS ABOUT TO SWING, BENNY PUSHES HER TO THE FLOOR AND BEGINS TO SWING AGAIN AT BJ, BJ CATCHES BENNY'S ARM, THEY STRUGGLE AND WITH HIS FREE HAND BENNY KNOCKS BJ TO THE FLOOR. LEELLA STRUGGLES TO GET TO HER FEET)

LEELLA
Benny please! BJ!

(BJ WHILE ON THE FLOOR GRABS A SCREW DRIVER FROM THE TOOL BOX AND AS BENNY PREPARES TO HIT HIM WITH THE TOASTER CORD, BJ QUICKLY GETS TO HIS FEET WITH THE SCREW DRIVER EXTENDED. BENNY STOPS SHORT

BJ
Come on. I did something Pop. Finally did something. Why ain't you jumping for joy? Put it down. Put…it…down.

LEELLA
Benny please.

(BENNY LOWERS THE TOASTER CORD)

BJ.

(BJ LOWERED THE SCREW DRIVER AND LETS IT DROP)

Neither one of you want peace in this house.

(LEELLA PICKS UP THE TOASTER CORD AND THROWS IT)

Fighting. Both of you can find time for that.

(BENNY WALKS TOWARD THE DOOR)

Benny, where are you going?

BENNY
You want peace in this house. I'll take care of Pete once and for all.

LEELLA
Again you are using Pete as—

BJ
Pop, don't do anything you'll be sorry—

LEELLA
Let him go! He always uses Pete as an excuse to cover up what he can't face.

BENNY
Let me tell you about your precious brother!

BJ
Wait a minute Pop, don't—

LEELLA
Get rid of this! This before you say anything to me about Pete or anything else. This is our damn problem.

(LEELLA PICKS UP THE SAXAPHONE CASE AND THROWS IT OUT THE KITCHEN DOOR)

Keep it out of here!

BENNY (ANGRY)

You're throwing out the wrong thing Lee. It should be Pete you take your hatred out on. Not a piece of metal.

LEELLA
MY BROTHER GOD DAMN IT—

BENNY
JUST LOVES US ALL! HE LOVES YOU SO MUCH—

(BJ TRIES TO STOP BENNY, BENNY PUSHES HIM OUT OF THE WAY)

BJ
Pop, there's no need—

BENNY
HE SENT BJ OUT TO BURN DOWN OUR BUILDING.

LEELLA
Liar. You just want to hurt P—

(LEELLA LOOKS TO BJ FOR A DENIAL, HIS SILENCE SAYS "YES.")

BENNY
But nothing I did was ever right for the boy. What I wanted for the boy, you always closed your eyes to. But Pete, your precious brother—

BJ
Shut up, Pop!

LEELLA
(TO BJ) You killed those children?

BJ
Moma, I didn't think anyone would get hurt.

LEELLA
Why would you even do—

BJ
Uncle Pete say they needed the money—someone to go along with this guy Bill. Insurance money and—

BENNY
That's what that Alton fellow was all about. I wanted no part of it. But I went along. But BJ was never—never part of the plan.

LEELLA
Where were you? Why didn't you stop him?

BENNY
I wasn't there. I okayed it, but wanted no part.

BJ
When I left Pop at that club, I came home and Uncle Pete was making the arrangements. Uncle Pete lied he said Pop was—

LEELLA
Here. (TO BENNY) You let him use our home to make plans.

BENNY
I'm not the one that gave him the key. Pete—

LEELLA
I don't ever want to hear his name mentioned in my house again, but you should of been here.

BENNY
I won't take the blame for this Lee.

LEELLA
You are all the blame. To be part of such a low life scheme for—for—

BENNY
God damn chairs Lee. Panty hose.

(LEELLA SLAPS BENNY)

LEELLA
Don't you dare try to make me feel guilty.

BENNY
How many times have you made me feel guilty for the boiler exploding? I couldn't prevent that anymore than I could of stopped Pete from carrying out his plan.

LEELLA
How in the hell do you know? You were never here.

BENNY
It's not my fault. Do you hear me Lee? NOT MY FAULT.

BJ
I killed those children. I did it. I can't stay here.

(BJ GOES TOWARD THE DOOR, LEELLA GOES AFTER HIM)

LEELLA
Stay inside.

BJ
It's no good Moma. I have to—

LEELLA
Sleep. Come on baby lie down. Rest.

(LEELA TAKES BJ OVER TO SOFA)

BJ
I got to think.

LEELLA
Yes. Rest. We're here.

BJ
I need money Moma. There're coming for me.

(BJ LAYS ON THE SOFA)

BENNY
Bill is dead BJ.

LEELA
Lay down. No one will know. We're here.

(LEELA QUICKLY GOES IN THE KITCHEN AREA AND GETS A WET TOWEL, AS BENNY STANDS NEAR BJ)

BENNY
I never wanted this for you.

BJ
I—I just wanted to help you Pop.

BENNY
Stop saying that.

(BENNY GOES INTO THE KITCHEN AND TAKES A LARGE KITCHEN KNIFE FROM THE KITCHEN DRAWER)

LEELLA
Benny what are you going to do with that?

BENNY
I'm gonna cut Pete's God damn throat.

LEELA
Benny no. There's been enough.

(LEELLA REACHES FOR THE KNIFE, BENNY MOVES AWAY)

We need you here.

BENNY
I have to do something Lee.

(BENNY EXITS OUT OF THE KITCHEN DOOR WITH THE KNIFE)

LEELLA
Benny!

(LEELLA TAKES THE WET TOWEL AND PLACES IT GENTLY ACROSS BJ'S EYES)
Rest. We're here.

LIGHTS FADE

ACT 2

SCENE 3

The scene opens in SMOKEY JOE'S club. SMOKEY JOE is prying open a can of paint with a spoon. On the floor are newspapers scattered around and old raggedy bar stools. There are a couple of chairs up stage right.

SMOKEY JOE
Hey, Pigmeat hurry up. Get those chairs up. A couple more can fit in here.

(SOUND OF A CHAIR FALLING)

PIGMEAT
Hey, Smokey. Come in here quick mann.

SMOKEY JOE
Must I do everything. Is that how it's gonna be? I got to buy the paint, paint the damn place myself—plaster and—

(SOUND OF GLASS FALLING)

What the—? Damn you Pigmeat. Ain't you good for nothing. We're surpose to be fixing this place up. Not—

(SMOKEY JOE PUTS DOWN THE CAN OF PAINT AND STARTS TO EXIT, BUT BENNY ENTERS. BENNY TOSSES A BILL ON THE TABLE. HE IS HOLDING A BOTTLE OF LIQUOR AND A GLASS)

BENNY
This should cover the glasses, my tab and any damn thing else.

SMOKEY JOE
Hey Benny. What's a couple of glasses between partners? We—

BENNY
Partners share in the lost and gain. Right? Good and the bad. The damn debts and the financial benefits. Responsibility—guilt. Right? Well damn it, ain't I right?

SMOKEY JOE
Hey, Benny what is this? When you get yourself straight I know your cash is good.
You'll pull your weight to help get ol' Smokey'sWeekend Din back on its feet.

(DRINKING FROM THE BOTTLE, BENNY TURNS FROM SMOKEY JOE)

BENNY
You know I'll pull my what? (LAUGHING) You're so damn sure.

(PIGMEAT ENTERS CARRYING BENNY'S SAXAPHONE CASE, PLACES IT ON THE
TABLE)

PIGMEAT
You didn't have to throw it at me man. Here (HOLDS IT OUT TO BENNY) Sorry.
Sorry man. Sorry. But—but we're gonna get along man. You'll see. We're gonna get
along.

BENNY
What did I tell you out there?

PIGMEAT
Nahhh mann nahhh. It's me Benny. It's me. You—you—you just don't think I'ma do
good, but man—

BENNY
It ain't got nothing to do with you! (POURING ANOTHER DRINK)
Now, let me drink this. I know what I have to do.

SMOKEY JOE
(TO PIGMEAT) If you've done something to—

(SMOKEY GOES OVER TO PIGMEAT, PIGMEAT GOES QUICKLY TO BENNY AS IF
HE HASN'T HEARD SMOKEY'S LAST LINE)

PIGMEAT
Nahh mann nahh. You—you don't waant to kill nobody man.

BENNY
Don't tell me what I want and what I don't want. I'm gonna kill the son of Bitch.

(BENNY HOLDS UP THE KNIFE AND CONTINUES TO DRINK)

SMOKEY JOE
What did he do man? This time.

(TRYING TO GET CLOSE TO BENNY FOR THE KNIFE)

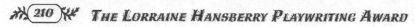

PIGMEAT
Us mann. What about us?

BENNY
Forget the trio. Look at you. One foot in the grave, the other almost there. And you think we could ever rise again.

SMOKEY JOE
You thought so one. You're letting that brother-in-law of yours—

BENNY
He ain't got nothing to do with this man. (POINTS TO THE SAX) We're losers man. All of us. We've missed the boat. The time has past.

PIGMEAT
Nahh mann. We man are—

BENNY
Nothing! Nothing. Tonight I was walking—just walking. There—there was an old man that use to walk up and down my block when I was a kid, blowing an old beat up trumpet. He—he would be blowing that thing 'fore day in the morn'n—bouncing up and down—doing the St. Vitus dance—singing—blowing, "When the Saints Come Marching In." "Til somebody would throw water down on him, then he'd move on. While I was walking tonight, looking for that damn Pete, I—I saw my face instead of his, as he looked one winter morn'n—he didn't move on. Sitting on the stoop— wet. His trumpet dangling from his hand as they placed his body on the stretcher. I guess they broke his fingers to pry that horn away from him. He just didn't know when to move on.

PIGMEAT
That won't happen to us man. Nahhh, we won't let it.

BENNY
Pigmeat don't you hear what I'm saying? It's not for me anymore.

PIGMEAT
You're—you're upset. Upset. Tell him he's upset Smokey Hey—hey Smokey, tell him he's upset.

SMOKEY JOE
Shut up Pigmeat. Go—go take the chairs down or something. Sweep up the glass.

(PIGMEAT TAKES DOWN ONE OF THE CHAIRS AND SITS IN IT, WITH HIS BACK TO SMOKEY JOE AND BENNY)

She was right. You ain't gonna play again.

BENNY
She?

SMOKEY JOE
Your wife called here for you tonight. She was relieved when I told her you weren't here.

BENNY
She's looking for me. Probably saw the sax missing. Maybe she warned him. Maybe that's why I can't find the—

(BENNY THROWS THE KNIFE INTO THE TABLE, SMOKEY JOE PICKS IT UP AND HOLDS IT IN FRONT OF BENNY. PIGMEAT TURNS AROUND)

SMOKEY JOE
Go ahead! You want to! Had enough drinks? (TO PIGMEAT) Pour him another one.

(PIGMEAT DOESN'T MOVE)

Put this in his gut. And while the worms and maggots devour him—in jail the roaches, rats and cheenches will feast on you. Move'n on. Ain't that what you call it?

(DISGUSTED SMOKEY JOE THROWS THE KNIFE INTO THE TABLE)

Move'n on Hell. And what then? I hope you're doing the steering Benny

BENNY
Who has there been? Who else is there? When you're the only one with the license. Always steady on that course. Slow down for all lights—no U-turns—no detours— and you can't afford to run into a dead end. Can't take the time to stop at a rest stop along the way. You got to be always full of gas. Taking them where they want to go—full speed ahead. Making sure they are able to handle things when they get there—and the ride has to be comfortable. You can't stop along the way to admire the view—because it pleases you. Man, I stopped twice and there was a collision.

SMOKEY JOE
Now, you want to end up a casualty.

BENNY
I've done things man.

SMOKEY JOE
What?

BENNY
Things!

SMOKEY JOE
Then hold the damn jailors key Benny, but even prisoners on the inside gets a rest break.

(SMOKEY JOE REMOVES THE KNIFE FROM THE TABLE, HANDS IT TO PIGMEAT, WHO QUICKLY PLACES THE KNIFE INTO THE PAINT CAN. SMOKEY JOE POURS BENNY A DRINK AND DRINKS FROM THE BOTTLE. HE PUSHES THE DRINK TO BENNY)

SMOKEY JOE
Blue is gonna look good.

(BENNY DRINKS FROM THE GLASS)

Hey Pigmeat, tell Benny about Barry Collins.

PIGMEAT
Ahhhhhh Benny. Ahhhhhhh Bennnnnnnny mann. I went—I went you understand down...town. Annd Collinss, you know Barry Collins was do'n the do. *Just* back from Eur—ope mann. I looked through—through the glass—the place was packed. He— he made a come back mann—he came back bigggerrr! Man, it didn't hurt his playing none, when he slatched up his wrist when he was doing bad. He was smoke'nnn. Sennnnd'nn viibess. He—he had them fly'nnnn. Like—like we was gonna do. Hey— hey Bennny mannnn. Heeey, you don't want to kill noboddy man. Nahhh. We'rre creeaaators mann. Creators of sound. Hey—hey (PIGMEAT SHAKING HIS HEAD, HITTING ON THE PAINT CAN) can't—can't you hear us mannn. Listennnnn.

(HEARING MUSIC IN HIS HEAD)

bop...bop...bop. Snow Job, Plaay'nn his baaasss mellloow. You—you whaaailling your horn...wa...wawa...wa...wawa...wa. Smokey sitting in sometimes burrn'nn that ivory, (WIGGLING HIS FINGERS) when our new guy is taking a rest break. Heeey Benny, Benny—Collinss was grooovve'nn. You know you want to mann. You don't want to hurt nobody. We'rre gonna make dream music bay—that burrrsst and minnggle in the aire—

BENNY
With us the conductors of sound.

(SMOKEY JOE POURING BENNY ANOTHER DRINK)

SMOKEY JOE
Taking them on magic carpet rides.

PIGMEAT
Yeahhhh. Bennny, can't you see us mannn. Weeee cannn doooo it mannn. Take a shot at it again. (PICKING UP A PAINT BRUSH) Heeey, (TAKING A SIP OF BENNY'S

DRINK) Heeey, look at us man. They're come'nn to see usss mannnn—us. And wee are good man. Just like Collins-you'rre back. And we are tooo-getherrr. Can't—can't you see us mannn.

BENNY
Go all they way this time.

PIGMEAT
If we try mann. We can try. And if our sound *clicks*.

BENNY
Maybe we'll get a chance to tour Europe—all over.

PIGMEAT
Eurrrrrr…rope alriiiiiigt.

(BENNY MOVES AWAY)

BENNY
No man, it would take too much time. We're talking again like a bunch of—

PIGMEAT
We'll make time. Playing in clubs we ain't never played in.

SMOKEY JOE
My offer is still good.

PIGMEAT
Then looook ouuuuut!

(BENNY TURNS TO PIGMEAT, THE TELEPHONE RINGS)

BENNY
If you and Snow Job fall man, I'm gonna leave you behind.

PIGMEAT
Nahhh Mannn nahhhh. Not this time. Weee'rrre gonnna do the do, 'til we can't do it no mo'.

(SMOKEY JOE IS WALKING TOWARD THE TELEPHONE)

SMOKEY JOE
Alright to the trio.

PIGMEAT
Triooooooooo!

SMOKEY JOE
Benny, your wife.

(PIGMEAT NERVOUSLY STARES AT BENNY. THERE IS A SHORT PAUSE)

BENNY
Tell her I'm rehearsing. (BENNY OPENS THE SAXAPHONE CASE)

Contact Snow Job.

(SMOKEY JOE WALKS BACK OVER TO THE TABLE)

Smokey, we're gonna need a two handed player.

SMOKEY JOE
I can sit in sometimes.

BENNY
Any damn time you want?

PIGMEAT
Alriiiiight!

(SMOKEY JOE PICKS UP THE CAN OF PAINT AND BRUSH FROM THE TABLE PLACING IT ON A CHAIR)

SMOKEY JOE
Ooooooooooweeeeeeee!

(BENNY IS PUTTING THE SAXAPHONE AROUND HIS NECK)

BENNY
We're gonna move on man.

SMOKEY JOE/PIGMEAT
Move on!

BENNY
No turning back this time!

(THE LIGHTS FADE TO DIM ON SMOKEY JOE'S CLUB AS THE LIGHTS RISE ON BENNY'S APARTMENT. THERE IS A FREEZE. LEELLA SITS ON THE SOFA WITH THE TELEPHONE IN HER HAND AS BJ STANDS IN THE KITCHEN AREA NEAR THE KITCHEN DOOR. BENNY IN SMOKEY JOE'S CLUB STANDS WITH THE SAXAPHONE IN HIS HAND WITH A CLOTH TO WIPE IT. SOFT JAZZ MUSIC IS HEARD WITH A SAXAPHONE SOLO AS THE LIGHTS FADE ON ALL SETS)

THE END

Strands

"Life's journey is circular... returning us to our fathers"

by

Eric Wilson

ACT ONE

Scene 1

   The following is a ceremony celebrating the birth of a manchild. The men have gathered in the meeting house, a private sanctuary for the men of the village. They are waiting... chanting... moving. We hear the sounds of a woman in labor and the voices of other women as they assist her in the delivery. The following is a voice over:

WOMAN 1: Allah help me! I can't go on
WOMAN 2: You must, the child will be born
WOMAN 1: Olorun Mimo---Holy God.......
WOMAN 3: The child will come and you must bring him...
WOMAN 1: I cannot.......Olorun Alaye ---
WOMAN 2: You must........

   More cries from the mother and then the crying of the newborn. The father exits. The men begin the ceremonial dance. The father returns with the infant wrapped in a kinte cloth, as two acolytes conduct an ancient ritual of blessing.

ACOLYTE 1:
        Olodumare, Seven heavens, Seven Earths
        Olorun Mimo, Olorun Alaye (Holy God, Holy Savior)
FATHER:
        The Heavenly Children offer this sacrifice.
        They are calling
        You are our helper and our lifter.
ACOLYTE 2:
        Hold all evil from us
        Make it blind, make it lame;
        Carry it to the spirit of the mountain
        Put it in a deep pit; place a stone upon it;
FATHER:
        Let the good wind from the North and the South
        From the rising to the setting sun blow upon it.
        Let it be so, for You are able to do this.
ACOLYTE 1:
        Olorun Mimo, Olorun Alaye (Holy God, Holy Savior)
        Fellow men, we shall all live.

   The men rise as the drums begin slowly, increasing in tempo and intensity.

ACOLYTE 2:

> We shall train him
> He will be us and we shall be him
> When we are old this prince will feed us
> Fellow men, we shall all live

The men move into position as a dance of confirmation begins. At the conclusion of the dance, the infant is brought forth.

ACOLYTE 1:

> This boy is yet a seed. If you wish that he grows
> to be a tree, we shall be ever thankful.
> He will grow to be like his stock

ALL:

> Warriors, Warriors, Warriors, Warriors, Warriors, Warriors

Scene 2

The chant continues. As the lighting changes, the father is left alone on stage holding the infant. The father disappears as we see the infant transformed into a young prince. As he walks forward, other young warriors appear carrying long sticks. A stick is thrown to the Prince, and they engage in a competitive dance of aggressive skills. Their play is stopped suddenly by the arrival of the elders and the acolytes. There is a dramatic change in lighting as the acolytes return with the strands of cloth to begin a second ritual; the initial phase of a rite of passage into manhood and the subsequent coronation ceremony for the Prince.

Scene 3

ACOLYTE 1:

> We stand that our collective spirits may be
> united with the Supreme One. Creators.
> May the spirits of our ancestors enter in so that we may create
> for them.

ACOLYTE 2:

> May our own spirits rise beyond, giving us the power to shape
> emotion, movement, time, space and life.
> Spirits come forth, spirits come.
> We call you by name.

They begin a libation ceremony, pouring the sacrificial wine on the ground.

MAN 1:
> Imhotep

MAN 2:
> Akhenaten

MAN 3:
> Shaka

MAN 4:
> Cinque

MAN 5:
> Du Bois

MAN 6:
> Garvey

MAN 7:
> Kenyatta

MAN 8:
> Nkrumah

MAN 2:
> King

MAN 1:
> Malcolm

MAN 3:
> Biko

ALL:
> Come forth.

The ceremony continues as the men begin to circle the Prince, each one extending a strand of cloth which forms a symbolic link to the Prince.

PRINCE:
> Whoever sees us with an evil eye, when he plants may the flood
> sweep his mounds away.
> Whoever wishes us evil
> May he break his fist on the ground.

ACOLYTE 1:
> We are broody hens, we have chicks. We do not fly up.
> We look after our brood.
> We do not eye others with an evil eye.

FATHER:
> (Giving him a ceremonial weapon)
> You are Prince, you shall
> rule over people. Always do what is right.

PRINCE:
> I am the Prince, I will be King, I will conquer
> my enemies. I will cut judgment with truth.

The Prince ends in a triumphant pose as the lighting changes. Suddenly, the drums stop, the men pause in their movement and then retreat into the darkness. The Prince begins to move as though he is surrounded by an unseen enemy and is finally defeated. He falls prostrate on the floor as the barely visible acolytes speak.

Scene 4

ACOLYTE 1:

Look into the eyes of time...... into the dream. Dreams
holding truth together.... Moving..... moving into an
unknown world. Look into the eyes of time. Sunrise and hot
days. Laying down in fearful nights... Trees bearing dreams you
cannot see and fruit you cannot taste. Look into the eyes of
time.

The weaver enters and removes the strands of cloth from the Prince.

ACOLYTE 1:

Your arms are strong as your soul is weak.
No breezes, nor waterfalls.... only bitter winds and rain.
Spirits see, know, reach, hold, feel your blood tears. We are
there in lay me down nights and gettin up days. In low
moans of love and the eyes of the newborn. In blood stained
cloth and burning. Yes we are spirits, seeing. Looking into
the eyes of time..... reaching, holding, feeling, knowing,
looking......

As the acolytes exit, the warriors enter. They, too, have been captured.

Scene 5

PRINCE:

I was born near the Gambia River in West Africa,
around the year 1729. My father's name was Kajali Demba, he
was a prince of the Mandinka tribe. My father had three wives,
I am the eldest child of his first wife. I was awakened one
morning by the crowing cocks and the familiar call of the
alimamo compelling the men of our village into the mosque for
the first morning prayer. I entered the sacred room, walking
behind the older men, unrolled my prayer rug to fall prostrate
before the righteousness of the one God, Allah. But my prayer
was stopped suddenly by a horrible uproar caused by the
screams of women and children and the smell of burning
thatched roofs. Our village was surrounded by the toubob--

slave raiders and their black slatee helpers. My brain screamed
for any weapon. Clawing, twisting, butting, gouging I fought to
protect the lives of my kinsmen and my children. But it was
hopeless, they attacked us without regard for man, woman or
child. I fell to my knees, my vision blurred by tears and blood.
All who were too old or too young were murdered before our
eyes while the young and strong were captured alive to be sold
as slaves.

WARRIOR 1:

Gagged and blindfolded, my wrists and ankles bound by a
knotted rope, we traveled long through the bush.
Prodded along by pointed sticks and the slatees whip until
we arrived at the bank of the river. We were thrown onto a
raft and descended the river for three days until one night we
came upon a vast dark vessel waiting in the distance.

WARRIOR 2:

We were forced to descend into the pitch blackness of the
ships hold. Where we were placed on rough and narrow
plank shelves and shackled side to side, spoon fashion.
Many died, their anguished cries to Allah disappeared into
the stinking blackness, but daily more captives were brought
down the narrow steps screaming in terror and chained into
the empty spaces abandoned by the dead. When our prison
could hold no more the ship began to sail.

Warrior 2 sings. It is a lament without melody.

WARRIOR 2:

Chains
Chains
Hold my soul and all its power in
Chains...............

PRINCE:

(Spoken)
Blinding darkness like a frozen night.
Will morning never come
This night has lasted 93 days
Each one linked
Welded tightly, locked together

WARRIOR 2:

Chains
Chains........

PRINCE:

Four corners of the room move closer
Still closer
Bodies move in

Bodies push back

WARRIOR 1:
Chains
Chains........

PRINCE:
Air tainted by the smell of burnt flesh
Pain
And death
Death that I am linked to............

WARRIOR 2:
Chains
Chains.......

PRINCE:
I was bought by a man whose name I did not hear. He took
me and I joined 51 other slaves whom he had bought in
Virginia. Thirty two of these were men, and nineteen were
women. The women were merely tied together with a rope,
about the size of a bed cord, which was tied together with a rope,
around the neck of each, but the men, of whom I was the
stoutest and strongest, were differently confined. A
strong iron collar was closely fitted around each our necks
and secured by a padlock and a chain of iron about a
hundred feet in length which was passed through the hasp of
each padlock. In addition to this, we were handcuffed in
pairs, with iron staples and bolts, with a short chain about a
foot long uniting the men alternately by the right and left
hand; the poor man to whom I was thus chained wept like an
infant when the blacksmith, with his heavy hammer,
fastened the ends of the bolts.

Scene 6

The Prince walks center stage and kneels. One of the warriors exits as the other
crosses upstage and pulls a strand of cloth from the backdrop, which becomes his
chain. He mounts the auction block.

VOICE OVER:
"Gentlemen step forward. This is a prime young
buck. Plucked from the trees. Good bones,
sinews... perfect for any kind of labor."

PRINCE:
Was it when I was snatched or was it my seasoning?

VOICE:
"Good strong nigga. Open your mouth nigga.
Look at them teeth."

PRINCE:

Or is it now on the auction block, where I lose my humanity?

VOICE:

"Who will buy? 100 pounds, 100, do I hear 100? Turn around darky....... NOW!"

PRINCE:

I must now be chattel, to be sized up and weighed.

VOICE :

"Good worker. Big strong nigga. Straight from the jungle. Keep movin' ya black bastard!"

PRINCE:

As...... if...... when I rise on..... 'dis'...... block I am reduced to mere property.

VOICE:

"Who will buy? 125, 125, 125 pounds. Look at him. I can hit him and he don't flinch. Look it. Look at him."

PRINCE:

I look at ya lookin' at me; who is best, who is worst?

VOICE:

"KEEP movin nigga or I'll break you now!! Do ! hear 125, 130, 130 pounds.

PRINCE:

I...... I...... I am king, a prince, a scholar.

VOICE:

"YES, 130, 135 do I hear 140. Shut up. Shut up. Get up you bastard nigga, NOW!"

PRINCE:

Please, no more, no more.
I am a Man.

VOICE:

"140, 145, Come on, this nigga's hung like a mule! Just right for breeding. Bend down darky. Look at that back. Good animal. Dumb as a ox, but strong as one too. Do I hear 150?"

The Prince begins to speak in a Black southern dialect.

PRINCE:

The longa I's up here the farther I's away from home.

VOICE:

"150 pounds do I hear 160. Look at that color. It don't rub off. Good strong bastard ape. Dance ya' goddamn ape, dance!!"

PRINCE:

> Not my dreams boss don't take dem.

VOICE:

> "160, Do I hear 165. Come on nigga dance.
> Keep jumpin' you sad ass bastard. JUMP! Yes
> 175, once, twice Sold! 175 pounds."

PRINCE:

> Not my land!!!!!!!!!!!!!!!!!!!!

The lighting changes. The weaver enters and removes the strand of cloth from the man on the auction block. The Prince retreats into the darkness, his enslavement is complete. We hear a work song. Out of the darkness, the men enter dressed in work pants and shirts, straw hats. With the sticks from the previous scene, they begin movement which represents repetitive manual labor.

Scene 7

WORK SONG:

> One day One day
> I was walking along
> Well you couldn't hardly tell
> Which a way I was goin'
> But I heard a little voice
> Didn't see n one
> It was long last John
> Said he was all alone
> And a'runnin real fast
> With his long clothes on
> And his satchel all packed
> Said they chained his feet
> Couldn't chain his heart

One of the men steps away from the group, looking towards the sun. He wipes hissweat as he begins to speak. The song and labor continues quietly underneath the monologue.

MAN 1:

> Mornin' reminds me of Pawpaw. Tell the truth thas da only
> time I'd see him. He was quiet like da mornin. Never said
> much but boy you sho' could see him and feel him. He was
> dere, no doubt. I'member one mornin that he call my name,
> grab me by the arm so tight I thought I might had done
> somethin' wrong. He look me in the eye and says, "Boy
> 'member, whatever you do, wherever you go, keep family
> together." That was the last time I saw him, cause that same

night, they come for him and Pawpaw was beat till dead.
The next day I was sold.

Since then I am de property of Mr. Newman. New
land.... new time. Dey say he alright to us. I don't know. I
keep thinkin' of Pawpaw and Momma...... me and my
brother Jesse playin' in the fields till they tell us to fetch
water. Lizabeth, my woman...... lookin' in her eyes,
seein' the pain, the love, the hate, but knowin' she doin' all
she can to live.

One of the men begins to listen to his story; he steps away from the labor and
moves towards him. He attempts to console him, but he rejects him.

Does it have to be this way, now, when I needs them the
most. It's hard to be a man alone. Ya needs someone to be a
man to......... a man for. I am sorry Pawpaw. I did
all I could, I heard what you said and..........I asked,
I begged, I cried, I promised, I fought, I fell down on my
knees but my Lizabeth and my boys was sold away
from me. They done gone without a Papa to look after them, hold
them, look 'em in the eye and tell them about family and
staying together....... They gone and I am still here. All in
one day....... well it's night now. I'll see you in the mornin'
Paw.

He exits as another man takes his place. The labor continues.

MAN 2:
It's so dark in a room you ain't ever been in. Her eyes in
that same darkness cried in the quiet. She didn't break the
quiet she jes breathed. It told me somethin'. I can't forget
that night. The overseer tells me, he say, go to Dinah's cabin
and lay with her now. I didn't know her cept by name, but
does I dare say no?

Her breath was scared, dreams born, died and born again
was in that breath. De breath trembled and shook, but the
breath understood. We touched that dark. The touch grabbed
my back bone and squeezed. Her hands were rough with
work, I could feel the creases and the scars, but the hands
was good........... they understood. The Mississippi heat
told our bodies to cry. Her tears mixed with the blood of my
brow and made me burn. Strong bodies move. Strong
bodies move, they move. She hurt. I felt the pains but was
it mines or was it hers? The smells of bodies soiled by the

work of the day filled the room, I held on, she held tighter.
We stopped............... does I dare go on?

Days pass... the time comes when I sees her workin' in the
fields. Full belly. Strong. I smiles, but she didn't know me.
I tell her to be stronger. Promise to help her through her
pains, pray about it bein' a boy child. I bring her
food, dream of the night we would steal away in the
darkness. Me, her, the baby. Cryin' and fightin' for life, but
does I dare?

The baby come, a boy child and I watches her and I see. I
see that strength washin' away. I sees the pains of holdin
another life in bondage. Like a flame not wantin' to give up
its heat to the cold. I want to yell out.... burn.... just so
I can make it anotha' day, just me, her and the baby. Massa
sees dis and gets colder. One day I see him push her and I
stand. Then he shoves her and I leaps up. He raise his
hand and I grabbed him but Dey hold me, tie me down with
ropes so's I can't move. 'Not her Massa....... not her.' I
fights and struggles as hard as I can. Dey hold me. Does I let
him or does I dare be a man?

Scene 8

Three men enter, who represent soldiers from World War I. They are distinctly
different. Man 1 is a proud "fighting man" from the 369th Infantry, Man 3 is a country
boy, illiterate, somewhat superstitious. Man 2, is the Prince, well educated and
articulate. His war experience has left him with a bitter awareness.

MAN 1:
There was a call to war and freedom.
MAN 3:
I heard it, with a loud midnight cry in Georgia, St. Simen Island.
President Wilson said America was goin' to war cause the world
had to be made 'safe for democracy.' It was gon take a "Great
American Army" and dey needed me. Ya' see I growed up on did
island. Sho' nuff, I know it like I knowed my momma. But, I ain't
knowed nothing bout no overseas and all dat other talk dey
was doin' bout the war, but I knowed bout hard work and scrapping
for food, and trying to squeeze a life out of this swamp land.
Ain't nobody even told me what day I was borned on, but I
remembers that day I heard the President. It was hot like always,
but it was making a different kind a heat. Da birds was talkin' too
much - trees wasn't the same green.

I walked deeper into da swamp to find a cool spot. It started to get dark, darker. As I sat down by the edge of the water I saw it again. The two of them was there like before--this skinny black boy in a worn out blue army uniform and a white boy dressed in gray. That Confederate soldier must a been scared, he was running and he run right into that black soldier hiding behind a bush. That white boy just started laughing I guess he though it was funny, seeing what he thought was a slave in a soldier suit. But when that colored soldier shot him, he stopped laughing and drop dead pretty quick. Then that black boy standing over him say, "Never mess with a man in his house." I been seeing dat vision ever since I was boy, playin in the swamp, but this time the meaning come clear. The old folks say dat black boy that I seen was my granddaddy, a runaway slave. This swamp land ain't much but my granddaddy died to claim it and it's all my daddy had to give me. So when I hear the call, I was the first in line.

MAN 1:

There was a call to war and freedom.

PRINCE:

I heard it. Like the horns of Jericho. My woman hear it too. She asked me did I have to go? Did I have to fight. Well I didn't know if I had to, but one thing I did know, to protect what is mine is a right not a privilege.

MAN 3:

There was a call to war and freedom.

MAN 1:

We started off as the old Fifteenth in the Harlem national guard, but when war came we became the 369th. Strong and proud. We were the first black unit to arrive in France and we had to prove ourselves. It all started on the night of May 13, 1918. The Germans sent a patrol of about twenty-four men and they was making their way toward the sector being defended by the 369th. The sector was made up by a number of 'group posts' as they were called. Private Needham Roberts and Private Henry Johnson were on guard at Post Number 29 when Johnson heard something move in the distance. The German patrol was cutting through the barbed wire. Grenades was raining on their post and the blasts wounded Roberts so badly he couldn't stand up, so he propped himself up against the door of the dugout and commenced to throwing grenades back at the enemy.

Johnson got wounded too, but not as bad. Man, he rushed the German firing all three cartridges in his rifle. One German fell. Then Johnson crashed his empty rifle down on the head of another German and knocked him out. Johnson looked back and saw two of them carrying Roberts off. Not that night. He charged them, pulled out his bolo knife and killed one of them. By then the man

Johnson had knocked out was on his feet again. He shot Johnson with a automatic pistol. Johnson fell, man he was wounded bad this time. But as the German closed in, Johnson leaped up and killed him with that knife. When the Germans saw this, they began to run like hell. Johnson was bleeding but he kept throwing more grenades until he got him one more. The French honored Johnson and Roberts--gave both of them the Croix de Guerre, or War Cross. Newspapers back in New York printed the story of "The Battle of Henry Johnson," talking about how a former red-cap porter of the New York Central Railroad had fought off twenty-four Germans. That was when the 369th became a legend.

PRINCE:

The United States knew it's sins and was afraid of sending armed black men into their midst. Camp Logan, outside Houston Texas-- the summer of 1917. Before the Twenty-fourth Infantry Regiment arrived this town was set for trouble. All public facilities in Houston, everything from streetcars to drinking fountains had "Jim Crow" rules. We were proud soldiers in training to make the world safe for democracy and we chose to ignore those rules. A policeman arrested one the soldiers using 'unnecessary violence' and this set off the riot. Fifteen whites were killed and twelve others hurt. All the Negro soldiers who had been in the riot were arrested and tried by a military court. Of the sixty-seven men in the first group to be tried, thirteen received death sentences and were executed immediately; another forty-one were sentenced to life imprisonment.

MAN 3:

There was a call to war and freedom.

MAN 1:

Armistice Day, November 11, 1918 was glorious. The black soldiers was the first ones to get back to America and we marched through the street of New York City. Stiff, proud, and Black. Strong, brave, Black warriors, some said they had never seen such soldiers. Cadence told of our victory. We were Negro soldiers. Armed to the hilt with lion's courage--bringing freedom home to all, for all. We knew too well what Martial Law was. We knew what "no entrance, not allowed" and "no you can't" was. The 369th knew damn well and we fought until all could breathe. People back home had to hear of the bravery, the gallantry of Negro boys fighting for liberty overseas, the color bearers carrying the regimental flag with the Crois de Guerre fastened to it. We walked in steady precision, ticker tape grazing our uniforms, medals gleaming for all to see. When the parade reached Harlem, we swung onto Lenox Avenue. Lt. James Reece Europe's sixty piece band struck up "Here Come My Daddy Now!" then we fell out into an open marching formation. Yeah, the 369th was back, Negro

soldiers. Yea, the ones you only heard about were here. Freedom,
was the battle cry and fried chicken our rations. Man we loved it.
Didn't want it to end but I knew it had to.

MAN 3:

When I come back down home from the war, it wasn't no party.
Prosperity was slow comin' to de swamp. Death followed me back.
No life in the people's eyes. I was assigned to the SOS troop,
'Services of Supply,' reburial squad. We buried the remains of
American soldiers. More than you could ever count.... more than
you would ever want to know. Days and nights... long, long rows.
You could hear the sound of the hammer, as they drove the nails
into each coffin. White crosses goin' on for miles, seem like...
White crosses. We was the last to come home... Home, to this...

MAN 1:

There was a call to war and freedom.

PRINCE:

I settled in for a long sit. A long ride. I fell asleep. It felt like only a
sound, and then I woke up in Tennessee. There had been no place
in New Jersey to change out of my uniform in the train station. I
figured it didn't matter, we had won the war and I had survived. I
thought things had changed.

I saw them when they came to the door of the "Jim Crow" car. I
was finally home and I got up to leave but they blocked my way.
The other riders left the train, but I stayed. Had to. Soldiers don't
retreat. The men surrounded me and laughed. It was the middle of
the day, these were not silent murderers, invisible in white sheets.

I thought, this is America. There was a call to freedom and freedom
is won. They pulled me from the train and dragged me to an open
field, a 2x4 slammed against the small of my back. One grabbed
my arm and thrust it up my back. Cold hands grabbed my head,
made me look into the faces my forgotten enemy as they stripped my
rank and destroyed my ribbons and medals.

I fought. I killed for you, for us. I layed in trenches and ate dirt for
you and yours. I have looked death in the eye, just like your sons.
No. Not now. Not like this.

Blood drenched, I stood two feet planted and assailed them for all
the hate, for all the bitterness until I couldn't see, couldn't feel a
thing, couldn't feel my legs. The rope fell around my neck and
death wrapped its cold claws around my neck. I heard the call to
freedom and the war was over.

The men stand in isolated pools of light, as Man 1 sings.

SINGER:
> Give me wings to fly away, fly away
> Give me wings to fly away, fly away
> The only thing I can pray
> Is Lord give me wings to fly away.
>
> Beat my weary body and curse my name, fly away
> Beat my weary body and curse my name, fly away
> The only thing that I can pray
> Only thing than I can pray
> Is Lord give me wings to fly away
>
> Wings to fly away, fly away, fly away
> Lord, give me wings to fly away, fly away
> Wings to fly away into your arms
> Fly away into your arms,
> Where I can be a man...............

The men move to other areas of the stage as another man enters.

Scene 9

MAN:
> I watched in cold dampness. I watched. We was all
> there. Me, Ray, Nat, Jefferson... and Mr. Scott. They got him too.
> Didn't make sense. Me and Nat I could understand. I get a little wild
> here and there. But not our Mr. Scott. He's a good man.
>
> But I had to watch when they took him out. I didn't get it. They
> know he ain't done nothin. Mr. Scott got a good job workin' at the
> university cleanin up and watchin' after things. Always smile and
> say "How ya doin'?" ...always. And had a good wife, a school
> teacher. Them folks know him. They know he wouldn't do it. It's
> just all that hate they got. They see him ridin in that shinin' car that
> he sweat for. Riding like a king with all that chrome, while they
> walkin'.... kickin dust. They don't like that.
>
> That lil gold hair gal start screamin rape and the whole town gone
> crazy cause her father was a teacher at the university. Their eyes
> were open wide and their lips were tight. They were screamin for a
> life. That lil gold hair girl, Regina Almstead was her name just
> singin. "Have you ever seen a dream walkin', well I did." She had
> to scream. Don't scream.........

I watched as they ripped the cell door off. The smell of the
blue light from the torch choked me. The sheriff told them not to do
nothing but he didn't get in their way. They just charged in asking
each one of us. "Nigga are you Mr. Scott?" "What about you
nigga, are you Mr. Scott?" "Are you Mr. Scott?" I watched him,
head up, eyes wide open. Not one tear as he said, "Yes." They
pulled him out. I could hear the blows. The bones. They came for
us...... me, Ray, Nat and Jefferson and took us to the trail.

The other men begin to enter, each one looking up as though he is watching the
event take place.

They wanted us to be there and watch. They pushed him up
and down the blood swept streets of this Columbia until they came
to the bridge. The bridge where I first saw that little gold hair girl
through the trees on the twisting trail. The dry oak bridge. I told her
to shut up. Not to say a word. But she had to scream.........

I had to watch as they beat him until the blood ran free. He just
kneeled down, still and silent. I began to scream, "I did it. It was
me. On this trail. ME, I did it. Stop, God, stop!" But they wouldn't
listen. "It don't matter as long as it's one of you niggas." One of them
big ol' boys lifted our Mr. Scott up in the air and I watched as they
threw this prince of a man off the side of this dry wood bridge.
I watched as his body crackled like a whip when the rope jerked
tight. I watched as Mr. Scott's body flew down through trees and
branches. His body hung not one foot from the ground. Dry wood
was his last home. No green grass. Silence poured over a thousand
screaming citizens. Watching as our Mr. Scott died in vain.

The men have dropped to their knees. The song begins slowly and then becomes
joyous.

Scene 10

MAN:
    I couldn't hear nobody pray Lord
    I couldn't hear nobody pray
    Down in the valley
    All by myself
    I couldn't hear nobody pray, Lord
    Down in the valley
    I didn't go to stay
    My soul got happy
    I stayed all day

I couldn't hear nobody pray, Lord
I couldn't hear nobody pray
Way down yonder all by myself
I couldn't hear nobody pray, Lord
I couldn't hear nobody pray, Lord
Way down yonder all by myself
I couldn't hear nobody pray
I couldn't hear nobody pray..........

PRINCE:
Black rivers flow through my veins
With a hallelujah chorus
Spit polish shoes and stiff-creased pants
Duke pomade and stocking caps
Rivers of wisdom . . .
In the hands of my grandfather
Hands that lifted the burdens of his cross
That touched fear and held the strength of peace
Black rivers flow through my veins

MAN:
Sunday morning with tambourines and fans, floor bowing
to rhythms of heaviness and joy.
Sisters in white dresses, gloves, and hats.
Giving soft cheek kisses to little boys in old mens suits
Strutting down the aisle with handkerchiefs lifted in praise
to a Holy God
Yes, Black rivers flow thru my veins

MAN:
The reverend, a mighty man walking and talking with God on
his lips, in his heart. His voice lifting burdens from
a mud soaked corner of the south
The brethren, feet firm and planted, arms crossed.
With hearts and heads bowed,
Praying, praying under the anointing

MAN:
O Lord,
We stand once more in your house of prayer.
Beginning to thank you Lord for the blessing poured upon this,
your humble servants.
We want to thank you for our living and lying down
last night.
Beside angels stood and kept watch over this old body as I
slumbered and slept in the image of death.

Early this mornin, you shook us with the divine fingers of love.
Had the curtain to rise over our weeping eyes
and I just got to thank you this mornin.

MAN:

Now Lord, no doubt there's someone here this morning,
Father, woke up with a dark cloud of despair hanging over
their life. Not knowing which a way to turn or where to go
O Lord, but you being God the Father, made them and you
know all about them, this morning. Asking you to walk into
their lives, Father. Search, research their heart this morning
Find anything like sin, harm or evil asking you to move it
just now, if such will be thy will

MAN:

Walk down the aisles in the hospitals this morning
O Lordy, touch and re touch the needy one
Now Lord, now my Father
We need you to go along with us and stand by us
this morning

MAN:

Now Lord, you brought us out of darkness and into
the marvelous light
O Lordy, through hell, hard times and tribulations
Meeting our name all up and down the highway
When I'm through being called everything but a child of
God. I'm asking you to meet me in my dying hour

MAN:

When we done gone the last mile of the way
Come in off the smoky battle fields
Set our swords up in the sands of time
Ain't gonna study war no more

MAN:

O Lordy, O Lordy close our weeping eyes no Father
Give us a resting place somewhere in thy kingdom
That's my prayer this morning, in my savior Jesus name
Amen.

MAN:

The brethren, uncles and grandfathers. Deacons with
shoulders bent and knees bowed.
Their hands, strong and black, like leather
Stiff from labor and laboring. Thick-jointed fingers

clasped in humble submission. Needing strength for another
week, a day. . . or an hour.

MARVIN:

> I've got a feeling, everything's gonna be alright
> I've got a feeling, everything's gonna be alright
> I've got a feeling, everything's gonna be alright
> Be alright, be alright, be alright.

MAN:

> Proud voices rising,
> Rising deep from centuries of despair and neglect
> Give me a new name
> Like Daniel, a mighty man
> Of peace in a lion's den
> Strength to know that
> There is power in the father's house

PRINCE:

> Black rivers flow through my veins
> Rivers of wisdom. . .
> In the hands of my grandfather
> Hands that lifted the burdens of his cross
> That touched fear and held the strength of peace
> Black rivers flow through my veins
> With a hallelujah chorus
> As a manchild, feelings rising, sneaking behind the church
> Being mannish
> With the pastors daughter
> And Momma say. . . if you don't stop eyeballin' them little
> gals, she gonna slap you all the way into next week

MAN:

> Sunday dinners and church anniversaries
> Feeding your spirit and your soul
> With Mother Johnson's chocolate cake
> And Sister Thompson's macaroni and cheese
> Miss Bertha's black eyed peas. Cousin Olett's fried chicken,
> collard greens, corn muffins, red soda water, and my
> grandfather's Bar-be-que, basted to perfection. . .
> Strands of communion and wisdom,
> From my father's hands to mine

The Weaver enters carrying a piece of cloth woven from the collected strands. He extends a piece of cloth to the Prince center stage as the others hold their positions momentarily. He points toward the future as the Prince follows in silence.

ACT TWO

Scene 1

   The stage is in darkness. The Weaver walks, quietly carrying the piece of cloth woven from the collected strands. He moves towards the back drop and pulls out a strand of cloth. As he exits, we hear a soft blues harmonica. Of the men enters.

MAN:
>   North bound. . . North bound to factories pumpin' out prosperity. No more burnin' winds. It's time to go, tired of share croppin'. Seemed to be doin mo' croppin' than sharin'. Ya' see a man's spirit got to go where the spirit has hope. Spirit needs to work, body needs food. Souls need a place to grow. My brother gone already. He came home from work. Sat down. Lit a cigarette. Took two puffs. Stood back up. Put five pieces of mamma's chicken and pecan pie in a shoe box and said good-bye. Wrote to tell me that he know what it's like to breathe now. Said things are a whole let better on the south side of Chicago than in this God forsaken hell of the south.

   The men enter speaking with urgency.

PRINCE:
>   Dear Sir, I read in today's paper that they need help up north. I want to bring a bunch of race men up north. Y'all need workers and we need work.

MAN:
>   It's hard in the darkness of the south. I got a wife and two children. They need food, clothes and a roof that don't leak over their heads.

MAN:
>   My littlest one shivers all night when the wind starts to blow. It scares me. I want to protect them. Watch my kids grow and understand this ain't the way things has to be.

MAN:

Me and my wife tryin to make it. She taking in laundry, but it
don't put food on the table. She strong, she just keep smiling.

MAN:

I ain't got no choice.

MAN:

If you need some strong backs or just some more hands, please
send passes for 8 or 9 men.

MAN:

No joking. I mean business because time is running out for us
9 good men. Sincerely, L. T. Jones.

The following is a procession, performed in the style of an African boot dance,
which should symbolize the rural to urban migration of black men.

MARVIN:

Has anybody seen my brother?
Has anybody seen my brother?
He went away long ago and I've got to find him.

ALL:

Here I am brother.
I been (pause) workin' real hard
And I need some inspiration (pause)
Just to move on
Work on brother
Work on
Work on brother, work on
Work on brother, work on, work on, work on, work on
WORK!

Scene 2

Man 1 gets his guitar and begins to pick out a melody as he speaks.

MAN 1:

Yeah, my daddy moved to Memphis when he was 19,
moved to Memphis with a tornado on his tail. Riding his
team of mules just as fast as he could, with Big mamma
crying and tumbling around all in the back of the wagon.
Just a screaming as that tornado kept on coming. Pots
clanging, boxes sliding back and forth. Anyway, Ol' Buck,

that was the mule, in his youngest day couldn't out run no tornado. The wagon flipped. Daddy picked up Big mamma and ran for cover as all their belongings flew to who knows where.

Man 2 and Man 3 enter as old blues men, they listen to the story.

MAN 1:

> After using all their strength to get between them and death, they set off to find the plot of land they bought. And wouldn't you know it, that hell wind touched down of their plot. Big oak trees pulled out of the ground. Trees that had been there for years ripped out of the earth. . . laying all around my daddy's plot of land.
>
> My daddy stood there. Seeing the tears congregate in Big mamma's eyes. Fighting back his own meeting. That man got up, got all them oak trees together, picked up a tornado bent hatchet and after three months of work, pain and Big mamma's bitching built two things. A feed store and out house. The two things every man needs. A way to provide for his family and place to take a good sh . . .

MAN 3:
(Singing, badly)

> My mind is weary and my feet feel so sore
> My mind is weary and my feet feel so sore. Cause you see I been walking since I walked out that door . . .

MAN 2:

> I met the blues 29 years ago in a field house outside of Hattiesburg, Mississippi. Yes Sir. Spent too much time working for the man. Got up. Dropped my hoe. Put my bag down. Went right over to my woman, Essie Mae Durham's house on Atlanta St. and slapped her. She had been sleeping with Rayford Williams for a month and a half. Slammed that rusty screen door and started walking. Had not a dime or destination, Only thing I had was a pair of brand new shoes. Brown soft leather. Won them in dance contest. Best pair of shoes I ever had. Didn't even have to break them in.

MAN 3:
(Singing)

> Well I got up one morning, Just wasn't feelin right
> inside. I got up one mornin, Just wasn't feelin right inside

I knowed I wasn't happy no more, so I got up and walked
out that door . . .

MAN 2:

They was good for walking. Had plenty of room for my
toes. Anyway, I met up with a fellow going to the city and
figured I was going that way too. Seemed like a nice fellow.
We walked. . . laughed . . . talked about life. He was nice
enough to teach me a lil' harmonica. We was some
walking/singing fools. Them hot roads with that smoke
coming off made for nasty traveling. But we did not stop.
Seemed like a real nice fellow. Two days away from
Jackson he beat me up and took my shoes. No dime,
destination or shoes. I had no choice but to sing the blues.

MAN 1:

I don't care what you say, there is something about the
blues.

A blues singer, obviously down on his luck, enter and begins his song.

MARVIN:

Well I gotta keep wallkin', walkin' down the line
I gotta keep walkin', walkin' down that line
I gotta keep walkin' an' singin' my song

Till I find a place where I belong.
My momma tol' me a story about a man they called my dad.
My momma tol' me a story about a man they called my dad.
Now I am walking in his foot steps
Hopin' my story don't come out so bad.

My gal she love, Love me more than I'll evuh know
My gal she love me more than I'll evuh know
She dream of me an her together
And I'm dreaming about there where I got to go.

Well I don't know where I am goin' but I
Hope the place bring me good news.
Well I don't know where I am goin' but I
Hope the place bring me good news
Well I hope I get there sooner or later
So I can get rid of these walking blues.

The other men join in as he exits.

Well I gotta keep walkin', walkin' down the line
I gotta keep walkin' an' singing my song
Till I find a place wheew I belong.

A young jazz sax man, portrayed by the Prince, enters.

PRINCE:

Well, if it ain't the fabulous trio of Leroy Chapman Johnson
Smith, Isaiah, 'T-Bob' Git-Tar Tompkins and the immortal,
incomparable and half-time incapacitated Tyrone 'Regal- Room
Red'. Ain't it past your bed time boys?

MAN 3:

We was about to ask you the same thing, little boy.

PRINCE:

Cool out daddy (Mocking the old men) "Don't want to get
your heart a racing. You know you ain't as spry as you used to
be."

MAN 3:

I can still kick your monkey ass. . .

MAN 1:

What you doing over this way, boy? Ain't you supposed to be
playing your jazz somewhere? What you want?

PRINCE:

Nothing much. Came to see how my old man is doing. Show
you my new horn. . . and tell y'all that this 'Blues Man' stuff is
real funny. (T-Bone jumps up. Regal-Room holds him back)
OOOOhhhh. . .

MAN 1:

I know we ain't wearing a pretty blue suit like you, but why
funny?

PRINCE:

Well all this talk about "Walking, walking, walking down the
line and she ain't do me right. . . " Its funny. Almost
embarrassing.

MAN 3:

Oh, we embarrassing now? (Jumps again)

PRINCE:

Yeah, embarrassing. Seeing grown men cry. Life ain't that bad, fellows. It's time to move on. Think about black kisses from a sweet chocolate gal instead of some trifling sister throwing bricks at folks. And besides that stuff is simple. "My gal she don't love me. I can't sleep at night. My gal she don't love me. I can't sleep at night. She a big fat ugly cow of a woman and she don't do me right." Ain't y'all never heard of variation?

MAN 2:

Did you ever think about the fact that it was all we had? Yeah, that's all we had. . . them three line. We had them lines and a whole hell of a lot a pain to put in them boy. See, you all in such a big hurry to judge what we do. Boy you ain't got enough bass in your voice or seen enough to know blue. That's all I need. That's it. . . three lines and me. I can tell you a whole story and have you cry in them few lines, boy.

NAT:

Cry? Cry? Get real man. See I may not have all your bass or even all your grey, but I have seen a couple things. Listen old man I seen Harlem at night. . . black folks scream for more as five men start chopping heads left and right as jazz woke up and stood. It's art. Listen. I can still hear it. Charlie Parker ain't never lied to nobody. Notes true. . . not hiding nothin.

MAN 3:

Well I don't know Charlie Parker. Probably a nice fellow but it sound like you talking about Mr. Elmore James. He ain't lie to nobody. The man would sing his soul. And for any man to do that he had to be strong.

PRINCE:

Strong? Crying the way y'all do?

MAN 3:

See, that's just it. You got to be strong to cry. You got to. See you had it too easy to know. . .

PRINCE:

Too easy? Naw, I didn't have it that easy. That sweet ass blues man over there kicked me out. A man that was at home 5 weeks out the year kicked me out the house. Left. Had to go. Left them damn blues. See that's why I am feeding my belly with pure sounds. Ain't nothing blue about jazz nights. Electric. Alive. Notes so tough. . . women so soft. . .

MAN 1:
> Why are you here, boy?

MAN 3:
> What you want?

PRINCE:
> Y'all still don't hear it to do you? Still hearing them hell hounds ain't you? Too busy frying fish and squeezing mud between your toes to hear.

MAN 1:
> Naw boy, I hear it. I hear a boy done got too big for his britches. . .

PRINCE:
> No sir, I ain't got that big yet, but let me keep talking I might. I can't look back there. Ain't nothing back there but burning memories. Yeah, that heat and that old leaning wood slat house. Do you remember that, Daddy? Can you? Try. I do. I also remember, "Boy mind your manners" and "Boy you can't do that" and "Boy you need to learn a trade." This from some shine-drinking blues man. I used to ask Momma where you were and why had to sing. She's say that's the only thing you knew. I guess she was right cause you didn't know she was sick. You didn't know we needed you. Is that when you started singing that great hit, "It's a low down dirty shame." Well it is and you are. A shiftless, blues singing, Son of a Bitch. . .

He slaps the mess out of him.

MAN 1:
> Boy don't talk about things you don't understand. Don't! I loved your momma till the day she died and I still do. Don't you think I asked myself them same questions? Huh? Why did I go? Was it the music? Was it the drinking or was it I was scared? I don't know but I am damned to think and wonder about it every day. Every day missing her. Every damn day seeing you standing there alone. I didn't know if you and your momma was dead or not and half the time I didn't know about myself either. . . Now all I can do is sing. . .

PRINCE:
> And all I can do is play.

MAN:

    What do you want, boy, an apology?

PRINCE:

    Naw old man I want to know why. Why I lay awake wanting
    you. A man I ain't ever know. Wanting you to tell me it's alright
    to fall and to be scared. Why? Why can't I love you. Can't talk. Only
    time I am saying something is on stage with my horn. Daddy is
    it the music?

MAN 1:

    Naw son. It ain't just the music. . . It's the soul.

    The Weaver enters pulling a strand across the stage. The Prince watched him. As
he exits another jazz man enters and begins to play. Two men enter dressed in
black. The following is a jazz narrative.

Scene 3

PRINCE:

    AAAUUUUUUUGH! BAAAAAD!!!!!!!!!
    We be bad
    Was bad
    We be a bad Black seed
    Black seed, Black seed
    Be growing 400 years
    400 years of planting
    Black seeds be growing

MAN:

    HEADLINE: "Local colored boy makes good"
    But he can't breathe

PRINCE:

    Black seeds be growing

MAN:

    "A credit to his race."
    "A honor to his people."
    Black seeds be growing

MAN:

    "Make his Mama proud"

PRINCE:

Black seeeeeeeeeeds. . .

MAN:

"Make his Daddy stand up straight"

PRINCE:

No more shoe shining rag popping
No more no-tip luggage carrying
Bending over back breaking
Elevator up/down

MAN:

Can I clear your table Sir?

PRINCE:

Where is my broom?

MAN:

Lord have mercy I declare I'm fresh out of Mr. Clean

PRINCE:

Drilling, toting, fetching
Machine making quotas on assembly lines
Swallowing my tongue to save my ass
"No sir I don't need no overtime, my family be doing fine."

MAN:

Black seeds be growing
In my heart
No more hush puppies, white socks, bow ties
And starched jeans
Holding my lips in to make myself pretty
Gassing my head--dyeing it red
Greasy do-rag
Hair so wavy it makes women
Sea sick. . .

MAN:

No more suicide thoughts

PRINCE:

Black seeds be growing

MAN:

No more killing thoughts

Murdering dreams and dreamers
Floating in red, white and blue nothingness
Black seeds be growing

PRINCE:

No more searching for last manliness
In wine bottles and roach clips
And wayside women

ALL:

Slapping, pulling, pushing
Clawing for life

PRINCE:

In alleys, juke joints
And flop houses

ALL:

No more

MAN:

No more Negroland
A place where they don't believe a thing
They just do your thing
When they really want a chicken wing
Raising their eyes to no-thing
No more Negroland
Black seeds be growing

PRINCE:

Bad black seeds be growing
Growing in my shoes--'tween my toes
Moving up my legs
Down my back

ALL:

400 years of ancient Black seeds
Be growing, be growing

MAN:

What was that? Did you hear it?
Feeeeeeed it?
LOOK OUT!!!!!!!

MAN:

Hair kinking

Lips unfurling
Noes spreading

MAN:

Oiling down
Stretching full body in the sun
Getting Black
Black seeds Black
Growing Black
BLAAAAAAAAACK

PRINCE:

Blacker than I was yesterday
Moving from out to in
Rising rage and revolution
Racing, running, revolution and ricochet
Look out!

ALL:

I'm coming to your neighborhood

Scene 4

Another man enter.

MAN:

BLACK POWER!!! Ya dig? I mean I was all in it. I
was a 'rally-going, dashiki-wearing, power fist Afro pick in
the back pocket', brother. I hung with the Nation, SNCC,
the Panthers and all other groups of that nature. Proud? You
couldn't tell me nothing. I was down for the cause and the
cause was most certainly down with me. 1970, I was
working with a very proactive militant group of brothers.
The A.A.C.F.D.T.C.D., you know the Afro-American
Council For Development Through Cash Donations.

I was on my first day of field work and walked
into this shoe factory, ya dig? You should have seen me. I
layed down this heavy rap about how the institution was
bringing down the brother man and elevating the other man.
How someday little black children and little white children
ain't gonna be able to play together cause the little black
children ain't got no shoes. And it would be in their best
interest to up some case before the revolution come. I must
have been convincing, because I got a fifty dollar
donation and a job offer. . . Shiiiiiiit, I took both.

So there I was. Seven inches cut off my 'fro'. Brand new
brown plaid suit. . . the first brother in a management
position. Yeah, things changed. I moved out of my
momma's house into this nice pad. Got a brand new lime
green Pinto. I mean out of sight. You couldn't tell me
nothin. I got there the first day and obviously was looking
good because I turned every head.

I even met the boss on the first day. They was treating me
good. They on saying things like: "So , this is Mr. Johnson"
and "I'm sure we will be doing a whole lot better now that
Mr. Johnson is here." The boss even called me 'Mr.
Johnson-Brother Man.' It was crazy. He winked, I smiled
and they showed me to my office. MY office. I was
tripping. I had my own office. . . OK it wasn't
so much an office as a really big closet, but it was mine.
They set me up with the company training books and told me
to start reading. Well I went to my office everyday and read.
And read and read some more. All day lone. I would hear
"Yes, this is Mr. Johnson." The only time I lifted a finger
was to get my paycheck.

One Friday I was standing in line to get my check when I
happened to hear some of the sales reps talking about how they
was happy they hired this one new guy in spite of the
fact that they were kind of upset that this 'Negro' was
getting paid to sit on his big black butt. Man, I started
sweating on my nose and getting edgy because I knew that
Negro was me and the big black ass they was talking about
was mine. I got my check, then headed back to the bosses
office to have a word with him.

I knocked on the door and he jumped and said, What do
you want, I'm a busy man, Johnson." I said, "I would like
to have a word with you if you might Mr. Charlie, I mean
Mr. Carlton. When am I gonna get some more responsibilities
around here? I mean I been here for a year and the only thing
I've done is make sure you all's pamphlets get read."

He said, "Is that all that's bugging you Johnson? Here,
take these papers and make me some copies." Then he went
to talking on the phone. I said, "EXCUSE ME, but I thought
I was MANAGEMENT." He told me to leave his office and
get back to work. I was mad now. I was about to show my
color, but I kindly said I really needed to straighten this out
today. He said, "Boy, you are here because the government

won't give us contracts unless we have coloreds in management. What's wrong with getting paid to do nothing. Isn't that all you people ever wanted? I thought you were different but you're all alike. . . never happy with what we give you. Well, you don't have to worry about responsibility any more. You're fired. I can always get another nigger." Man I was dumbfounded. I stood there and looked at him. He said, "What do you want now, Johnson?"

Man I stepped back, you dig? And put one hand in my pocket and with the other hand pointed him dead in his face and said, "You know what I want. I want my afro back and my pick with the little fist and my damn dashiki!! And I want you to take your coffee, them pamphlets and shit and kiss this Mr. Johnson's big black ass."

Scene 5

We hear a familiar rhythmic pattern prevalent in rap music. As it builds, the entire ensemble enters (including the Prince, who does not speak during this segment), they have become angry young men, disenfranchised--they are a roving street gang. They work the audience over before they begin to speak rhythmically.

MAN:
You know where I come from by the rhythm I keep. You hear the pavement, the projects and the brothers on the corner downing the eight ball. You see in my walk that I was born with a dirty spoon in my mouth and did not like the taste. You all know but think I don't. But I am here to tell you . . . I can kick a little ass if I have to.

MAN:
My knowledge goes beyond the slave shores of 1619. My knowledge was born in the womb of an African star that enlightened civilization lasting more than 200 years guiding man to spirit and spirit to man. A light so bright it blinded man's eyes so that he could see his true and righteous nature. And still . . . I can kick a little ass if I have to.

MAN:
It's not just in my head. It's in my hands than can pound gold into jewelry and blanket a caress. It's in my walk that proclaims defiance yet begs humility to God. It's in my voice screaming pain while singing of love and loves lost.

It's in my eyes. Take a look. Do you see anger or pain? I
see the burning of knowledge giving strength to each man
to stand up and shake the walls down of ignorance forcing
injustice to fall at its feet. In spite of all this... I will kick
a little ass if I have to.

MAN:

I understand the plethora of idiosyncrasies in man's
innermost existence. The complexities of time and space. I
know Darwinism first hand. I understand iambic pentameter.
I scream in sonnet form. I've heard Ravel's Bolero and
understood and dissected the beat. In fact "To be or not to
be" ain't no question; it's a hypothesis of being. And that is
why . . . I can kick a little ass if I have to.

MAN:

I understand the flood of emotions that come from the
realization that knowledge without the love of a black
woman means nothing. It has filled me up and has stripped
me down and has filled me up again. I have tasted a passion
so strong that the Almighty God had to step back and trip out
on his creation. So, believe me when I say I can kick a little
ass when I have to.

MAN:

All of this knowledge has lead to a self-fulfillment and love. I
want to hold you. Touch. Understand. To teach you.
Let's hold hands before they become clenched fists. Love me.
Don't force me to kick a little ass if have to.

The men confront the audience again. The Prince has become violently angry.
The group persuades him that it's not worth it. Believing that he had calmed down,
they exit; leaving him alone.

Scene 6

As the lights fade, we hear the sound of an approaching storm. The Prince is
wearing a strand of cloth tied around his head as a head band.

PRINCE:

Yeah, I'm cool . . . I'm alright . . . Naw, I'll catch up
later . . . Peace out, yeah I'll see y'all at the center. Peace . . .

Singing to himself "Me and Eric B. was Coolin at the Palladium"
See a fly girl all world I say hey lady I'm

Sorry if ya in a rush
I don't mean to be mean
Or intervene or interrupt . . .

Shit it sho has been good. We been together for awhile, you
and me. Yeah I was down. You either got it or got your ass
kicked. They had to recruit some young ass brothers. They
asked my boy Kenny that. See Kenny thought he was the
hardest brother this side of hell. He told them, "Naw I ain't
down with shit." They beat Kenny down so bad, they
came up to me. Shit what was I supposed to say? Next thing
I know, I'm hanging tough. Moms didn't like that too much.
We was runnin' shit. My initiation, petty theft. I got caught
and got eight months in the county jail. I ain't gonna lie. I
was scared. That shit wasn't no joke. You could get all the
speed, crack, weed, coke you wanted. I didn't have nothing
else. My old dude . . . that crazy bastard disowned me. Shit, I
was lucky my Moms came. At least it was one person that
didn't forget my ass. When I got out, my Moms took me in,
fed me, took care of me. She was always working. My old
dude ain't had a job for 10-15 years. He got fucked up in
Viet Nam Always flashing back like he was back in the
jungle and shit. Come home catch that old man jumpin out
of bushes and shit. I thought it was funny at first.

I came home one morning, had to be about four. I hear my
Moms crying. He had beat the shit out of her. Almost broke
her jaw. I found her in the corner of my room tied up with a
telephone cord. Dripping with blood and tears. I hunted that
mutha fucker down for a week . . . for a week.

I came home from my girl's house and I seen him. Yelling
about shit that happened 20 years ago. He had this gun in
my Momma's mouth, screaming about shit ain't been FAIR. I
shot him so many times the police thought five people
attacked him. I couldn't let him take the only thing I had.
NOT MY MOMS. They let me go cause she told them what
happened. But she don't talk to me no more and I ain't seen
her since. Shit, it don't matter. SHIT AIN'T SUPPOSED
TO BE FAIR OL' MAN. I tell you what ain't fair. God I hate
this shit. I can't do no more. I ain't got nothing. Nothin I
have looked my life in the eye and cried.

Sensing that something is wrong, he grabs his arms and feels it burning.

Shit. NO . . . OH GOD NO . . . I ain't gonna die in

a pile of nothing . . . Like this . . . But it hurts so bad, so bad,
so bad. GOD, God . . . God help me . . . Save me . . .

Scene 7

   The Prince falls to his knees, collapsing. The lighting changes, We hear the
African drums. The men enter, followed by the Weaver, wearing formal African
ceremonial attire. A robe made from the collected strands of cloth is carried on.
During the ceremony, the robe is placed on the Prince, liberating him from his
turmoil. The men chant.

ALL:
> Drums, hear the drums
> Drums, hear the drums
> Hear the drums, hear the drums
> Hear . . . etc.

WEAVER:
> Once there were plains of sand
> And silence of a million years
> Until a pyramid was built
> So perfect that every night your star fell on its point
> And your people celebrated your existence with drums . . .

CHANT:
> Drums, hear the drums
> Drums, hear the drums
> Hear the drums, hear the drums
> Hear . . .

WEAVER:
> At nightfall you danced love
> Consumed spirit and sand the song of your fathers
> Dreaming life
> With family and strength you slept

CHANT:
> Drums, hear the drums
> Drums, hear the drums
> Hear the drums, hear the drums
> Hear . . . etc.

WEAVER:
> At the break of day a different sun rose
> To strangers in your world

Slave nets dragged you
Running
Fighting
Holding on to an almighty God
Brave men
Hear the drums
Sing the song of your fathers

The chant stops.

WEAVER:
No silence
Only shouts of lost men
In damp stretch filled holes of
Ships where death crawled
Screaming
In tongues only you understood
Brave men
Hear the drums
Sing the song of your fathers
Full of your history

CHANT:
Drums, hear the drums
Drums, hear the drums
Hear the drums, hear the drums
Hear . . . etc.

WEAVER:
Stripped
Bought
Beaten
In unmerciful rhythms
The whip rising, falling, rising, falling
Thrown on never seen shores
Where spirits left
Once dreamed songs dying in the sun.
Life pouring down your shoulder
Tears and pain clinging to your throat

The chant stops.

Your women,
In the white fields of remorse
No longer at the river gathering water for the day
Wiping sweat with callused hands

Lying numb . . .
Tears falling on linen pillows
Brave men
Hear the drums
Sing the song of your fathers
Full of your history and purpose

CHANT:
Drums, hear the drums
Drums, hear the drums
Hear the drums, hear the drums
Hear . . . etc.

WEAVER:
Working until they thought you couldn't
Tortured by lies and half truths
Brave men, hear the drums
Sing the song of your fathers
"No more auction block for me"
"Steal away, steal away . . ."
"I ain't gon'let nobody turn me 'round"
"Free at last, free at last, thank God almighty . . ."

Brave men
Hear the drums
Sing the song of your fathers
Full of your history and purpose
Rise again
Build again
Yell the battle cry

The chant stops.

For once a pyramid was built, so perfect
And a star fell on its point
And your people celebrated your existence

CHANT:
Drums, hear the drums
Drums, hear the drums
Hear the drums
Hear the drums, Hear!

THE END

UNION STATION

A Drama In Two Acts

by

Marta J. Effinger

CHARACTERS
(in order of appearance)

Chloe Avery. 10-year-old very curious daughter of Rutherford and Cecilia Avery.

Rutherford Avery. 33-year-old attractive Black male of medium build. Works as a parking lot attendant while aspiring to be an entrepreneur (*own a bakery*). Cecilia's husband.

Hamlin "Golden Lips" Warden Jackson. 63-year-old, Black male. Widower, employed at Union Station as Red Cap. Plays the harmonica.

Booker Avery. 13-year-old son of Rutherford and Cecilia Avery.

Cecilia "Cil" Avery. 32-year-old, Black female, dark and beautiful with full features. Tired from working routine office job for the government. Mother of two children (Booker and Chloe) and Rutherford's wife. A sculptor.

Nate. Rutherford's friend.

Alberta Jean Jackson-Collins. 45-year-old Black female with graying hair, full Black woman. Hamlin's daughter who works with Cecilia. Widow.

Jacob "Jellybean" Douglas. Hamlin's old buddy, drives his own cab. Plays the guitar.

Vernon Taylor. Howard University student, Big Brother/Mentor to Booker.

Radio Disc Jockey. Female or Male.

Radio Listener. Female or Male.

Time: The summer of 1978. Place: Northeast section of Washington, D.C. off of North Capital. All action occurs in the jointly occupied home of the Avery's and the Jackson's. Act I: Thursday, early evening. Act II: Saturday around noon.

ACT 1

SCENE 1

(Lights rise on the outside of the house where Chloe Avery is jumping rope alone. Lights then rise on the inside of the house that is filled with different styles of furniture. Pictures, antiques, and a few large and small sculptures also fill up the area. Cecilia Avery is standing at the dining room table decorating a cake. Hamlin Jackson is seated at a smaller table in the room folding boxes and placing tissue paper inside of them. Rutherford Avery is standing behind his son, Booker Avery showing him how to stir something in a bowl. Other smaller cakes and pies are sitting around the room in bunches.)

Chloe

I like coffee, I like tea, I like the boys and the boys like me. Oh, yes, no, maybe so. Oh, yes, no maybe so…

D.J.

Hey, soul sisters and brothers. It's Thursday afternoon and the rush hour traffic is almost ovvvvveeeeerrrr. I know all of ya'll are ready to party. Listen now, I know some of you are still stuck on the road, but for the rest of you that are at your cribs mellowin' out I've got a tune for you that's goin' ta' get you in the mooooooood. If you know it, give me a call at 90.3 FM.

(Song plays and Chloe still outside at the window anxiously begins to listen attempting to remember the title)

Hamlin

(Rubs/plays his harmonica that is placed on the table)… Well you know I sleep with my harmonica, playin' a little tune at night helps me to sleep better. Whatever ailment I ever got, I believe my harmonica do the trick better than any doctor's concoction cause back in…

Cecilia

(Continues to decorate the cake slightly ignoring Hamlin) Umm, hmm, Mr. Hamlin, umm, hmm…

Rutherford

(Standing behind Booker, his hands over the Booker's hands) See you have to stir it like that. You got It? (He pats Booker's head)

Booker

Yes sir.

D.J.

(*No one has given the D.J. the name of the song*) Citizens of the chocalaaaaateeeee ciiiiityyyyyy, I want your calls. You all know the tune.

(*Music continues to play and Chloe continues to listen and think at the window*) Rutherford crosses to Hamlin and places hand on his shoulder)

Rutherford

Mr. Hamlin, you need some help with them boxes?

Hamlin

Makin' out fine. It's up to you if you wanta' help me. Just don't come messin' up my system.

(*Rutherford exits to the kitchen*)

Booker

(*Continues to stir*) Mr. Hamlin can you pass me that cinnamon?

> (*Hamlin passes him a grater, plate, and cinnamon sticks, he places bowls down and begins to grate. Fire alarm heard outside. Chloe stops jumping for a second to try and see where the fire engine is going*)

Hamlin

(*To himself*) More sirens go down this street in the summer than the law should allow. Man can't think with them things interruptin' all the time.

Rutherford

(*From kitchen*) How you all coming along out there? Cil, you all almost finished? Booker you need some more help?

Cecilia

(*Moving to the window to check on Chloe*) Relax, Rutherford. We're almost done?

Booker

No sir.

Rutherford

Anybody know what time it is?

Hamlin

(*Slowly moves to pull something out of his pocket*) You ask that just awhile ago.

D.J.

Who do I have on the phone?

Radio Listener

(*Loudly*) This is Patrice Brown of Northwest D.C.

D.J.

Okay, Patrice. You tell me the name of the tune I just played and I'll give you $100 in cash.

Radio Listener

Okay, is it umm, umm, "You've Met Match" by Stevie Wonder?

D.J.

That's right, and you just got yourself some cash.

Chloe

(*Chloe disappointed starts to jump rope again*) I like tea, I like the boys, and the boys like me, Oh, yes…

Cecilia

(*Crosses to the window*) Chloe Avery, what is that I hear you sayin'?

Chloe

(*Startled*) Nothin' mommy.

Cecilia

It better be nothin'. Come on in here and help us with all of this work.

Chloe

(*Running up steps to house*) Yes mam.

(Door closes)

Hamlin

(*Looking at a watch taken from his pocket*) It be about 6:45.

Rutherford

(*Entering*) Cil, is that Nate?

Cecilia

No, baby. He's not here. (*to Chloe*) Go on in the kitchen and wash those hands. (*She moves back to decorate cake*)

(*Chloe exits*)

Rutherford
(*Moves to window*) He was supposed to be here twenty minutes ago. He's gonna make us late.

Hamlin
I would hate to be dyin' and have to depend on that boy, Nate to save me. Late all the time. Umm, umm.

(*Noise heard from kitchen, everyone turns around*)

Cecilia
Booker, go see what your sister is doing in there.

(Booker exits)

Rutherford
(*Opens the door. Nate enters*) Hey, man you're late.

Nate
(*Slaps Rutherford's shoulder*) No I'm not.

Rutherford
You were supposed to be here at 6:00 p.m. to help finish some of this baking.

Nate
Man, I can't bake. I can't even cook an egg really good. And anyways, my watch says five minutes 'til 6:00. (*He taps watch*) Oh, it stopped running. (*He laughs lightly*) Well if I got paid a little then maybe I could afford a watch. How's everybody doin?

(Cast responds to Nate)

Hamlin
See this watch here Nate, been gettin' me where I wanta' go on time for nearly forty years. Yep. Know where I got it from?

Nate
From one of your earlier customers at the Union Station.

Hamlin
Yes sir, from being one of the best red caps they done ever seen. Folks know to call…

Nate
(*Interrupts Hamlin. Smells.*) Umm,umm. What is that I smell?

Rutherford
(*Proudly*) I've been teachin' my son how to make lemon pound cake.

(Nate continues to smell)

I've got an order for tomorrow for apple crumb cake and I'm lettin' him start it.

(Nate moves to Booker looking over his shoulder.)

You pick up them items from the warehouse?

Nate
(*Pulls out a list from his pocket*) Stuff is in the truck, 15 pound bag of flour sugar, pecans and whatever else you had on the list (*He pulls out the receipt and places it on a table, Cecilia looks at it*) Oh, you didn't have any change.

Rutherford
I bet. I'll see about that later.

Booker
(*Enters holding Chloe's shirt*) Here she is?

Chloe
Get off of me Booka? Daddy tell Booka' ta' stop pullin' on me.

Rutherford
(*Crossing to Chloe*) Why don't you come over here and put your hands to some good use? (*He picks up some napkins and leads her to the living room near the pieces of art*)

Cecilia
Rutherford, don't put her near my art work.

Rutherford
Baby. We need more room. Chloe knows not to bother it. She's only folding napkins. (*He tickles her and she laughs*) Right Chloe.

Chloe
Right daddy. (*She turns radio dial*)

(Cecilia has a blank expression on her face and continues decorating the cake)

Nate
Rutherford cornered you into helping again too, huh?

Hamlin

No. I offered. He's been baking since I went to work this morning and he's been at it all this afternoon. I thought I could at least lend a hand.

Nate

What?

Rutherford

See man, some people offer. You don't have to twist their arm.

Nate

I'll try and remember that. (*Pause*) Hey, man whose anniversary is this for again?

Rutherford

The Williams' over on Road Island Avenue. It's their 40th anniversary.

Nate

(He *shrugs his shoulders as if he is jokingly fearful of the idea*) Ooww. I can't see being married that long.

Rutherford

(*Pulls Cecilia to him*) I can man. Right about the time I set my sights on a bakery in high school, I set my sights on this woman.

Cecilia

Rutherford I have to finish this.

Rutherford

I want to be with this woman until they put me in the grave. Umm, umm, umm.

(Hamlin looks up smiling)

Hamlin

(*To Alma*) Alma, we nearly reached our 40th anniversary, didn't we girl, five years ago. (*Pause*) I was just showing them my watch, still can't go nowhere without it, you need…

(Everyone stares)

Rutherford

(*Interrupts*) Nate, why don't we start packing the cakes up now?

(Nate pats Hamlin on the shoulder)

Booker

Ma that looks good. (He *exits to kitchen*)

Nate

Cil you got a gift for decorating cakes. Look at this Rutherford.

Rutherford

(*Barely noticing, but hugging Cecilia's shoulder*) I know. I know. I hope I made enough pies. (*Pause; checks something in a box then reaches another to hand it to Nate*) Nate can you get the packages out of the truck so we can start loading up?

(*Nate exits outside and Cecilia exits to kitchen*)

Nate

(*Appears outside with a large bag of flour, Rutherford crosses outside to help him*) What did the boss man at the parking lot say when you told him you'd be late tonight?

(*Rutherford doesn't respond. They enter house and quickly drop bag of flour at the feet of one of Cecilia's sculptures in the living room*)

You know he don't like ya'll guys askin' to leave early…So what he say?

Rutherford

(*Motions for him not to talk loud. Nervously looks to make sure Cecilia isn't listening*) Not much.

Nate

What you mean, not much I know that boss wouldn't let you come in late without havin' a few words to say. He always makin' sure he get every minute of work out of you and then some. (*He exits outside with another box*)

Hamlin

(*Overhearing and looking down*) Don't never hurt to tell somethin' to somebody twice. That's what I say. Then the folks who in charge ain't got no need to go wonderin' and suspectin' that you doin' somethin' that ain't got no purpose. (*He looks up slowly and directly at Rutherford, who looks back with a slight smile*)

(*Rutherford crosses to the phone and dials. Alberta coming from work appears outside*)

Nate

(*To Alberta*) Lord, I done died and gone to heaven. He sure been lookin' out for me.

Alberta

Don't you ever know how to greet anyone with some sense?

Nate

(*Bowing to her*) You know I just fall to pieces when I see ya'.

Alberta
(*Walking up the steps*) Ain't you got something... anything to take care of?

Nate
(*smiling broadly*) You the only thing I want to take care of.

(Alberta exits inside)

Rutherford
This is Rutherford Avery...Yes, I know I'm supposed to be workin' tonight, but like I explained to you before I might be a little late. I know there's a shortage on Thursday's...I know, but... listen, why are you giving me a hard time?

(*Cecilia and Booker enter, she begins to place more items in the dining room while listening to the phone conversation, she then pushes Booker to the front door with items, he exits*)

I told you before I have to take care of some important business...I'll...I've...been working for you for enough years. You can't...I know that...(*Angrily*) I know that too. And I said I would make up the time...Whatever. (He slams down the phone)

Alberta
(*Enters and sinks down into the sofa*) Lord, that Nate is a nut and a half. (*Noticing Chloe*) How you doin' today Chloe?

Chloe
I almost had $100 Miss Alberta.

Alberta
(*Rises to touch her head, then looks around the house*) See that's why the electric bill so high cause don't nobody know how to economize around here. (*She moves to turn off radio, another light, and then crosses to Hamlin*)

Rutherford
Don't look at me like that Cil

Cecilia
Like What?

Rutherford
Like I just shot somebody.

Alberta
(*Kisses Hamlin's forehead*) Evenin' daddy. How ya' doing?

Hamlin

Alright, baby. Why you so late, why didn't you come home with Cil?

Alberta

(*Turns out lights in dining room while he is still sitting there*) I had to finish some typing before I left the office. (*Pause*) How was work? Was Union Station crowded today?

Hamlin

Commuters and tourists were coming in and out of town. It seems like they multiply by the thousands each year. (*He crosses to the living room to turn on television, Chloe joins him*)

Cecilia

(*Moving to clean up area*) What's the problem with you and your boss Rutherford?

Rutherford

He's just mouthin' off 'cause I'm going to be a little late for work tonight.

Cecilia

Oh, Rutherford. Why didn't you tell me this? Nate and I could have handled the delivery for that anniversary.

Alberta

(*Wiping up dining room table. To herself*) Ya'll seem to waste more and more of the ingredients each time I turn around. Don't ya'll know how to save the flour that might fall on the table for later?

Rutherford

(*Pause, begins to make sure he isn't leaving anything behind*) Why are you startin' to worry again, Cil, huh? I told you I'll go park them cars after I finish. They aren't going anywhere, and neither is the boss man. And you saw for yourself I tried to be polite about it, but he just won't let me be

Cecilia

Rutherford, one day you'll turn around and you won't have a job parking cars.

Rutherford

Won't need it because we'll have the Avery Family Bakery. (*He moves to pick up a box, then to kiss Cecilia*) We'll talk about it later okay, now give me some sugar. (*She pecks him on the cheek dryly as Booker enters*)

Alberta

(*Looking at receipt on the table*) By the looks of this receipt if you keep spending like this, you'll be spending more than you be saving.

Rutherford

Alberta, how long have we been livin' together?

Alberta

(*Jokingly*) You know it's been a long year and a half.

Rutherford

I keep tellin' you over and over all these ingredients are necessary, to make everything perfect. I can't skimp on my customers.

Alberta

Suit yourself. (*Continues to clean*)

Booker

Dad, you didn't forget about the meeting tomorrow at Howard University did you? It's an open house for the mentor program.

Rutherford

I've got an appointment at the bank tomorrow Booker. I don't know what time I'll be finished.

Booker

(*Disappointed*) But, I'm suppose to bring somebody along with me. I can't go by myself. I told you…I might be included in their Saturday science and math workshops for Jr. High school students in the fall.

Nate

(*Nate enters*) Everything is in the truck.

Rutherford

This meeting at the bank is very important Booker. Okay? (*He answers for Booker*) Okay, now why don't you come along with me and Nate? He'll drop you off after we're finished.

Booker

But, I really didn't…

Cecilia

Go on with your father Booker. It might be fun. (*Booker looks disappointed*)

(*Nate and Rutherford move to exit*)

Nate

(*Winking*) See you later Alberta.

Rutherford

(*Laughing*) You two got something going on here?

Hamlin

(*Still looking at* TV) That's what I'd like to know.

Alberta

You all get on out of here with your crazy selves.

(Rutherford and Nate exit)

Rutherford

(*Rutherford yells back*) Booker grab my uniform out of the closet.

Booker

(*Gets uniform out of closet*) Ma, what about the meeting?

Cecilia

I'll go with you.

Booker

But you've been goin' all along to meet Vernon. (*Pause, disappointed*) I don't even want him to know about it anymore. He doesn't care.

Cecilia

When things calm down around here, I'll mention it to him.

Booker

I don't even care anymore. (*Pause*) You know I asked him to take me to that lecture at the college…He was busy. I asked him go to that exhibit with me…he was bakin', and made me do that instead too. Only time he wants to talk is to bring that bakin' up. (*Pause*) That's right don't mention it. You know what he's gonna say. He's probably gonna blow up, I bet ya.

Cecilia

Don't bet me. (*Pause*) Booker things have been looking up for your daddy. He might be glad to see somebody takin' you out to places and all.

Booker

Ma' you're gonna' take care of everything, right. Even if daddy doesn't want me to, you're gonna let Vernon be my Big Brother/Mentor aren't you? The people down at the program have already set everything up. I can't leave the guy hangin'. Ma he's real nice. He gets good grades from Howard and all. He's studying Black studies and everything. I never met anybody in college who majors in studying their own people. Now that's bad. He's even…

Cecilia

(*Smiling*) I've heard the entire plug for Vernon Taylor. I know it back and front now. You want me to repeat it to you? He's real nice ma, he gets good grades from Howard ma…(*She moves over to playfully hug him*)

Booker

Oh, ma, I don't even sound like that.

Rutherford

(*Eagerly offstage*) Come on Booker, we've got a delivery to make.

Cecilia

Oh, ma — yes you do. Don't worry, now go on before you all are late.

> (*Booker exits. Cecilia reenters the house and looks at big bag of floor in living room near her art work*)

Alberta will you help me lift this flour into the dining room? Rutherford can put it where he needs to when he comes back.

Alberta

So how far in advance did you tell Supervisor Jenkins you had to leave early today?

Cecilia

Last week. You know that.

Alberta

I know. I just wanted to make sure, 'cause he came by after you left. He say he don't remember you askin' nothin' like that. I know he was wrong, and I told him so. That I did. You always tellin' Rutherford to make sure he tell his boss that he's not gonna' be at work, so I know you wouldn't forget to do somethin' like that.

Cecilia

I can't...

> (Hamlin looks at his watch)

Hamlin

(*Interrupting*) Ya'll need some help?

Alberta

No, you stay right there daddy.

> (*Jacob "Jellybean" Douglas, an older man in his early 60's is seen walking up to the house humming. He has a guitar strapped around his body. A straw hat on his head and a brown paper bag in one hand*)

Hamlin

If I lift heavy suitcases everyday, I can lift an ole' bag of flour.

Alberta

We have it don't worry.

(*He exits to the front porch with an old wooden crate and his harmonica*)

Hamlin

Right on time man. Right on time.

Jacob

Hey, man what it be like?

Hamlin

(*Crosses to sit*) Can't complain Jellybean, just hangin'. What 'bout you?

Jacob

(*Sits*) Hey, Golden Lips you know when the sun rise I do the same, keep on movin' everyday. (*Pause*) I was up your way yesterday. Had to drop somebody off. They said they were catchin' that train goin' to Memphis.

Hamlin

Yeah, that one was crowded. It was suppose to leave the station at 1 p.m. didn't get outta' there 'til quarter pass three.

Jacob

Now, I know folks must have been steamin'. (*He wipes his forehead with a handkerchief*) Why did it leave so late?

Hamlin

Some rich ole' thang, who looked like she had more money than them Kennedy's and Rockfella's put together, well they was holdin' the train for her. She was runnin' late.

Jacob

(*He shakes his head*) Ummm, umm, umm that don't make a bit a sense.

Hamlin

That's what I say. Don't care who she is, they should have left her, long with them furs, and luggage, and all right here in D.C.

Jacob

I hear ya'. Things ain't like they use to be. I know if I'd paid all that money to ride the liner they best leave when time say leave.

Hamlin

If we had any say so in the matter, folks would still be gettin' their money's worth. (*Pause*) When I first started workin' at Union Station, I did more than was asked of me, and still do. Customers always make sure they call on Hamlin Warden Jackson when they come to town. Yes Sir. They were and still are guaranteed to get the best service they've ever had.

Jacob

You know I'm just the same. Folks get in my cab, I'll take them wherever they wanta' go. I ain't like most of them guys now, who claim they ain't gonna' be caught dead in some of these neighborhoods around here, especially Southeast. I tell them young guys ain't a soul gonna bother them in Southeast 'cause some of the finest folks live there. And I tell all my customers too, I'll take 'em to Anacostia, Georgetown, Benning Road, 14th Street. I know these neighborhoods like the back of my hand. I'll even drive 'em all the way to Memphis. May take a few days longer than that train but, as long as they pay the bill when it comes time—I'll get 'em there. (*They both laugh in agreement*) See that's how me and Ma Douglass raised them children of ours—and they done turned out fine. We say ain't nothin' like some good hard work to make a person successful. I look at that boy of mine practicin' law and all. Yep. Elliot know some hard work. Make me proud.

Hamlin

(*Laughing*) Make me proud too. I believe that's what Rutherford want to make somebody proud. You know, I talked to Alma 'bout investin' even mentioned it to Berta a few times

Jacob

Now you know, Berta ain't gonna' have none of that…she'll squeeze a nickel until the buffalo shits.

> (*They laugh hysterically. Alberta appears on the porch with a tray, with 2 slices of pie, and 2 glasses of lemonade/milk*)

Alberta

What are you two carrying on about now?

Hamlin

(*Still chuckling*) Aww nothin'.

Alberta

How you doin' tonight Mr. Jake? Has it been hot enough for you?

Jacob

Yes, indeed. I'm cool though, now that I see your pretty face.

Alberta

Mr. Jake, you need to go somewhere with your bad self.

Jacob

You know Ham, your daughter looks as sweet as this pie she's brought us. Yes, indeed, ummm, umm. Child you almost as sweet as your mama was. Yes, indeed, your mama's pretty face sure kept my eyes a jumpin' and you're the spitting image of her you know Alberta

(*Alberta has a blank look on her face when he says this. Jacob tastes the pie and kneels one knee on the crate*)

I do believe if Ma Douglas ever starts to actin up I'm come up here and ask Alberta if she'll take my hand in marriage and bake me a pie until my time on this earth is up. Your ma was the finest woman I ever saw, next to Ma Douglas of course.

(Alberta exits abruptly)

Hamlin

Fool if you get stuck down there don't start yellin' for me to help you up now.

Jacob

(*Rising*) It's been five years, why she so touchy when anybody bring up her mama?

Hamlin

I don't know Jellybean, I just don't know. (*Pause*) You recall how Sister Especulia used to show Alma how to make up them pies. Man, them women must have been whippin' over a hundred of them apple, blackberry, peach, and cherry pies a night.

Jacob

You talkin' bout Blades Joint again...best joint in all of Alabama. Yep. Sister Especulia told me that after we got them folks in her place so happy we deserved to have anything to eat in the joint.

Hamlin

I couldn't wait to get some good ole' pies and some good ole lovin'.

(They both laugh)

Jacob

I hears' ya'. Only reason Alma picked you over me was you could put down them pies faster than me.

Hamlin

Sister Especulia knew that if Alma wanted to win my heart she'd better move to my stomach first. Guess Sister Especulia was right. (*He pats his stomach*)

Jacob

Yeah, cause everyone in Sister Especulia place, including the band knew that I was the handsomest of us two. (*He rubs his chin proudly, and sticks out his chest*)

(*They laugh hysterically, holding stomachs, rubbing their eyes*)

Hamlin

What was that song we use to play that sent all them women yellin? We were playin' it awhile back.

Jacob

Umm, was it "St. Louie Woman?"

Hamlin

Naw, that ain't it. It was the one that Alma didn't like 'cause sisters wanted to get fresh with me.

Jacob

Who ever wanted to get fresh with you in Blades Joint? I never saw nothin' like that.

Hamlin

You must be losing your memory. Remember Savanna Savage?

Jacob

Who?

Hamlin

You knew Savanna. Her father use to own that shoe repair place over on Rawson Road. She always went to that salon over top of her father's place to get her hair straightened as hard as she could. Girls use to say, that if Savanna Savage saw one kink in that head of hers she would go crazy. They use to say that that straightening comb had burned all the sense out of Savanna's head.

Jacob

Golden Lips, I remember the salon and the shoe repair store, but I don't remember no Saphonia woman.

Hamlin

(*Raising his voice*) Her name was Savanna Savage. Alma swore she was gonna sock her in the mouth when she tried to get fresh with me one rainy night in June.

Jacob

When on God's green earth did Alma ever claim that she was gonn' sock anybody in the mouth?

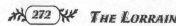

Hamlin

Well, she told that to Savanna Savage and then gave me a piece of her mind. Said that if I was encouraging her in any way that she was gonna' beat both of us to a pulp.

Jacob

Man you crazy, when all this happen? Where was I

Hamlin

You were there. I told you, you're getting senile 'cause there's no way a soul in this world could forget Savanna Savage and her famous walk. (*He gets up and mimics a walk, stands over Jacob, and shapes out a female body*)

Jacob

(*Looks closely for a moment*) Ohh, ohh, I know who you talkin' bout. Savvaaaannaaaaaa Saaaavaaaaagge! Umm, umm. Umm. Yes indeed. If that wasn't a woman I don't know what was.

Hamlin

I don't know about all of that. I thought she was always loose upstairs myself too.

Jacob

I declare she had that body in place though. But I guess all that hot pressing and straightening almost everyday did have an effect on her in some way or the another…

Hamlin

(*Impatiently*) Jellybean, I was tryin' to remember that song, and the only reason I thought I could is because Savanna Savage used to go wild when we started to play it at Blades Joint.

Jacob

Well, I don't know. Was it Ma Rainey's "Ya Hear Me Talkin to Ya?"

Hamlin

Naw, that wasn't it at all. It was—(*He plays a little bit of a tune and realizes that is not the song*) No that's not the one either.

Jacob

(*He plays smoothly begins to smile*) I got it.

Hamlin

Yeah, yeah. I remember, "There'll Be a Hot Time in the Old Town Tonight." Give me a little bit of it.

(*The men play, "There'll Be a Hot Time in the Old Town Tonight"*)

Jacob

Umm, umm, umm.

(They speed up their playing)

Hamlin

Yes, indeed, yes, indeed. My, my, my. *(They continue to play)*

> *(The men continue to play the song. Cecilia is in the living room attempting to wipe flour off of her art work that sits over in the corner and begins to mold clay. Chloe runs down the steps in a night shirt, with a comb and a jar of hair grease in her hand. Alberta enters from the kitchen and sits)*

Chloe

Miss Alberta you gonna' still plait my hair?

Cecilia

(Interrupts) Chloe I said you could stay up, but I didn't say you could bug everybody.

Chloe

But Miss Alberta said she would plait my hair on Thursday. And today is Thursday.

Alberta

Come on around here child. Don't you ever get tired of flittering around?

Chloe

(Sits on the floor between Alberta's legs) What's flittering?

Alberta

Jumping all around. *(She jerks her shoulders back and forth)*

Chloe

(Laughs) Nope.

Cecilia

No mam.

Chloe

(Looking up at Alberta) Sorry, no mam.

Alberta

Hand me the grease. *(Pause)* Now remember Chloe you're going to have to hold still or somebody else will have to do your head.

Chloe

Well mommy can't do it because she pulls too hard.

Cecilia
If Chloe held still sometimes mommy wouldn't have to pull hard.

Alberta
You hear that?

(*As she parts Chloe's hair the truck is heard*)

Chloe
Yes mam. (*She is moving her head around*) Ooowww. I bet you that's Nate bringin' Booka' back? I wanta' go see.

Alberta
You just sat down here.

Chloe
(*Anxiously*) I can go...(*Pause*) Oww!

Alberta
See, I told you to stay still. (*Rubbing Chloe's scalp*) You can see your brother when he comes in. Anyway this is a sudden change. Why you so anxious to see Booker, you never been before?

Chloe
"Cause he might be bringin' back some leftovers.

(*A truck is heard pulling off. Booker appears outside carrying a cake box*)

Jacob
What's new with you brother? (*He gives Booker a cool hand shake as the boy reaches the steps*)

(*Booker and Jacob smile as though this style of greeting one another is a ritual between the two of them*)

Booker
Same old thing brothers.

Jacob
When you gonna' join us to do some jammin'?

Booker
Oh, I don't know, one day I guess. I'll be around.

Jacob

Okay, I guess you think you too smooth for us old timers? We done played up and down this city and these here states. We was one of the coolest acts at the Howard theater.

Hamlin

Yep. That's right he think he too bad for us.

Booker

No, I couldn't touch you all. (*Pause*) But, umm I'm into books... I want to go to college.

Jacob

That's good, but what has you jammin' with us got to do with you goin' to college?

Booker

(*Innocently*) That's my point, what has it got to do with me goin' to college? (Quickly moves towards door)

Jacob

(*Looks at Hamlin*) You can join us when you ready anyway though.

Booker

Okay, thanks. (*Booker enters house*)

Jacob

Stay cool. (*To Hamlin*) He's young.

Cecilia

How did it go?

Booker

(*Uninterested*) It was fine, I guess. We really only stayed to make sure everything was alright with their order. (*Pause*) Where's the food?

Cecilia

Everything is in the 'fridge Booker, and clean up after yourself.

Chloe

(*Excited*) Booker was there anything left?

Booker

Why you concerned?

Chloe

'Cause if there is, I want some.

Booker

(*Taunting Chloe*) It just so happens that daddy made a few more of them tiny cherry cakes than he needed, so he set them aside and that's just what I got in my hand. (*Holds cake box with one hand*)

(*Chloe licks her lips and attempts to rise*)

Alberta

I thought you were so anxious to get your hair plaited?

Chloe

Can we do it later?

Alberta

I'll think on it. (*As Chloe rises she shakes her head*)

Booker

Wait a minute, who said you were gonna' get any?

Chloe

(*Surprised*) What?

Booker

(*Licking his lips teasingly*) I said, who said you was gonna' get any of these cherry covered cakes?

Cecilia

(*Still molding clay, not looking at the children*) Booker, how many times have I told you not to tease your sister? I've got eyes in the back of my head. You two go on in the kitchen. Booker you share or neither one of you will have them.

Booker

Come on big mouth? (*He pushes Chloe, but she laughs*)

Chloe

(*Whining*) Mommy.

(*Cecilia gives Booker an evil look and the children exit to kitchen. Hamlin and Jacob finish a song and the two men slap hands*)

Jacob

I'll be checkin' you later, don't want the little lady to start worryin' none. Ma Douglas always worryin' 'bout me ya' know?

Hamlin

Stay clean man.

Jacob
(*Walks down steps*) You know I try, you know I try.

(*Jacob exits, Hamlin enters the house with crate/dished. He sits in his chair*)

Alberta
(*Pulls out pieces of newspaper and magazine*) Daddy, look here. (*She attempts to show Hamlin, he shows little interest*) These little houses they got over in Northwest, ain't they nice? They was just built a year ago.

(*Hamlin appears to be dozing off*)

Daddy you awake?

Hamlin
Yes, I'm always awake.

Alberta
See? (*Pushing them in his face*)

Hamlin
They alright, I guess.

Alberta
Just alright? (*Shows Cecilia*) Cil, ain't they cute?

Cecilia
(*Continuing to mold clay*) Hmm, hmm. Look real comfortable. (*Pointing*) That one seems nice.

Alberta
Some of them are two, even three bedroom places. Some of them got patios, I could start us a little garden daddy. Wouldn't that be nice?

Hamlin
Yeah, I guess…

Alberta
That's all you got to say? (*Pause*) These look like we just might be able to use our little savings to afford one. It ain't easy finding places like this that's so cheap.

Hamlin
Well, I like where we are just fine. I don't like movin' around every time I turn around. I'm comfortable here.

(*He leans back in his chair. Cecilia smiles attempting to stay out of the conversation*) Ole' folks use ta' say you put a seed down somewhere, you ain't suppose to go back the next day and try and dig it up when it ain't even grown into a plant yet.

Alberta

Daddy, now you know we wasn't gonna to be staying here forever. You know gettin' this house was just a way to keep both of our families off the street for a while. I sure don't want to go to my grave knowin' that I died in a house that the government had me on a waiting list for. (*Pause*) We been wanting a house for a long time. (*Thinking to herself*) We were almost there, almost had enough money and then we got sidetracked. (*Directly at him*) We need to get back on course Mr. Hamlin Jackson.

Hamlin

(*Upset*) You tryin' to call Alma's death a sidetrackin'?

Alberta

Aww, daddy please don't start it, please…

Hamlin

Oh, you don't want to talk about your own mama or even your husband leavin'. You blamin' them cause we ain't got no house?

Alberta

Daddy, now you know that's not what I was sayin' at all. You know… (*She doesn't know what to say*)

Hamlin

Cil, she always at a lost for words when it come to them. Ain't that right Alberta? I can't even talk to you about them.

(*Cecilia looks surprised that he has made her a part of the brewing argument*)

Alberta

(*Begins to place magazine and newspapers in a stand*) Daddy day in and out…

Hamlin

Alma, day in and out she has yet to recognize the loss of flesh and blood. (*He pulls out his harmonica and begins to play*)

Alberta

You are impossible Mr. Jackson. I want to talk about makin' our lives better and all you can do is pull out that harmonica. (*She sits in silence*)

(Rutherford enters)

Rutherford

(*Moves to put a bag in the closet, crosses to Alberta and touches her shoulder*) What you do now Alberta? I can hear Mr. Hamlin playin' all the way outside.

ased
Alberta

(*Slaps his hand off of her shoulder, jokingly*) Oh, hush up.

Cecilia

Rutherford, what are you doing here?

Rutherford

(*Crosses to kiss Cecilia*) No good evening, how are you Rutherford?

Cecilia

Good evenin', how are you Rutherford? Now, what are you doing home?

Rutherford

The boss man got a replacement for me tonight.

Cecilia

He did what?

Rutherford

When I got there, only 'bout 20 minutes late he'd already gotten a replacement. Isn't that some stuff? He could have said that to me over the phone. (*To himself*) Naw, he wants me to come all the way down there and show me that somebody else was doin' my job tonight. Wanted to try and show me up.

Cecilia

What did you do?

Rutherford

Picked up my bag. Stuck out my chest…(*He sticks out his chest*) said see ya' Mr. Boss man and left…(*He laughs*) Cil I've learned how to be a good boy for the master, didn't even talk back.

Cecilia

See Rutherford, all you doin' is provokin' the man. He's got the power. He determines whether we eat or not. (*Worried*) What happened, Rutherford…(*Crosses back to her art work*)

Rutherford

(*Sits next to Alberta on the sofa, leaning forward, excited about his plot*) I'd been waitin' for the day though, when I could go up to Mr. Boss man and say, you can take this uniform, this lot, and these cars, and shove 'em all up your…

Alberta

(*Interrupts*) nose. (*Placing her hand on his shoulder*) his nose Rutherford.

Rutherford

(*Laughs*) Whatever, but I wanted to shove them somewhere. I'm not going to have to ride all the way across town anymore to have him get on my damn nerves. No sir. Rutherford Avery isn't takin' that any more. (*He rubs his hands*) I quit.

Cecilia

Oh, my Lord. Oh, my Lord.

Rutherford

Baby before you even think about sayin' it, I'm not apologizing to that man. I'm not goin' back. He thought he was going to get a chance to try and make me seem like a fool. Like I needed him more than he needed me. I have better things to do than park cars, and be treated like a nobody at the same time.

Cecilia

(*Angrily*) It's money Rutherford. How do you expect us to live?

Rutherford

We did well tonight. And it's going to get better. I made a few contacts tonight. See when folks like or don't like somethin' they talk. And folks like our goods. That's what advertisin' is all about. That reminds me, it's about time I got some business cards made up. (*He pulls out a note pad and pen*) I can see us now, baby. Booker handlin' most of the orders, you workin' the cashier, Chloe…

Cecilia

(*Interrupts*) Are you listenin' to me Rutherford Avery?

Rutherford

I'm listenin'. You all don't need to worry, everything will be fine. Don't I always come through?

Alberta

(*Rises*) Are you crazy? Are…

Hamlin

(*Interrupts intentionally*) Alberta can you grab me some water?

Alberta

(*Crossing to Hamlin, pointing*) Did you hear that?

Hamlin

And make sure you put enough ice cubes in there. (*Hands her a glass, she moves slowly.* Go on now my throat is gettin' real dry. (*Alberta exits to kitchen continuing to look back*) I've been tellin' you to come down to the station. I could fix it up where the boss could give you a good job with good benefits too.

Rutherford

Thanks but, I told you all the bakery will be the job where I'm the employer and the employee. I've gone into business for myself.

Hamlin

Well, seems to me if you doin' somethin' like that you need to have some money in your pocket to start with, maybe I'm wrong.

Cecilia

Mr. Hamlin, you're right. Rutherford thinks he can just up and start a business without anything.

(Alberta reenters with water for Hamlin)

Rutherford

Why do I want to work for the rest of my life parking cars—takin' orders and jumpin' for folks who can't do a thing for me nor respect me as a worker? When was the last time a red cap got promoted? That's what I'd like to know? The man who owns the parking lot, in charge of all of us, knows nothin' about me or what I want to do. He's just like the cow that dishes out milk from it's tits.

Alberta

Hold up. (*Laughing*) Now what has that white man got to do with milk? How did you come up with that analysis Rutherford?

Rutherford

(*Attempts to draw a diagram on his pad of paper*) A cow dishes out just as much milk as it wants you to have. You keep squeezing on it's tits tryin' to get a full bucket, thinkin' all along some more is goin' to come. (*He grabs a stool in the living room and begins to act as though he is milking a cow*) You sit there like a fool pullin' and pullin', but that cow knows from the start it isn't going to give you anymore. See that's just like the white man you keep workin' for. Each week he gives you a little bit a pay like he's doin' you a favor. You feel you're gettin' closer and closer to somethin' you think is goin' to be all good. As soon as you get almost there, he stops giving what's really yours—what you've earned. You shouldn't have to beg no damn cow or no white man for a little bit of milk when it is supposed to be yours.

(*Everyone looks confused. Chloe and Booker can be seen peeping through the kitchen door*)

I give Mr. Boss man 8 hours of sweat and blood. I want decent benefits, job security, and good pay. I don't want any hassle. If I started workin' at the Union Station, I'd work and work. Just when I think I'm gonna' have enough for Cil, me, and the kids, it'll be snatched away. It's happened to me before. Boss man wants to see me break, wants to see me crack. I don't want him to give me a damn handout. Just pay me what I'm worth.

Alberta
That doesn't make a bit of sense.

Rutherford
Yes it does. You all just haven't been listenin' to a word I've been saying.

Hamlin
Yes we have. You just said you was sittin' milkin' a cow and 'cause it ain't give you no milk it's just like the white man 'cause he don't give no milk either.

> (Alberta laughs out right and Cil covers laughter with mouth so she won't upset Rutherford. Hamlin looks perplexed, not realizing he's said something funny)

Rutherford
(Shakes his head in disgust) Excuse me, but I've got to get ready for my appointment in the morning, good night. (He collects papers and exits upstairs)

> (Booker and Chloe continue to attempt to peep their heads through the kitchen door)

Chloe
I wanta' listen too, let me listen Booker.

Booker
Ssshh!

> (All of a sudden both children come tumbling out of the kitchen door. Chloe has crumbs all over her face)

Cecilia
You two wanta' be into adult conversation, I think your behinds are tired. (Pointing) Go on upstairs and get ready for bed.

Chloe
But, mommy it was…

Booker
You gonna' get us in more trouble. (He leads her up the steps)

Hamlin
Children always gonna' be like that Cil. They always think they missin' something. (Pause, thinking) But what I was about to say was sometimes things ain't got nothin' to do with nobody else. They just come up.

Alberta
Daddy you just as confusin' as Rutherford.

Hamlin
(*Ignoring Alberta, to Cecilia*) But sometimes it's like two forces workin' against you, and you can't fight 'em. Alma and me, had been savin' up, started payin' on that house that we found when we come up from Alabama. Then Alberta come along here, and marry. (*Pause*) You know weddings and all seem to make a day perfect.

(Cecilia puts the unfinished clay away)

Cecilia
(*To herself*) that's for sure, weddings make everything perfect for that day, then reality comes and slaps you in the face.

Hamlin
Well, I had been playin' with Jellybean at the Howard Theatre and workin' at the station too. Then the theater close down—after some years Alma and me get it in our heads we wanta' go on back down home, let Alberta and her new husband, Malcolm take on that mortgage. But Alma take ill and that money went to bills, bills. Lost the little house, lost Alma. (*Pause, to Alma*) But you back with me now, forever. Baby, I wonder who livin' in our house now? (*Pause*) Even Malcolm got sick, all of this stress I guess wasn't no good for that boys' heart.

(Alberta looks extremely uncomfortable)

Seem like around that time death come our way every which way we turn. (*to Cecilia*) But see, Cil we couldn't control that, it just happen.

Alberta
Daddy, I think Cil has heard this story before. (*She collects her papers and turns out a light*)

Hamlin
I would have thought you had remembered how me and your mama taught you how to respect folks. I guess not.

(*Alberta exits upstairs*)

Cecilia
It's cooled off some. Guess, I better get to some of my ironin'. (*Crosses to get an ironing board, iron, and laundry basket with clothes*)

Hamlin
I wonder when you ever goin' to slow down, looks like you always runnin' somewhere to do something.

Cecilia
Well, if I keep busy runnin' I won't have time to worry about anything.

Hamlin

You think that's always the best thing?

Cecilia

What do you mean?

Hamilin

You know Alberta does the same thing. She'll never admit it, but I can see that she's runnin' away from somethin' all the time. I believe though, with Lord's help folks can always change, all of us have room for improvement. We can't never be satisfied. We all gotta' keep workin' to change for the better.

Cecilia

That's the problem Mr. Hamlin, it seems like I've become satisfied. You know what I'm trying to say?

Hamlin

Kind of I guess, but explain it to me.

Cecilia

(Begins ironing clothes) I've become satisfied with not being able to buy my children what they want, satisfied cause no matter what I do I can't seem to convince that man of mine that he needs to take a steady job. Any job right now—so that we can pull our weight around here. We've gotta' do our part. He has got to understand that at least when he's parkin' cars and I'm workin' in that government office we can to put food on the table. (Pause) Maybe I need to start thinkin' a little more about the future than about now. Mr. Hamlin I don't know if tomorrow I'll have a home to call my own, I don't even have one today.

Hamlin

What do you mean you don't have a home, what do you call this? As soon as our name came up on that government housing waitin' list we had another home.

Cecilia

Mr. Hamlin we don't own this. I can't call this mine—two families with no connection sharing a house.

Hamlin

(Surprised) I thought we had a connection. We might not be a blood family, but there is blood between us. I care about you and them kids like you all were my own, like you were another daughter. I believe no matter how much Berta or even Rutherford denies it they know there's blood between the two of them somewhere too. I don't give up hope on them and you neither.

Cecilia

I'm scared Mr. Hamlin that I'm gonna' grow old, and I'm not gonna' have anything to show for my life because I stay satisfied. I haven't learned how to stop being satisfied. That's why I stay busy, so I won't think about the pain of it all, won't have to think about giving those children or myself anything extra. (*Pause*) Today I looked in Woodies window downtown like I always do on my way home. And like always, I see that suit that I know would look so fine on that man of mine, but I know all I can do is look. I can't go in the store and smell the material. I know just by standing at that window that I can't afford it for him. So, I keep on walking for blocks taking care of my business like I'm supposed to. But you know Mr. Hamlin bein' busy— that doesn't even work all the time. Some way that pain seems to seep into my veins anyway. And I don't know how to make it go away. I'm beginnin' to start believin' that nobody can make it go away.

Hamlin

Cil, what do you want? What do you need?

Cecilia

I need to feel like all of this is worth it.

Hamlin

All of what?

Cecilia

Livin' Mr. Hamlin, livin. Sometimes when I see those children of mine I sit down and wonder why they were ever born?

Hamlin

What are you talkin' foolish like that for, you are glad they were born?

Cecilia

I'm serious Mr. Hamlin. Why are we put here? Why were Black folks created anyway —to suffer each and eveyday of our lives? Black folks can get away from the white man as much as we want, but things still ain't gonna' get no better. I use to think that I could change things for myself, my family, and even maybe someone else. If I would have known this was how it was gonna' be when I was born I would have jumped right back into my mama's womb and told them to send me back. And when I had Booker and Chloe, I asked the Lord to send them back … but he wouldn't. He let them come on out, and get bigger and bigger, and suffer and suffer.

Hamlin

(*Angrily*)You need to stop right there 'cause you know those children of yours are a blessing. (He begins taking down the it ironing board and ignores hanging up the pressed article on the board the ones around here that keep all of us grown folks sane and laughing. I don't see them starvin' and eatin' off of the ground, or wearin' dirty dingy clothes. I don't see them without the love of everyone in this household.

Cecilia

See Mr. Hamlin, they aren't doin' that, but—

Hamlin

Alright, they ain't sufferin' then. (*Exits to kitchen 'for a moment to put away board.*)

Cecilia

(*To herself*) Does that mean I'm supposed to be satisfied with what I can provide my children?

(*Hamlin reenters*)

(*Sadly smiling to herself*) Rutherford and I, when we were younger after school we made out a check list of the things we were gonna' accomplish as a couple. (*Imagining*) Have children. . We've done that. Not live in the projects and have our own place. . Not really. . Have that bakery. . .We haven't really gotten that... (*She crosses to her art work touching it*).. Make somebody notice my work. Ain't done that, Rutherford hasn't even...

Hamlin

(*Attempts to in interrupt*) Cecilia Avery.

Cecilia

You know, I even feel ashamed every time Chloe and Booker ask me can they have something and I say no because I don't have the money to give. Their daddy can't even buy it for them. (*Pause, holds out her hands*)I use to think these hands could mold my life so perfectly. Mr. Hamlin, when I was younger I said it wasn't ever gonna' be like this. It was never gonna' get to a point where I get sick to my stomach of livin.

Hamlin

(*Reaches out to Cecilia*)You need to stop thinkin' like that, it's gonna get you nowhere.

Cecilia

(*Angrily, pulling away*) Well forget the thinkin' then. I feel like I'm about to vomit each time I think 'bout life. What's the use of hopin' anyway? I've been listenin' to Rutherford ever since I've known him talk about if Black folks do for themselves then everything will be okay. Rutherford say, if you depend on yourself, then you ain't gotta worry about the rest of the world messin' with your mind. After some years, I want to tell him he's wrong— that no matter how hard you try it ain't gettin' any better. He think he's gonna' have that American dream. Mr. Hamlin, how dare they fool my man like that. (*Pointing upstairs*) How dare they tell that Black man upstairs if he work hard and do what he suppose to do that he'll get ahead just like any other man. Rutherford has bought into it, but it ain't the same for us. (*Pause, picks up Chloe's clothing or toy*) My baby, she was in my belly when this city burned ten years ago. It's been ten years since Black folks got so angry. We was tired 'cause we knew then that we wasn't gettin' any part of that so-called dream. Is folks sleep walkin' or somethin'? Things ain't changed. (*Emotionally, she begins to cry*) There's no use in typin' any more letters to the bank. There's no use in me makin' sure that those two damn black and blue suits of Rutherford's have those perfect creases in them. We'll be doing these little deliveries and getting nowhere. We'll never have the bakery, we'll be talkin' 20 years from now about how it's goin' to be. Something somewhere somehow is never goin' to let you have what you need, much less what you want.

Hamlin

In my day—

Cecilia

Mr. Hamlin I don't mean any disrespect, but it isn't your day anymore, we're some years pass that. Look at us, look at us, look at me, at my family, your family, look right outside this door; there's still nothin', nothin'. Nothin' Mr. Hamlin.

(*Cecilia exits, Hamlin pulls out his harmonica and plays*)

ACT I

SCENE II

(It is Friday afternoon. Booker is on the front steps reading his books. Chloe is playing hopscotch on the sidewalk)

Chloe

You know what Juanita told me over in the playground Booker today?

(Booker ignores her and she yells)

Booker.

Booker

What Chloe?

Chloe

Guess what Juanita told me in the playground.

Booker

I don't care what Juanita had to say really.

Chloe

Well, she told me how we got here.

Booker

What?

Chloe

She told me how a woman has a baby before she has it.

Booker

(He puts down his book quickly and moves closer Chloe) What do you mean she told you about what happens before a woman has a baby?

Chloe

(Laughing) You know Booker, don't act dumb.

Booker

(*Angrily*) What has Juanita been telling you?

Chloe

First she said that a man and woman is made differently. She said that they got things and a woman, like her, has things. She said that that's good cause then one thing can fit perfectly into the other.

Booker

(*Booker rubs his head fearful of what Chloe is saying*) What?

Chloe

She said it's like puttin' dressing into a turkey. I told Juanita that didn't make no sense, but then she went on and told me more. She told me that next time the holidays come around look where everybody puts the dressing into that turkey. And she said see how that bird lays there with its' legs all folded up waiting for the dressing

Booker

Be quiet I don't want to hear anymore.

Chloe

But Booker then she said that you all put the turkey in the oven and the dressing and the turkey gets all hot and it's done. Is that how it is before a woman has a baby Booker? Is that how the man and woman do it? I told her I was gonna come and ask you, and she got mad and said she wasn't gonna speak to me anymore if I did. I told her that I didn't care. I was gonna ask you anyways. Was Juanita right Booker, huh?

Booker

Chloe I don't want you listenin' to nothing that girl Juanita has to say. She's stupid and she shouldn't be tellin' you things like that.

Chloe

Well, she said that's how a woman has to do it. The woman is the turkey and the man is the dressing (*Excited*) She even told me that she's a woman, but I tried to tell her that she can't be woman 'cause she's not really old yet, she's just 13. But she said that she was a woman 'cause she's been a turkey and had all the dressing (*Laughing*) She said she wouldn't mind being the turkey again either, if you were the dressing Booka'.

Booker

What? Why me? Why me? (*Pause*) I don't want you repeatin' this. You hear me!

Chloe

Why?

Booker

'Cause if you do you're gonna get a beatin'. (*He begins to reopen book*) Man, Chloe why do you hang around with that Juanita anyway, huh? (*Silence*)

Chloe

(*Proudly*)She said I could be a woman when I get ready.

Booker

(*Angrily, closing his book*) Well, you aren't going to be a woman anytime soon. You hear me? I better not catch you thinking about being any turkey. You hear me? Don't you listen to Juanita ever again.

Chloe

But she knows so much about being a woman.

Booker

Ma and Miss Berta are the only ones you know who can tell you about being a woman. And you don't even need to think about being one for a long time anyway. I don't care what Juanita says. She's no woman—she's a fool.

Chloe

(*Angrily*) No she ain't Booker. She's seen a lot and been through a lot too.

Booker

Juanita can't teach you anything, but trouble. You hear me? (*She looks down at her game as if she is ignoring him. Pause*) I said do you hear me, Chloe?

Chloe

Yeah, I hear you. So Booker tell me then, what does the woman and man do before she has a baby?

(*Chloe begins to play with her game again and Booker begins to read his book. She puts her hand on her hips; Cecilia can be seen coming to the house with a bag. Alberta appears in the window*)

Alberta

Ya'll children help your mama with her bag(s).

(*The children help Cecilia lift her bag up the steps*)

Cecilia

How are my babies today?

Chloe

Good. What you bring home? (*Looks in the bag excited*)

Booker

Ma you don't have anymore babies. (*Head in his book*)

(*Alberta moves from the window and exits upstairs*)

Cecilia

Booker, you and Chloe finish those list of chores I left for you?

Booker

Yes, we did.

Cecilia

(*Looks at Booker*) You sure you don't want me to go with you to the meeting? I'll drop these bags inside...

Booker

I'll be fine ma Vernon's comin' by.

Cecilia

Okay. Now you got your bus fair put away? (*Booker shakes his head*)
Don't you go sittin' in the back in no bus either. (*Booker shakes his head*)
Soon as you see that sun goin' out of sight you better...

Booker

Yes. I know ma.

(*Vernon Taylor, a young attractive male about twenty-one walks up the steps
He is dressed in jeans and a t-shirt*)

Cecilia

Boy, you better get your head outta' that book. How do you answer me?

Booker

I'm sorry, yes mam.

Vernon

Hello, Mrs. Avery. (*To Booker*) Hey, man how are you doing? (*They shake hands*)

Chloe

(*Whispering to Cecilia*) Is that him?

Cecilia

Shhh. (*To Vernon*)Good to see you again. This is my daughter Chloe.

(*Chloe giggles as he extends his hand to her Booker looks anxiously*)

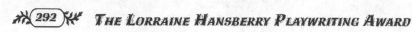

Booker

You ready to go man?

Vernon

Yes, I thought we could grab something to eat on our way.

Cecilia

Vernon, I'd like to talk to you a minute before you all go. (*Vernon moves to door with Cecilia, Booker begins to follow*)

No, Booker you stay here.

> (*Booker looks worried, Cecilia takes the bags from Chloe, and enters the house with Vernon*)

Vernon

Mam, you need some help?

Cecilia

No thank you. I've got it. I'll be right back (*She exits to the kitchen,*)

> (*Vernon is left in the living room looking around the room he notices the art work and looks at it closely*)

Vernon

You're very good.

Cecilia

Excuse me.

Vernon

(*Pointing to her work*) As Booker told me your work is very good. It's different, each piece says something different—seclusion, rebirth, age.

Cecilia

(*Surprised*) You know art?.

Vernon

I've taken some classes. (*Pause*) Did you study anywhere? You must have sold a lot of pieces by now?

Cecilia

No, I never got the chance to study. I learned it all on my own. The furthest place most of my work has ever gone is in this living room. I get donated materials from wherever I can. I always... (*Changing the subject*) I wanted to talk to you about Booker.

Vernon
(*Looks puzzled*) Alright.

Cecilia
Vernon, Booker has a father. He lives here and all. I don't know what the situations are for other boys in the program, but I wanted to make sure you weren't gettin' the idea that my son is one of those abandoned Black children gettin' some service.

Vernon
No, I wasn't thinkin' that at all, I -

Cecilia
I just wanted to tell you that his father doesn't know about Booker participating in this Big Brother/Mentor program yet, but he will know.

Vernon
You don't have to give me any explanation.

Cecilia
I know, but you see, I believe Booker needs someone who's gonna have time to take him out and have fun, and me doin' it is different than a male doin' it. Mr. Avery, you see is somewhat preoccupied these days, let me change that he's always preoccupied with gettin this bakery that he wants to open off the ground. And I don't want Booker to be waitin' around day after day until there's some time for him. He needs to be around young men like yourself-in school and all. I don't want you to take the place of his father. 'Cause his father loves that child (*She seems to think to herself*) He loves him, he is just preoccupied like I said, but you could talk to Booker when he needs things like that. Do you understand what I mean?

Vernon
Yes, mam I do. I don't want to take anyone's place, I want to be Booker's friend. I joined this program so that I could give back to someone like Booker, who needed attention at different times. And—

Booker
(*Yelling through the window*) What are you all doing in there?

Cecilia
You all better get goin'. (*She leads him to the door*)

(*Alberta comes from upstairs and stops on the steps, Cecilia doesn't see her*)

Vernon
(*Turning to her*)You should let the world see your art Mrs. Avery. (*Exits to porch*)

Chloe
Why can't I never come along when you take Booker out?

Vernon
Well, we do a lot boy stuff, and you'd probably be bored anyway.

Chloe
No, I wouldn't I like boy stuff. What kind?

Vernon
We go to meetings, play ball and sometimes hang out with others guys I go to school with at Howard.

Chloe
I think I'm startin' to like boys. I wouldn't mind being around them. I told you, Juanita say it's good for a girl like myself to be exposed to the opposite sex. (*She pronounces opposite incorrectly*)

Booker
(*Interrupting angrily*) Chloe.

Chloe
(*Interrupting Angrily*) How are old are you all?

Vernon
Twenty-one, twenty-two...

Chloe
(*Yelling surprised*)Twenty-one, twenty-two. Ya'll ain't boys, ya'll old men. (*She stands on her toes raising her hand above her head*)You almost up there in daddy's and Mr. Hamlin's age. Dag.

(Booker moves to exit)

Booker & Vernon
(*Booker is shaking his head Vernon is smiling*) Bye Chloe.

Chloe
(*Almost ignoring them*) See ya. (Plays on steps)

(Chloe enters the house and exits upstairs)

Alberta
Was that that Vernon boy? (*Doesn't give Cecilia a chance to respond*) Shouldn't he be spendin' time with them fatherless boys?

Cecilia

See that's what people think this mentor program is for fatherless boys, but that's not how it works. The older young man acts like a buddy, someone to hang out with.

Alberta

Yep, the same things a father's supposed to be. (*She crosses to the dining room*)

(Cecilia begins feeling and looking at her all work closely)

(*Alberta is sitting at the dining room table with papers that look like bills She looks frustrated. She then opens her Bible and pictures fall out onto the floor. She is frozen, Cecilia crosses to the dining room*)

Cecilia

Berta.

(*Alberta does not respond*)

Berta. (*Raising her voice*) Alberta Jackson-Collins.

Alberta

Yes?

Cecilia

Somethin' on your mind, you rushed out of that office so fast today. (*Notices the photos and bends to pick them up, cautiously looking at them*) You miss them? They were two beautiful people. I wish I could've had the chance to know them both a little better but, I guess through Mr. Hamlin, I feel like I've known your mother all along She must have been a remarkable woman? And Malcolm Collins sure was a fine man. Child, it sure is funny how styles change. One minute we all got our hair slicked back or conked, next minute we got afros. (*Thinking and handing photos to Alberta*) Wonder what we gonna look like in the 80s? (*Cecilia laughs*) Wonder what he would have looked like…

Alberta

(*Interrupting*) I thought I was the one who's supposed to try and give the advice; bein' in everybody's business. You tryin' to take my job Cecilia Avery?

Cecilia

No. (*Crosses to get a magazine*)See, I been readin' in Ebony how heart problems all over the Black community. It really ain't nothin' new. Malcolm just needed to take…..(*stopped by Alberta's stare, puts down magazine, pauses*) I thought you might want to talk about him.. about them both.

(*silence*)

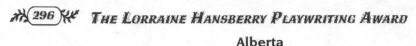

Alberta

What makes you think that?

Cecilia

Because the photos seem to have accidentally fallen from the Bible, and so you saw them. I guess that accidentally brought up some memories, or— (*She attempts to pull more from* Alberta) So you never answered my question, do you miss them? (*silence*) Okay, I get the picture sister, this is one thing you're not going to talk to me about. I'll leave you alone.

> (*Alberta moves the shelf and looks at the pictures again. She crosses to the stairs. She holds onto the banister tensely, and begins to cry looking upward. Cecilia crosses to get dinner dishes unaware of her presence. Alberta wraps her arms around herself, rocks, and runs upstairs. Chloe is now upstairs. Cecilia begins setting the table. She exits to the kitchen. Rutherford enters cheerful, she reenters does not see him. He attempts to hide as she goes back to the kitchen He sneaks up on her at the table*)

Rutherford

Baby, baby umm, umm have I got some news for you.

Cecilia

Oh Rutherford, I hate when you scare me like that.

Rutherford

Listen now, I've got to tell you something important. (*He leads her to the sofa*)

Cecilia

You sure are in a good mood. Did you get your job back?

Rutherford

No, but I talked to the bank today about getting the loan again.

Cecilia

Yeah, I know. I've gotta' tell you about Booker and the ...

Rutherford

(*Interrupts*) Yeah, yeah but wait, I went down there early this mornin' and waited for them to open the doors. And usually when I go down weekdays I see that McIntosh guy.

> (*Cecilia looks puzzled*)

You know the bald headed one who's always hunched over that desk. (*He mimics*) The one that always tries to give us the third degree— making it sound like we were some family on welfare with 50 children living in the projects.

Cecilia
Oh, yeah. (*She sucks her teeth*) Go on.

Rutherford
Well this time, I saw somebody else. (*He looks at papers to read her name*)A Ms. Dorsey, a sista Dorsey. (*He laughs*)I let her taste them pecans pies the children had helped me make. She was smilin' and tastin' and smilin'. Well, she had me fill out some forms, and said she'd try and arrange a meeting to discuss more details about the loan and leasin' a building.

Cecilia
(*Excited*) And?

Rutherford
What do you mean, and?

Cecilia
So what else did she say?

Rutherford
Cil, why are you asking, "What else did she say?"

Cecilia
Didn't Sister Dorsey say anything else, did she give you anything?

Rutherford
Cil, this was the first time in all the times that I've gone, and someone seemed sincere when they said they'd set up another-meeting or even try and help. It's always we'll get back to you and they never do.

Cecilia
(*Rises*)So what makes you think Sister Dorsey is any different?
(*Silence Rutherford begins to look angry*) Baby did she put anything—any promises in writing? When you filled out them forms did she fill out anything?

Rutherford
No, but she said she would try and set up another meeting Haven't you been listening to me? Nobody in the whole damn bank has ever done that before. Baby you listenin' to me?

(*Cecilia looks as though she is in another world*)

Cecilia
You always sayin' don't believe everything you hear, people will dish out as much bull as they can to ya'. Look at you, you believe the first thing somebody tells you that sounds good. Did she promise you?

Rutherford

No, but-

Cecilia

Because she's a sister you believe her too. Don't stake our lives on her so easily Rutherford. We've got bills to pay.

Rutherford

(*Pulls her gently back on the sofa*) I know that. You don't have to remind me Cil.

Cecilia

Seems to me you sometimes forget. We've got to help with the light bill, the rent, we haven't finished paying the hospital bill when Chloe was sick this winter, not to mention-

Rutherford

Okay, Cecilia, okay.

Rutherford

We'll be real quiet. (*He kisses her again, laughing*)

Cecilia

You're never quiet. (*Breathing heavily*) Baby, I've got dinner on the stove.

Rutherford

How long ago did you put it on? (*kissing her neck*)

Cecilia

'Bout 15 minutes.

Rutherford

(*Leading her to the steps*) Then we've got a good half hour before it's done.

Alberta

(*Coming down the steps*) Rutherford Avery what have you got that big grin on your face for?

Rutherford

(*Startled then relaxed looking at Cecilia*) I've gotta' take care of some business. (*Lightly pushes Alberta out of the way*)

Cecilia

(*They run up the steps, laughing*) Berta will you check the pot on the stove it should be...

(*Rutherford continues to pull her up, the steps they exit*)

Alberta

(*Shaking her head, looking around, crossing to the kitchen*) At least they turned out the lights. (*Exits*)

(*Jacob helps Hamlin through the door*)

Hamlin

All I need to do is sit down for a brief spell.

Alberta

(*Enters worried*) Daddy what happened to you? (*She moves to help Hamlin. to his chair*) Oh, hi Mr. Jake.

Jacob

He's gonna' be okay Alberta.

Hamlin

I fell at work.

Alberta

Why didn't you call me? I would've come to get you.

Hamlin

They said you'd already left when I called, and Jacob said he wouldn't mind comin' to get me.

Jacob

I didn't mind goin' to get my ole' buddy. (*He slaps Hamlin's hand*)

Alberta

Oh, thank you', I'll give you the money for it.

Jacob

No, no. Alberta, I think of you all as family.

Alberta

Daddy I've told you about racing against time. People at the Union Station will get where their goin' soon enough. Is your leg broken? What did the doctor say? (*She moves towards him and he stops her with his stare*) Let me get one of these pillows so we can put your leg up.

Hamlin

I don't need anybody fussin' all over me. I'm gonna' be fine.

(*Alberta puts the pillows from the sofa under his leg and behind his head, Jacob chuckles to himself*)

Alberta

So who got you the hospital daddy?

Hamlin

Union Station called an ambulance.

Alberta

I hope that boss of yours plans to pay for it too.

(*Rutherford comes down the steps with shirt undone, standing by listening*)

Jacob

(*Notices Rutherford*) Where you been hidin' son? Ain't seen you around.

Rutherford

Trying to take big steps with my business. (*Looks to Hamlin*)

Hamlin

I ain't even thinkin' about it.

Alberta

What you mean, you had better think about it.

Hamlin

Berta you know what my supervisor had the nerve to say to me while I was sittin' waiting for the ambulance to come and get me?

Alberta

What?

Hamlin

He says to me, "Hamlin, I hope that leg of yours is feeling much better soon." He talks a little small talk. Then he starts to askin' 'bout how I been. Even asked, "How is that daughter of yours doing I haven't seen her in awhile."

Alberta

(*Suspiciously*) What else did he say?

Hamlin

After all that, he finally says to me, "Hamlin, when you get a free moment to think, why don't you consider retirement?"

Alberta
(*Angrily*) That bastard had the nerve enough to say that to you after you just fell and injured yourself on the floor.

Jacob
Don't get yourself all worked up now Berta.

Alberta
What does that stupid supervisor think? He thinks employees, trusted, loyal and steady ones are like warn out engines. When something is wrong with them and they get a little age on them then you just throw them out.

Cecilia
(*She runs down the steps in a house dress, to Rutherford*) Baby, it don't take that long to check... (*She realizes everyone is in the living room and stops*)

Hamlin
Yes sir. Said it right to my face and didn't even flinch once.

Alberta
If that don't beat it all. If that ain't the devil I don't know what is. Daddy what did you tell him?

Hamlin
I told him my leg would be back as good as new in a couple of days.

Alberta
Well, daddy it does take a little longer than that for your leg to heal.

Hamlin
Now, Alberta you know better than anybody I ain't one to be sittin' around playing cards and all in the day, I got to keep busy.

Jacob
That's for sure... we have our jam sessions, but Hamlin Jackson, I know ain't one to be in the house all day.

Alberta
I know daddy.

Hamlin
And I'm not one for retirin'.

Alberta
Daddy, I'm not saying you should retire, that's the last thing we need. You need to let the leg heal correctly. I know the doctor told you that.

Hamlin

(*Puzzled*) What do you mean that's the last thing we need?

Alberta

I just mean, I can't be taken off work to...

Hamlin

(*Finishes*) To take care of me.

Alberta

Daddy, bills need to be paid.

Hamlin

Did I ever ask you to sit here and nurse me?

(*Cecilia motions Rutherford to come with her in the kitchen, he is continuing to listen until she actually pushes him. They exit. Jacob motions to leave.*)

Where you goin' Jellybean, thought we was gonna' jam? (*Puts his hands to his lips to imitate harmonica playing*)

(Missing page 49)

Alberta

Oh, daddy, please. You sit around here tellin' all those damn stories like everything is all perfect—how you all always tried to make my life perfect, when all you did was take away my dreams. . take away my husband. So whatever, I learned I got it from you and her.

(*Hamlin raises his hand to hit her*)

Hamlin

(*Attempts to reach out to her*) I'm sorry, I'm sorry.. Baby.

Alberta

It's funny, I hear the kids always tell Cil... (*She grabs her purse*) you ain't go not more baby. (*Exits*)

Hamlin

(*Crosses to the dining room, pulls out his harmonica to play and wipes his eyes*) Alma, how you doin' baby? (*Pause*) yea, I hurt my leg. It'll be ok I guess... You heard us? All these years I've been sayin' takin' to one another like that isn't right. It doesn't help none. (*Pause*) I didn't mean... We was both upset, but the child knows what she feels. Things ain't as good as they seem Alma. Times seem like they get harder each and every day. Rutherford quit his job. I'm hurt. (*A little upbeat*) I been thinkin' bout investin' In the bakery. Yep, that's just what I'm thinkin'. What you say about it?

(*Pause*) What we gonna do? (*Pause*) I know I know me and ole' Jellybean was discussin' in the cab how things ain't like they use ta' be. I look on them days when I was playin' over at the Howard theater.

> (He *smiles softly. He plays a chord on harmonica. Chloe appears on the steps listening. He does not see her*)

Those weekends were the best times. You'd come back stage and bring Alberta with you to heat me play. Folks loved me. Everywhere I went around here kids was askin' me to play somethin'. They couldn't get enough of me. Now, it isn't like that Alma. Folks don't wanta' here no song; no stories. Alberta don't want to hear… (*Stops*) Alberta, if I could just go back down to the Howard Theater far a night or even to Alabama to play at the joint—Naw—I know the joint is probably gone now, Sister Especulia probably up there somewhere with you. We all had good times then, happy times. You know I miss you too, I'll be joinin' you soon. (*Pause*)What you mean stop talkin' that foolishness? Ever since you went away, things ain't the same. You always fixed things, I guess that's that southern comfort in ya'. We did alright by Berta didn't we? (*Lightly cries and crosses to his chair*) Alma, Alma you still there? I thought you'd gone again.

INTERMISSION

Act II

Scene 1

(It is Saturday around noon. Rutherford and Nate can be seen coming up the front steps with a dusty dough machine. They are sweating and struggling to get it in the front door. Hamlin is in the living room chair snoring)

Nate
(*Stopping in the living room*) Let's sit it here for a minute. (*Standing up, rubbing his back*) How low did you talk that man down for this pile of mess?

Rutherford
He dropped it to $75 bucks, (*Proudly*) This dough machine is power. (*Pointing*) Let's move it in there.

> (*They cross the dining room with the machine. Hamlin is awake, but does not let them know it*)

Nate
This thing? I bet it don't even run right. I don't want to be around when your woman finds it in her dining room.

Rutherford
See Nate, you're wrong. This will make things easier for Cil. She won't have to do all that mixin' by hand. (*Daydreaming*) This is gonna' increase our capital overnight.

Nate
(*Excited*) Then maybe you'll start to pay me? (*Looking at him*) I doubt it. (*Nate examines the machine*) Rutherford, all this machine reminds me of is an evil woman.

Rutherford
You tryin' to call my woman evil?

Nate
Naw, naw, man. It remind me of all other evil women. (*He whispers because of Hamlin*) Like Berta for instance.

Rutherford

My machine don't remind me of no Alberta.

Nate

See the way she is all stuffy and tight, that's how this machine looks now. It ain't gonna' get you no money—what it'll get you is trouble. (*Grabs a rag out of his pocket*) But you see, you put a nice cool rag over it, rub it a little, (*He begins wiping the machine*) it'll begin to shine and purr, and get this fine, fine rhythm to it. (*Puts his arm around Rutherford's shoulder*) See all Berta need is a rag like me to rub her the right way.

(*They laugh*)

Hamlin

(*Letting them know he's awake*) You better, put that rag right back in you pocket 'cause Berta ain't gonna' give you the time of day... Talkin' 'bout she some machine.

Rutherford

He was just jokin' Mr. Hamlin.

Nate

Yeah, Mr. Hamlin I didn't mean no disrespect.

Hamlin

I know, all I mean is you gotta' get on her good side. See, ya'll young guys don't know how to do that. (*Aside*) Some of us old guys don't know how neither. Come over here and take a seat.

(*Rutherford and Nate cross to Hamlin looking at one another*)

You gotta' talk to her nice, but don't use none of them lines you got Nate. She catch on real fast to them. Yes, indeed... And you can't be late. Lord knows she hate somebody who ain't never on time or early.

Nate

You really think your way would work?

Hamlin

(*Calmly*) Who's to say—may, may not.

Rutherford

(*Encouraging*) Hey man, Mr. Hamlin knows Berta better than anyone around here.

Nate

Hey, what have I got to lose?

Rutherford

Your front teeth. (*Laughs*) We got an order to fill.

(*Rutherford exits to kitchen, Nate follows holding his teeth worried*)

Hamlin

Alma, Alma. Somebody interested in Berta You here that Alma? Yep, ole' Nate got eyes for our girl. (*Laughs*) Hope she don't mess it up. You know he thinks she evil... Think he gonna calm her down. Say he can get her under control, make her relax. I told him don't be talkin' 'bout my daughter like that. Yes, I did... Oh, she ain't really evil. She got a temper, got that from you. Yes indeed. Oh, baby don't it take the wrong way. I always liked when you got hot, umm, umm, umm. Yep, especially when women started gatherin' round me when I played. When Bessie Smith came to town, the guys in the band say she could be an eeeevvviiilll woman. You could tell that when she sang.

(*Alberta and Cecilia enter with bags, laughing*) Now that was a big woman, I would have loved to see somebody like Nate try and handle her... Baby my eyes was only on you, always, always.

(*Cecilia sits on sofa and Alberta looks distantly at Hamlin and crosses to the dining room*)

Cecilia

Afternoon Mr. Hamlin.

Hamlin

What's in the bags?

Cecilia

We ran down to see if they had any halfway decent vegetables left at the market. Seems like everybody had the same idea, to go today. It was crowded as I don't know what down there.

Alberta

(*To Cecilia*) And it seems like they want to charge an arm and a leg for the stuff. (*Continues to take items out of the bag*) A woman was just sayin' to me that it's gettin' so bad that folks can't even afford to put scraps... (*Turns to see the dough machine, raising her voice*) What on earth is this? (*Finally beginning to speak to Hamlin*) What is this daddy?

(*Rutherford begins to peep his head through the kitchen door, Hamlin shrugs his shoulders as if he knows nothing about the machine. He exits to the front porch accidentally forgetting his harmonica*)

Cecilia
(*Crosses to the dining room calling out*) Ruuuuutherfoooord.

Rutherford

(*Enters with Nate*) So you like it?

Alberta

What is It?

Nate

Power! (*Laughs lightly*)

Cecilia

Power? What kind of damn power, and…

Alberta

What is it doin' in the dining room?

Rutherford

Isn't it a beauty?

Nate

Yes it is. (*Referring to Alberta*)

(Alberta glares back at Nate strangely)

Rutherford

This dough machine is our first major investment. Picked it up today for only… (*Proudly*) baby, I want you to guess how much I got it for.

Cecilia

I don't even want to know. (*Rubs her hand over her forehead*)

(*Alberta moves behind Cecilia's chair*)

Rutherford

Seventy five dollars is all I paid for it. (*Moves to go pat it*) That's all, this is the best deal I've ever gotten. (*Pause*)The old man who sold it to me wasn't real eager to part with It either.

Cecilia

(*Angrily*) You wasted our hard earned money on this thing. What has gotten into you Rutherford? Are you the only person in the Avery family now?

Nate

(*Looking to Rutherford*) I guess I'll be checkin' you all later. (*Begins to exit*)

Alberta

Nate, were you there when Rutherford bought this so-called machine?

(*Alberta and Cecilia look at him accusingly, Alberta exiting upstairs*)

(*To herself*) I sure hope you didn't spend any rent money or grocery...

Nate
(*Holds up his hands to Cecilia*) I'm innocent. I just helped him bring it in here. Tell 'em Rutherford.

Rutherford
This was my idea. I'm a business man. I can make decisions. I checked out a few vacant spaces for the business, then I got this beauty.

Cecilia
(*Angrily*) You've done some wild things, but this one tops them all.

Rutherford
What do you mean? No one has to sit around gettin' tired from mixin'.
(*Reaches for Cecilia's hands*) Those hands can take a rest.

Cecilia
(*Exhausted*) Rutherford, you know I support the bakery, you just can't do things like this. You can't go buying dough machines, and all when you feel like it. I'm not...

Rutherford
Baby, I told you I'm gonna make it all better. (*To Nate, handing him an apron and an index card from the dining room pause. Notices a pie box on the table. Impatiently*) Where's Booker. He was supposed to take a delivery around the corner for me. (*To himself*) Gotta' do everything myself. (*Cecilia is about to speak, but he continues*) Nate grab those apples out of the 'fridge for me, then you can start gettin' the rest of the ingredients for the cobblers out for me.

(*Nate looks nervous*)

It's all here on the card man. Cil will come in to check on you.

(*Nate exits to kitchen*)

(*to Cecilia*) I feel like the banks gonna' give us the money any day now. Trust me.

Cecilia
Rutherford I ain't goin' out buyin' art supplies 'cause I think I'm gonna be able to sale my work tomorrow. I've borrowed them, I've...

Rutherford
(*Innocently*) Baby, but that (*Pie box in one hand and points to art work*) isn't gonna' make us any money... (*Excited, points to the machine*) That is. I'll be back. (*Exits*)

(*Hamlin is talking to Alma on the porch, Cecilia goes upstairs, Chloe appears outside and stands watching Hamlin*)

Hamlin

(*To Alma*)... Jacob say, Ma Douglass been spendin' a lot of time in the garden of hers. He say...

Chloe

(*Sits*) Who ya' talkin' to Mr. Hamlin?

Hamlin

My wife, Alma?

Chloe

(*She looks around*) Where she at, I don't see her?

Hamlin

She's up there. (*He points and Chloe looks up*) Ya' can't see her, I can hear her.

Chloe

What ya'll be talkin' bout?

Hamlin

Everything... my harmonica, ole' times, (*Pause*) you.

Chloe

Me? What ya'll be sayin'? (*She anxiously moves to his ear*) Can I listen?

Hamlin

Why don't you talk to her?

Chloe

(*Giggling*) I don't know what to say?

Hamlin

Tell her anything you want. She a real good listener.

Chloe

(*Excited*) Okay. Hi, Miss. Uh, umm (*She whispers to Hamlin*) What her name again?

Hamlin

Alma. Miss. Alma.

Chloe

Oh, yeah. Hi, Miss. Alma. This is Chloe Avery. I don't know what Mr. Hamlin told ya' but I'm ten and a half. Mommy say I'll be eleven in 'bout 10 months. (*Thinking*)

Umm, you know I'm gonna win this contest they been having on the radio, (*Curiously whispering again to Hamlin*) She know what a radio is? (*Hamlin nods his head*) Well I'm gonna win $100 dollars for that contest, I'll be rich. I'm gonna take everybody out to dinner one day. You can come along if you want ta'. And I'm gonna...

Hamlin

(*Smiling*) Hold on, now Chloe, don't tell her everything all at once.

Chloe

You ain't jivin' me Mr. Hamlin, is you? She heard me didn't she?

Hamlin

She heard every word. (*Pause, listening*) She say she'd liked to talk to you again.

Cecilia

(*From upstairs*) Chloe... Chloe come up here and clean up this room, you know better.

Chloe

(*Opening front door*) Aww mommy.

Cecilia

Chloe Avery, what did I say?

Chloe

Yes, mam... Mr. Hamlin, remember you said I could talk to her...

Hamlin

Whenever you want.

Chloe

(*Hugging him, she looks up*) Talk to ya' later Miss. Alma. (*She exits*)

> (*Hamlin smiles broadly, he laughs. Alberta crosses to come downstairs, bumps into Chloe who is hurrying upstairs*)

Chloe

Sorry, Miss. Alberta. (*Exits*)

Alberta

(*To herself*) One day, just once, I'd like to come home to some piece of mind. (*She begins cleaning up the room*) I don't understand it one bit. They think money come fallen out of the sky.

Nate

(*Enters from the kitchen, wearing and apron and covered in flour. Alberta does not see him, he glides over to her and he looks as though he is tempted to touch her buttocks, but decides against it.*)

I wish I had myself a camera, I'd hold this moment forever.

Alberta

(*She turns to see him, embarrassed*) What?

Nate

Berta you know you a fine woman? My Lord.

Alberta

Don't you be usin' the Lord name in vain in this house. (*She becomes very serious and moves to finish straightening up living room*)

Nate

You know what I mean, the Lord just blessed you, with certain attributes. (*He stares at her behind*)

Alberta

Oh. (*She looks uncomfortable*)

(*Nate moves to turn on radio. Marvin Gaye songs are playing. He shakes his head listening to the music, she looks at him strangely.*)

Nate

Dance with me Berta? (*He reaches out his hand*)

Alberta

You gotta be crazy?

Nate

I guess I am. (*He pulls her to him, Marvin Gaye's "Let's Get It On" is playing*)

Alberta

(*She attempts to pull away*) I ain't dancin' with you.

Nate

Come on lady just relax.

(*She stares at him suspiciously and begins to dance along with him, but her arms look limp. They dance awhile his eyes are closed. He is really into it. She keeps eyes open still suspicious*)

Berta when the last time you had a man treat you right? (*No response*) Treat you like a queen? I believe in treatin' a woman just like that. Hold her tight, pamper her.

(*He rubs her back, she doesn't back down, her arms wrap around him. Chloe appears at the steps looking. They don't notice her. They continue to dance heads changing sides. Nate kisses Alberta, she squirms less. Her clothing is covered with flour. Cecilia appears at the steps embarrassed*)

Cecilia

Don't you remember you manners girl. You don't go spying on folks in your own house.

(*They come down the steps where Nate and Alberta stand startled. Chloe is grinning. Cecilia smiling, but still embarrassed, Hamlin enters*)

We didn't mean to walk in…I was…umm.

Hamlin

(*Smiling broadly*) Well, I'll be. (*Grabs his harmonica and exits outside again*)

(*Alberta's clothing is completely covered with flour prints she stares at Nate, she exits upstairs, Nate looks at Cecilia innocently*)

Nate

I really better be checkin' you all later now.

Hamlin

(*Calmly to Nate*) You sure is a fast one that's all I can say.

(*Nate does not look back and exits. Cecilia is crossing to the kitchen*)

Chloe

Mommy, is Miss Alberta and Nate what you call turkey and dressing?

(*Vernon and Booker can be seen coming up the steps, Vernon has a bag in his hand and Hamlin shakes hands*)

Cecilia

(*Looking puzzled*) Huh, what are you talking about baby? (*Exits*)

Chloe

(*Nervously*) Never mind.

(*The song "Dance to the Music" begins playing on the radio. Chloe then jumps up and is in the middle of the floor with two of her crayons acting as though she is playing the drums. Booker enters with Vernon who is carrying a bag*)

Chloe
(*Continuing to dance*) What's in the bags?

Vernon
Art supplies for your mom. (*Begins dancing with Chloe*)

(*Booker looks at them strangely*)

Chloe
(*Still dancing*) She's in the kitchen.

Booker
(*To Vernon*) She's a nut

(*Vernon continues to dance, Booker taps his shoulder to go to give Cecilia the supplies. Vernon exits to the kitchen with bag. All of a sudden the D.J. voice is heard on the radio announcing a contest*)

D.J.
Hey, all you brothers and sisters this is the soul man on 90.3 FM in the heart of your chocolate ciiiiityyyy. That was Sly and the Family Stone. It's muggy outside, but that' doesn't mean we can't keep Jammin' in here and if you're hip I've got a trip for you

Chloe
Booker, Booker, he's gonna announce the contest again.

D.J.
Now I've got some cash here that I'm itching to give away. So if you're my ninth caller I'll fill your pockets with $100.00.

Chloe
You hear that Booker?(*Jumps around and runs to the phone*)

Booker
You're not supposed to use the phone without permission, Chloe.

Chloe
It's only one call.

DJ.
You cool cats know the number. Give me a call, remember be my ninth caller and the cash is yooooooouuuurs. (*Music can be heard*)

Chloe
(*She pats her foot impatiently*) Come on, please answer.

D.J.

Yeah, 90.3

Chloe

(*Anxiously*) Am I your ninth caller?

DJ.

Sorry soul sister you're the eighth caller.

Chloe

Shoot. (*Slams the phone down*)

Booker

(*Crosses to the dining room, where more of his books are placed*) See I told you to stop calling them anyway. People have their numbers dialed before you even pick up the phone.

Chloe

Oh be quiet (*Pause, crosses to Booker*) You tell daddy yet about Vernon?

Booker

(*Covering her mouth*) I told you mama was gonna tell him.

Chloe

(*Moving his hand*) How you know?

Booker

'Cause I asked her.

Chloe

Then I dare you to go say something about it to him when he comes home.

Booker

No.

Chloe

Why?

Booker

Because I told you, ma already told him about it, so I don't need to say anything else about it.

Chloe

(*To herself*) Well I would ask him. (*Crosses to the living room*)

(*Vernon reenters and notices another book that Booker has picked up in the dining room. Chloe moves back to listen to the radio*)

Vernon

I see you've been readin₈ those books I gave you on Frederick Douglass (*Pause*) You anything about him?

Booker

(*Attempting to show him*) It was sayin' how he was a slave and was runnin' away. They beat him real bad, but then he got his freedom and started himself a newspaper. (*Thinking*) It was called.. The North Star. (*Excited*) He had this quote that said, There Is no progress, without struggle. See says it right here I didn't look first though. (*Smiling broadly and turning to the page*)

Vernon

(*Smiling*)That's right, now what does that mean for us?

Booker

Well, for Black folks it mean that we can't get anywhere, without hard work We might even face some obstacles—like racism and all. Nothin' gonna come easy. . that's how you become successful, when we keep goin'. . it's like Douglass was doin', he was speakin' out against slavery and all, and even riskin his life, but he didn't stop, he kept…

(*At that moment Rutherford comes in the door, Booker looks nervous. Rutherford stares from the other side of the room at Booker and Chloe*)

Chloe

(*Looks up*) Hi, daddy.

Rutherford

(*Stares at Booker*) Booker ain't you donna' to explain to me why you wasn't here to do the delivery like I told you to?

Booker

(*Nervously*) Umm, I'm sorry.

Rutherford

(*Notices Vernon*) Booker, ain't you goin' to introduce me to your friend?

Vernon

Evening sir. (*Extends his hand to Rutherford*)

(*Rutherford does not shake hands with Vernon, he only stares at him*)

Chloe

(*Runs to Booker, teasingly*) This is Vernon.

(*Booker kicks her*)

Oww, (*Confused*) Why you kick me Booker? (*Pause*) See, daddy Vernon is from the Big Brother/Mentor program. (*Pause*) At Howard University?

Rutherford

(*Angrily at Booker*) No, I don't see. (*Begins to yell to Cecilia*) Where's your mama? Cil, Cil. (*Walks to the staircase*)

Vernon

(*Confused*) I think I better go. I didn't mean to 'cause any trouble here. I was just trying to show Booker…(*Extends book to Rutherford*)

Booker

Daddy, I ain't doin' nothin' wrong…

Rutherford

Let's stop all the crap…I know what you're tryin' to do…let this Vernon take over…(*Snatches book from Vernon*)

Booker

No, dad. Ma was gonna tell you…see, it's like Chloe said Vernon's been teachin' me a few things…

Rutherford

(*Opens book angrily*) There is no progress, without struggle. (*Smacks it shut*) There is no progress, without struggle.

(*Cecilia enters from the kitchen and stands startled*)

Vernon

(*Moving to the door*) I'm going Mrs. Avery.

Cecilia

(*To Vernon*) Thank you, and I'm sorry.

(*Vernon does not turn back, he shakes hands with Hamlin on the front porch and exits quickly*)

Rutherford

(*Angrily*) What you sayin' that to him for? (*Crosses to Booker shaking him, Booker attempts to get loose*) See boy, you been learnin' the wrong thing. I won't get a substitute father. (*Suddenly looks up at Cecilia*) Cil, look here what I've been teaching my son…I won't get a substitute. Say it son, say it for daddy…

(*Cecilia attempts to pull Rutherford away from Booker who finally breaks loose. Chloe runs up the steps frightened*)

Cecilia

Stop it Rutherford, you're hurtin' him.

Rutherford

(*Pulling away from Cecilia*) I'll do what I want. I'm his father.

Booker

You don't understand. Vernon will tutor me and take me to the football games at Howard.

Rutherford

(*Suddenly turns angrily to Cecilia*) You never talked to me about getting him some damn big brother.

Cecilia

We tried. I was gonna' mention it to you.

Rutherford

So you start makin' decisions round here and haven't even discussed them with me.

Cecilia

I didn't know I had to report to you on every decision I make? You sure don't. This was important to Booker, so I said yes.

Rutherford

I'm Booker's father. I was goin' to teach him how to become a business man—own his own business—hire and fire people—build him a chain of bakeries. What is that wet behind the ears college student gonna teach him, huh? I know, he'll teach 'em how to be late for doin' his deliveries.

Cecilia

It was only one delivery, Rutherford. (*Pause*) Vernon can help him prepare for college.

Rutherford

There are plenty of boys around here he can hang out with. College?—tell him about the 8 guys who work at the Union Station with Masters degrees. They can't get jobs in their fields. They have been laid off from their other regular jobs so much that Mr. Hamlin calls them regulars.

Cecilia

That's not the same thing and you know it.

Rutherford

(*Starts pacing the floor*) While I'm out busting my butt...

Cecilia

(*Interrupts*) Hold it right there Rutherford, you certainly ain't the only one out here bustin' your butt to keep food on the table and a roof over our head.

Rutherford

(*Long pause, curiously*) You act like you're the only parent these kids got sometimes. like I don't even exist, like I can't and haven't ever taken that boy anywhere or helped him with nothin'. (*Sadly, but proudly*)I taught him how to bake it was me, Rutherford Avery. (*hitting his chest*) Me. All I ever ask is for my family to help me get OUR bakery together. Ya'll act like ya'll don't care, when it comes to the work that needs to be done, ya'll drop off like flies.

Booker

(*Tries to intervene*) Mama wasn't trying to do nothin' like-

Cecilia

Booker, go on upstairs.

Rutherford

(*Blocks Booker from exiting*) No! Let him stay, let him hear it all. Booker's suppose to be the big man now. He thinks you and he can make decisions without even asking me my opinion. (*Face to face with Booker*) I want him to explain to me why he needs this from someone else. (*Pause*) I'm waiting, I'm waiting.

Booker

You're never home. And when you are you're bakin' and never have time to do anything else. Yeah, I didn't want ma to tell you. (*Turns to Cecilia*) told you he was gonna act just like this. (*Back to Rutherford*) You don't ever listen to me, you always so busy, you're never around. I ain't never asked you for nothin, no money-I was just askin' you to be my father and you can't even do that cause you so busy. I didn't get a substitute father. I got someone who listens to me dream about going to college. I don't know what I want to become—maybe a doctor or maybe a business man. I don't know. But I do know, I ain't given him up—not for you or nobody else. Not for you to feel good and look good. I'm not giving Vernon up for anybody. (*Runs upstairs*)

(*Rutherford stands startled*)

Cecilia

(*Tries to call after him*) Booker, come back here. You come back here. (Back to Rutherford)

Rutherford

(*Depressed, he slowly moves behind Cecilia putting his arms around her. She is motionless*) You can't take him away from me...I need...

(Cecilia quickly moves from Rutherford after Booker upstairs)

Cecilia

Booker…Booker…*(Runs upstairs)*

(Hamlin enters from the front porch, Checker board is nearby on the coffee table)

Hamlin

Come over here and play checkers with me Rutherford.

Rutherford

I don't feel like it Mr. Hamlin.

Hamlin

(Sitting) I ain't askin' all that. *(Sets up the game)*

(Rutherford sits near Hamlin)

That Booker sure is gettin' big, hmm, hmm, that's for sure. Got his head in a book all the time. Always thinkin' 'bout school even when it ain't session. *(Silence, Hamlin makes a move with checker piece)* He was probably like you when you was a boy?

Rutherford

I doubt it…I *(Stops when he thinks Hamlin is cheating)*

Hamlin

He want ta' go places that we ain't never even thought about. I wouldn't stop him— boy should be able to dream.

Rutherford

(Beginning to get angry) What are you gettin' at Mr. Hamlin?

(Long pause. Hamlin changes the subject)

Hamlin

You know I always been interested in investin' in somethin', just don't know what? I ain't no millionaire, but I do keep some money put away. I was thinkin… yep, boys always need help in realizin' a dream

Rutherford

Mr. Hamlin I don't need no handout. I'm gettin' that loan. . .I don't need any favor.

Hamlin

I ain't talkin' 'bout no handout.. You wouldn't have to go down to that bank all the time and you could spend more time with them ….. all they need is a little time.

Rutherford

You tellin' me I don't do enough for... that I don't provide for them...

Hamlin

You readin' too much, Into what I'm tryin" to say (*Long pause*) Checker game remind me of... (*Jumps Rutherford*)

Rutherford (*Frustrated, places checker piece on the board hard*) Life. You make a move and you keep gettin jumped.

> (*He crosses away from Hamlin, who begins to rest his eyes. Rutherford stands in the middle of the dining room floor. He plugs in the machine, it runs. He stands beside the machine crying. Lights are only on Rutherford and the machine.*)

Act II

Scene 2

(It is Thursday early evening. Cecilia is looking out the front window. Alberta is in the area looking over a pile of bills. She is singing a spiritual, "Soon I Will Be Done with the Troubles of the World.")

Cecilia

Where is Booker, Berta?

Alberta

Don't you know?

Cecilia

(*To herself*) Vernon will be here to take him to the movies in a little while. (*Crosses from the window*)

Alberta

Vernon, Vernon, Vernon. That's all I ever hear when It come to Booker Avery. You better stop worryin' about that Vernon, and get your mind on some other things—-like your work in the office. (*Pause*) I ain't never seen folks who's attention focus on a boy in college as much as you and Booker's does.

Cecilia

Well, ain't you ever thought about goin' to college?

Alberta

Yeah, I thought about it. But, now my mind on that job of mine. And Supervisor Jenkins been mumblin' that you better get your mind back on the job too.

Cecilia

What did I do wrong now?

Alberta

Nothin' really girl, he just noticin' that your mind been somewhere else. You know he always watchin' us. He's been doin' it ever since we asked to leave early when we wanted to come look at this house. You went in his office beggin' and sayin' that you and I had found this low priced house where the two of our families could live

together and share the rent. You almost told that man your whole life story sayin' that you couldn't live In the place where you'd been livin'. Yep, I remember it all. And so do Jenkins.

Cecilia
You think we did the right thing?

Alberta
About leavin' early. That man better not have said anything to me about leavin' that job early after I've worked overtime so often and ain't never really gotten a dime for it. He better..

Cecilia
No, no Alberta. I mean about us livin' together. You think we've done better for ourselves? You think we've 'caused more problems for everybody. (*Pause*) We should've stayed where we were. (*To herself, looking out the window again*) We should have stayed where we were.

(Long pause)

Alberta
(*Patting Cecilia's' shoulder*) Cil you think too much, you just think to much. (*Begins singing again "Soon I Will Be Done with the Troubles of the World"*)

(*Hamlin enters with paper*)

Hamlin
Ya'll I want you to help me draft up this letter to my supervisor. I been workin on it, but it just don't sound right.

> (*Rutherford enters looking exhausted, he throws down his briefcase and papers fall out, he exits to the kitchen for a glass of water, and reenters*)

Only after a little fall they want me to call it quits just like that. I still have some good years left in me to keep on workin'. I've been fine and I'm gonna' keep on doin' fine. They can't get rid of me that easily.

Rutherford
The man don't need you around anymore. You, well you didn't go when you were supposed to go. He didn't get you in the war. You ain't been in jail. You're just an old man who worked his body and soul out for the Union Station for 40 years. See, you and me is what they call a high risk A high risk (*To himself*) We're just takin' up too much space.

Hamlin
Boy you are talkin' nonsense. All I've gotta do is draft up a letter tellin' them how

much service I've given over the years and they'll see that they can't let me go. (*To Alberta*) You'll type it up for me at work won't you Berta?

Alberta
Yes, daddy I'll type the letter and every thing will be fine, don't worry, everything will be-

Rutherford
There's no use typing up any letter. What you've gotta do Mr. Hamlin is sit back in that chair of yours and wait for the gates of heaven to open. What you goin to say, "It'll be okay I'm waitin for those pearly gates. Life is gonna' be much better up yonder. You better call Alma up now and say, "Here I come Alma, here I come. I don't care what the man do to me down here 'cause here I come." (*Starts singing*) Amazing grace how sweet the sound that saved a- (*Forgets rest of words and laughs*)

(Cecilia stands startled)

Alberta
Only cause you're tired and seem to be hurtin' don't take it out on daddy, Rutherford. Don't be blaspheming, don't do it, it ain't no need for it.

Rutherford
You are the last person Alberta who needs to give advice on how to talk to folks. You don't know a damn thing about what I'm feelin', and neither does the Lord. You all lyin' to ole Mr. Hamlin tellin' him things are gonna' get better. Tell him the truth.

Cecilia
What are you talkin' about?

Rutherford
Tell him Alberta—Cil tell him that when and if he gets back to work they'll be nothin' there for him— no job, no nice shiny quarters. Tell him that boss of his that he's been so loyal to all these years will have forgotten his name by the time he gets back. Tell him that all those folks who claim that he's given them such good service for all these years won't even remember that his Black face ever existed.

Cecilia
(*Pulling on Rutherford's arms*) Rutherford don't do this.

Rutherford
(*Pulls away from Cecilia*) You all are afraid to tell him, but I'm not cause I know. I know how It feels to have them spit In my face like I'm some dog out of an alley. I know how they laugh behind my back when they turn me down after I beg them for a loan day in and out. Tell ole Mr. Hamlin that he's gonna' die with nothin' right there in that old chair. (*To Hamlin*) If they aren't gonna' tell you Hamlin Jackson, I will. Your time is up. (*Leaning over into Hamlin's' face*) You're old, you're Black, you're

a male— (*Standing straight up as it he has discovered something*) You Are Worthless. Somebody tell him tell him, tell him before—

Hamlin
(*Rising half way' out of his chair*) Shut the hell up, just shut the hell up. Why are you sayin' all that? You don't know what you're talking about.

Rutherford
(*Leaning back over Hamlin his harsh words push him back into his seat*) Like hell I don't. Don't worry though I'm worthless too. Hey, Alberta isn't that why Malcolm died cause you couldn't give him nothin.'

> (*Alberta turns her back as if she can't believe that he is saying this, Rutherford moves behind her back*)

So what you say to the Lord about that one? I would have loved to hear him explain that. You can't even figure that out yourself, can you? (*Laughs sickly*) I ain't got nothin, you ain't got nothin', we all ain't got nothin. So we're all gonna die with nothin-

Cecilia
Damn it Rutherford stop it or get out, I mean it.

Rutherford
(*Holds Cecilia's arms*) See I'm nothin' to them out there. (*Points outside*) I'm nothin to you all in here. That's why you want me to get out. You never thought it would turn out like this huh, Cil?

Cecilia
(*Begins to cry*) I can't take it anymore Rutherford, I'm too tired.

Rutherford
I'm tired too. Cil I'm real tired. (*Exits*)

Cecilia
I'm sorry he didn't mean what he said he's just upset. (*Exits*)

Hamlin
Maybe he's right, I don't have to go back to that job. I'll have my retirement money. I can find something else to do. We can talk about investin' again.

Alberta
Daddy, don't bring up that bakery… after what he just said to you—to us. I've heard it all now.

Hamlin

(*Changing subject*) Alma young folks think they know everything it was like I was sayin' yesterday…

Alberta

(*Frustrated*) Daddy, why do you keep doing that?

Hamlin

Doin' what?

Alberta

Sittin' there like you're havin' some deep conversation with her.

Hamlin

'Cause I am.

Alberta

Daddy this needs to stop, you know there isn't a soul in this room except you and me.

Hamlin

And your mama. Her soul is here with me when I wake up and when I go to bed.

Alberta

Daddy it doesn't do any good— you hanging on like this. Sitting here like she's in the room with you isn't doing any good. You act like she's talking back to you.

Hamlin

Just like the Lord talks and listens to us when we pray, your mama's doing that very same thing

Alberta

You know that's not the same thing Daddy let her rest in peace will you?

Hamlin

You gotta say somethin' to her sometime Berta.

Alberta

I've said my goodbye's. I said them a long time ago. I said them when that man left me. There's no need in me holding on. She's been dead almost five years and you are still here talking to her like that woman was up and kicking Just like anybody who walks this earth.

Hamlin

That's how you've been thinking of her, as that woman? You can't even call her name can you? When you go to church and pray to the lord you don't even call her name do you? Your own mama's name.

Alberta

I can call her

Hamlin

You haven't said her name in years. You don't ever move an inch to sit down here with me and even discuss how it was when things were good when she wasn't sick, when she was taking care of everything, and when we all was taking care of each other. (Pause) Say her name, Alberta. Please just say your mama's name just for me, just once?

Alberta

I don't need to prove anything to you.

Hamlin

Seems you need to prove something to yourself more. You act like you can't hurt Alberta. You're always relieving everybody's pain except your own. Take some of that advice you give Cil and Rutherford sometimes. You hear?

Alberta

Daddy what are you talking about? I'm fine.

Hamlin

Berta you can't fool me. I'm your daddy. You miss your mama and you Miss Malcolm too.

Alberta

Daddy don't start it please. You're tired, you need some rest.

Hamlin

Call it what ever you want. I ain't gonna' stop on account you don't approve. and you won't face reality yourself. Malcolm and your mama lives in us everyday. (Pause) Her birthday's coming up soon you know? Helping Rutherford could be her birthday present I was thinkin' we could spend the day together. (Alberta does not reply) Take some flowers to her grave. We could have lunch together.

Alberta

Daddy-

Hamlin

Don't give me your answer now, you think on It some, I know you're busy and all, but it would mean a lot to me. (Pause) Berta, It would mean a lot to your mama. Go on, I have talk to her about these few pennies.

Alberta

(*Kisses Hamlin on the head as if there is no use arguing with him over the situation*) I'll think on it daddy.

(*An hour has passed, Chloe and Booker enter, Cecilia has also returned to the living room*)

Chloe

Mommy, you know where daddy went away to? He comin' back?

Booker

Ma don't know Chloe.

Cecilia

I thought you were supposed to be getting ready for Vernon. (*Pause*) Listen to me Chloe. Things haven't been going too well for your daddy and me, so he might be gone for a little while. He just needs to get some business taken care of.

Chloe

Daddy said we were going have the bakery real soon. Juanita told me that I was telling a story, so I hit her. She said that I was making up the whole thing and that we were never gonna have anything

Booker

(*He stands defiantly looking at his mother, behind Chloe*) For once ole' Juanita was right.

Cecilia

Don't start it boy, not today. Chloe listen to me, every time someone tells you something or promises you something, even though they try and try, they can't always give you what they say they're gonna give you.

(Chloe stands quietly confused)

Chloe

I know Mommy. But you the one who say you can't never go back on a promise.

Booker

Why don't you tell her the truth?

Chloe

Mommy, what is Booker talking about?

Cecilia

Baby sometimes we think we can make things happen. No matter how bad you want things, that doesn't mean you can have them, at least not when you want them.

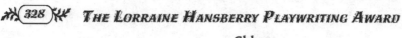

Chloe
No, mommy. (*She pulls away*)

Cecilia
Chloe, listen to me please. We'll have that bakery someday, but not now. Things aren't right at this moment.

Booker
When is the time ever right ma, huh? Nothing ever comes at the right time. I don't want to wait on you and daddy's promises anymore. You keep filling our heads with all these promises. Daddy's been messin' with those blueprints, and papers for as long as I can remember; but you don't ever see anything really come of it. You know ma, like I know, that ain't nothin gonna come of it.

Chloe
(*Suddenly starts hitting* Booker) Stop sayin that. You're lying.

(*Cecilia pulls* Chloe *off of* Booker)

Booker
Tell her ma, that we ain't gonna have nothin', no surprise today or tomorrow. I hate this place, and Chloe and you are gonna' start hating it too.

Cecilia
Booker, look at you, listen to you. You sound like a person who doesn't know a thing about love

Booker
I—

Cecilia
You sound just like me and your father. You can't take it. You're the spitting image of most adults in this world, me and your daddy included. When life becomes difficult we act like we can't pull ourselves up or anybody else for that matter. You're sayin' the same thing I said to Mr. Hamlin. You want to give up too, but no matter what you do and say, I still keep loving you. I still keep hoping that you'll come back the way you use to be. You have become bitter just like your father and me too. You spend 40 hours with Vernon, and you can't understand why two families not connected by blood share a home together.

Booker
(*Angrily*) This is a home?

Cecilia
Yes, I said a home with love. You get all those meanings from those books he gives you, but you forgot about family and what that means. You forget the good times

you've had with your daddy. Maybe it's all my fault? Maybe you two are strangers because of me? All I have to say is don't let it hurt you and this family Booker like it seems to have hurt him. You're probably saying to yourself with your eyes all cocked and lips all poked out, that ma don't know nothin'. Ma don't know how I feel. (*Touches Booker's head, and he pulls away somewhat*) You think that ma is never going to let things get better, daddy neither. They are just crazy right. Isn't that what you're thinkin' Booker Avery? You hate ma don't you?

(Booker's face shows surprise that his mother would even say that)

Huh? Say it Booker Avery You hate this house, hate ma, daddy, Chloe, Miss. Alberta and Mr. Hamlin. Even hate yourself. Say it!. They don't know how to do nothin'' right, isn't. that the truth? They all make me sick. Things would be better if they would all just leave me alone.

Booker
I haven't even said anything like that. (*Looks to the floor*)

Cecilia
Baby you didn't have to. I can see in it your eyes and can hear it these days each time you open your mouth. But you know what? (*Lifts his chin*) You can hate ma and be mad at Ma all you want to, but you know what? Ma and daddy are gonna' always love you anyway, and we're gonna' to keep telling you, that maybe not today, but tomorrow we'll be able to give you what you've always wanted.

Chloe
I love you mommy.

Cecilia
I love you too baby.

(Vernon knocks at the door)

I love you Booker.

(*Booker moves to exit*)

You have a good time. (*Easily slides by Booker and places something in his hand, Cecilia turns to exit*)

Vernon
(*Doesn't enter the home, looks slightly uncomfortable*) I'll have him back at a reasonable time Mrs. Avery.

Booker

(*He opens the door and opens his hand, there are three crumbled dollar bills, he finally turns to her*) I love you ma (*Pause*) and daddy too.

(*Booker and Vernon exit. There is a slight smile on Cecilia's face, she exits. Chloe kneels in Hamlin's chair. Alberta appears at the top of the stair case, but Chloe doesn't notice her*)

Chloe

Miss Alma? . . . Miss Alma.

(*Alberta listens*)

Why we can't never have anything Miss. ..... Do you know? I say my prayers and yes sir and no mam like I'm supposed to. (*Pause*) Miss Alma my daddy gone. don't know when be comin' back. He sad 'cause he can't get no money for the bakery. My mama sad too. She don't say It though. Everybody mad at each other. Juanita say, I ain't got no real family with us, Mr. Hamlin, and Miss Alberta. (*Mimicking*) She say, "All you got is a mess." What you think Miss Alma? (*Pause*) Why my daddy don't say he don't got a surprise for me anymore? (*Pause*) I can't even win that stupid contest on the radio. I stopped tryin', just like my daddy.

(*Alberta remains and Chloe sways in the chair*)

(*It is another Monday afternoon. Booker is on the porch reading a book. Rutherford appears and is wearing his parking lot uniform, stares at Booker for a moment*)

Rutherford

Got your head in that book again, huh?

Booker

(*Looks up*) Yes sir.

Rutherford

(*Nervously moving closer*) How's your mama doin'? Your sister?

Booker

They good. Chloe keep askin' where you go?

Rutherford

(*Still calm, but curious*) What you all tell her?

Booker

Ma, say you out takin' care of business.

Rutherford

(*Sighing to himself*) Takin' care of business. (*Pause*) So you waitin' for Vernon?

(A fire alarm is heard Rutherford and Booker look)

Booker

No sir. I better get inside. (*Rises uncomfortably with his books*)

Rutherford

Yeah, I guess so…don't want to take up your time. (*Pause*) Booker.

Booker

Yes sir. (*Long pause*)

Rutherford

(*Innocently, holds both of Booker's arms*) I didn't mean to hurt you all. (*Pause*)You know, when I was younger I said I was goin' to be the first Black kid in my neighborhood to have somethin' of his own..... I was (*Light laugh*) Lord sound like Mr. Hamlin. (*Pause*) I was just trying to make things better for ya. Let you all experience the good life for a change. That's all…

Booker

I know. (*Begins to exit again*)

Rutherford

I failed, but I was just tryin' to. . well you 'know. Will you let your mama know I'll be back later? (*Silence*)

(*Rutherford exits. Hamlin, Jacob, and Chloe are in the living room. She is intrigued by the men's playing. Booker enters and crosses to the dining room*)

Chloe

Mr. Jacob where you get the name Jellybean? Your mama give it to you?

(Hamlin and Jacob look at one another)

Jacob

Naw, baby my mama sure didn't give it to me?

(Jacob and Hamlin laugh)

Hamlin

(*Instigating, starts to play a tune*) Tell her where, man…

Jacob

The ladies.

Chloe

(*Confused*) What ladies?

Jacob

(*He pops a jellybean in his mouth and hands one to Chloe*) The ones that was sweet on me...

(*The phone rings, Hamlin who is near it answers*)

Hamlin

Hello... He's not here right now... I don't know... Oh, you want to place an order. (*Pause*) Well, Mr. Avery, I think he said he wouldn't be gone for long... I can take down the information... One of ya'll pass me some paper and a pencil... Okay, you want four dozen of them oatmeal raisin cookies, chocolate chip, hmm, hmm... two of them pecan pies, yep, everybody loves them... And three of them custered... umm, umm... what does he call them? (*Pause*) I think he calls that... Chloe's Custered Surprise... So when do you want all of this... (*Raising his voice*) Tomorrow?... You, say he always gets an order to you on time... umm, umm, that's right, 'cause we aim to please... (*Continues to write*) Yes, I have it all... Thank you. (*Hangs up*)

Chloe

Why you tell that person that order could be done?

Hamlin

'Cause it will... (*Booker enters*) Booker. Come on in here boy, and don't drag your feet. Now we're gonna' get this done on time. (*To Booker*) I want you to run down to the market to get these things. (*Extends list and money to Booker who remains still*)

Chloe

But Miss Berta says we suppose to buy everything from warehouse to say money.

Hamlin

I would agree but we ain't got time, not today. (*Continues to extend list and mone to Booker.*)

Jacob

What's a matter with you boy, we got an order to do?

Booker

What's the use in...

Hamlin

(*Interrupting*) Sometimes you gotta' stop thinkin' so much and show some action.

(*They all wait for Booker to finally take the list and money, he does, and Hamlin pats him on the back, Booker exits*)

Chloe you go in that kitchen and show Mr. Jellybean where everything is.

(Chloe and Jacob move to exit to the kitchen)

(To himself) I'm gonna' try and get this machine to workin'.

(It is a few hours later and lights rise on the dining room where Hamlin, Jacob, Booker, and Chloe are folding boxes and napkins, putting sprinkles and other designs on baked goods, the dough machine is running. Alberta enters with a Bible and wearing a church ushering uniform. She is in a good mood and is singing a gospel song)

Alberta
Ya'll should have been at revival tonight, pastor was lit up with…(*Stands looking at all of them, she does not turn out any lights and slowly walks towards everyone in the dining room*)

(Everyone speaks to Alberta, but she does not respond, they all look puzzled)

Jacob
You all right Berta? (*Feels her head*)

(Alberta does not respond)

Hamlin
(To Alberta) What's a matter child, cat got your tongue?

(Alberta slightly smiles, hugs Chloe and the child continues to work. Alberta then crosses to exit upstairs, but she pauses sits on the couch and begins to dial the phone. Nate can now be seen coming up the steps with some flowers he continues to wonder if he should go into the house)

Alberta
Elliot…hello this is Alberta…am I disturbing your dinner? (*Light laugh*) Yes, your daddy's over here with my father again…You always said to call when that roommate of mine needed an attorney to discuss tightening up the ends of that business…You said when he finds some backers…some investors—to call…

(Jacob and Hamlin have moved behind her to listen)

I never thought I'd say this, but Elliot I'm callin'. I know it's late, but I was wonderin' if you could run over here tonight to…Thank you, God bless you. I'll see you in a little bit. (*She hangs up, and turns around surprised to see Hamlin and Jacob*) Why are you two staring?

Hamlin & Jacob
(Surprised) You?

Alberta

Yes, me the woman who's tighter than a head band on a hat would like to invest. (*Putting her arms around their shoulders, crossing to the dining room*) Let's see what I can do?

(*Nate knocks at the door, Alberta crosses to it. Nate stands grinning, Alberta steps outside*)

Nate

Umm, umm, I just thought I'd bring you some of these to brighten up your day. (*Silence, he hands them to her*) I was wonderin' maybe we could spend some time together. Get to know one another. We could take one step at a time. (*Nervously*) Alberta, I ain't Malcolm. (*Silence, he begins to speak in a stronger voice*) I mean to do right by you Alberta.

Alberta

(*Smiling*) You just gonna' stand there talkin' or are you gonna' come in here and help us. (*She grabs his hand, leading him into the house*)

(*Rutherford in his uniform appears again sitting on the porch, waiting for Cecilia. She is now coming up the walk pauses and looks at Rutherford who rises. Inside, Hamlin pulls Jacob aside*)

Hamlin

(*To Jacob*) I taught him all that. Yep. Jellybean, he might turn out like us after all.

(*They laugh*)

(*Cecilia stands in silence, then she quickly begins to move to the house*)

Rutherford

I know I haven't always listened and been there for you and the kids. I've been thinkin' that to be a good father all I needed was to provide a steady income from something I owned, like that bakery. (*Slightly smiling*) I guess Booker really showed me that you all need more…I do too. Cecilia, all this time I been tellin' you you can be the cashier, you can be the cashier, (*To himself*) but you have hands for makin' art not pushin' numbers…that doesn't matter much now, with everything that happened with the bank, but I'm sorry. I'm real sorry.

(*Silence, Cecilia moves even closer to the house*)

(*Touching his shirt*) See, I got my job back. (*Silence, confused*) Baby, isn't that what you wanted?

Cecilia

(*Calmly*) But, it was never what you wanted Rutherford.

Rutherford

Baby? Baby, I need you.

Cecilia

(*Long pause*) Rutherford Avery I have always needed you, your support...real support for my dream.

(*Long pause, Rutherford reaches out his hand to her, she responds, they hug and kiss. Cecilia leads Rutherford into the house*)

Hamlin

I'm tired of repeatin' myself...everybody that comes in here needs to put their hands into this work in the dining room...(*Mimicking Rutherford from past moments*) Rutherford you need some help findin' somethin' to do?

(*Alberta and Hamlin move to the door, they touch Rutherford's hand in forgiveness. Cecilia begins looking around the room*)

Alberta

I've pulled out my box and Hamlin and Alberta got some money to put into that business. (*Long silence*)

Hamlin

I guess I get a kick out of these anniversaries and parties. I like using my hands like that, that's why I spent so many years at the station. It's time to move on, this something different. (*Pause*) Rutherford got good ideas, good plans I can't take that away from him.

Cecilia

After all you've worked for all the years Mr. Hamlin. (*To Alberta*) What about your dream house? The house that you could call your own? (*To Hamlin*) What if the business doesn't work? What if you lose all of that money? What then?

Hamlin

What if? What if? What if I get hit by a car tomorrow I would never be able to find out how this all turned out. (*Putting his hand on Cecilia's shoulders*) Cecilia sometimes we've got to take chances and this is one of those times.

Alberta

Daddy's right.

Hamlin

We trust you and Rutherford. We don't think we're throwing our money away into some stupid get rich quick scheme. The bakery is going to benefit everybody. (*He crosses to the window*) Your family, my family, this community. We need something like this in the community...

Jacob

...to bring back the hope, to bring back the life into folks.

Alberta

We need something to bring back the life in us. I need to learn about giving again. My mother would want me to give again. (*Looks to Hamlin*)

Cecilia

But—

Nate

Listen Cil. Doesn't Rutherford always preach, do for ourselves, be independent?

Hamlin

And in the end the banks name won't be on the papers—ours will. We would have pulled in the resources. We would be what he calls the employer and the employee. We would be—

Nate

Bad!

(All laugh)

Chloe

(*Chloe has been listening*) Mommy?

Cecilia

Yes Chloe.

Chloe

Are we gonna be partners with everyone in the bakery? Huh mommy... daddy?

Hamlin

Ya'll better answer that child, 'cause we got work to do. Ya'll we've got our own Union Station right here.

Booker

Daddy, Mr. Hamlin and us have been makin' up names for the goods. (*Crosses to show him a list*) Chloe's Custard Surprise.. Alberta's Angel cake...

(*They laugh but, Nate laughs the loudest, Alberta looks at him*)

Rutherford's Raspberry tarts...

Chloe

(*Pulling on Booker's shirt*) Don't forget that one for Miss Alma...um, um, apricot rolls.

Hamlin

Yes indeed, the Jackson's want to really be a part of this business. I can do some of the mixin', Cecilia can do…

Rutherford

(*Adds*)the decorations. (*Smiling at her*)

Alberta

It's not like you're gettin' money from the bank or strangers. You're gettin' money from folks you know. (*Pause*)You're gettin' money from family. And that's what we are a family that fusses a lot sometimes, but loves a lot all the time. And family has got to stick together In all of those times no matter what.

Hamlin

(*Proudly*) That's what me and your mama taught you

Alberta

(*To Hamlin*) Yes, that's what you and mama taught me.

(*Everyone looks surprised*)

No matter what happens when one of us Is gone the others have got to stick together and help one another through.

(*A knock is heard at the door, Alberta moves to it*)

Rutherford

Berta stay where you are. I'm closer. (*Begins to move towards the door*)

Alberta

(*Raising her hand*) No, I wanta get this one.

Rutherford

I'm closer.

(*Alberta continues to move to the door anxiously*)

Cecilia

What's the matter with you Alberta? We're not expecting anybody.

Alberta

Yes we are, (*Rubbing her hands*) we gonna' make some deals tonight. Now, shall I let the attorney in Mr. Avery?

Rutherford

Let him in sister. Let him in, so that our family bakery can open for business.

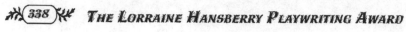

Hamlin

Alma....everything is gonna' be alright, Alma.. everything's gonna' be okay.

(Alberta reaches the door. Everyone looks in excitement. Lights fade down)

THE END

The Scenes

This section of the volume introduces the reader to 6 of the national Hansberry playwrights by way of brief scenes from their winning dramas. The scenes are selected to reflect the thought, action and characters of the plays and to provide actors with scenes for the classroom, for auditions, and for competitions.

A Star Ain't Nothin'
But a Hole in Heaven

by

Judi Ann Mason

SETTING/TIME: Beckett's farm house, Elm Grove, La., May, 1969

CHARACTER: 1 man, 2 women

    Lemuel Beckett: Aged, blind man; Pokey's uncle
    Mamie: Pokey's senile, dying aunt
    Pokey: High school senior living with Uncle and Aunt

A poignant folk drama of rural southern life in which a young girl, (Pokey) about to graduate from high school, struggles to overcome the inertia of tradition and "southern brainwashing" in order to realize her dreams and aspirations-to go North for a good education. The immediate conflict is with her guardian (Uncle Lemuel) who believes that"all education is for white folks because they ain't got skills in they hands like us." In Pokey's search for her own truth, she discovers numerous lies, fears, and 'little holes in heaven' - and ultimately decides to live her own life.

Scene 1

(Pokie crosses to Mamie's bedroom. She disappears a moment and re-enters with Mamie. She takes her toward the bathroom and guides her there. She then crosses back to the kitchen, preparing the oil for her uncle.)

Mamie: Pokie?

Pokie: Yessum?

Mamie: Is it hot outside?

Pokie: It's sticky. I think it done cooled off a little. The sun is gone down.

Mamie: Feels real hot.

Pokie: I'll turn the fan on. (She crosses to the fan and turns it on) This should cool things off a bit for you.

Mamie: What time is it?

Pokie: Almost 9:15.

Mamie: Nights are gettin' as long as the days. It takes so long to get through one or the other.

Pokie: It's summertime. Days are longer in the summer.

Mamie: I'm finished.

Pokie: Okay. (She crosses to the bathroom to get Mamie.)

Mamie: It's nice to have a bathroom on the inside. I remember when I was a little girl, I always had to go outside or behind a tree.

Pokie: What did you do when it was raining?

Mamie: We had a jar. But you still had to go outside to empty it. Didn't have toilet paper either.

Pokie: What did you use?

Mamie: Newspaper. Paper bags.

Pokie: You want me to help you back to bed?

Mamie: I think I'll sit out here for a while. I ain't botherin' you huh?

Pokie: Bothering me how?

Mamie: I thought maybe you had to do some school work.

Pokie: No mam. (She starts to hum)

Mamie: What you hummin'?

Pokie: Just an old song I usta hear when we lived by that church.

Mamie: What is it?

Pokie: "Do Lord, Remember me."

Mamie: Real nice song. They sho' did usta sing that song. Every Sudnay. I thought they didn't know but one song.

Pokie: Maybe they didn't.

Mamie: (Singing.) Do Lord, Do Lord, Do remember me. Do Lord, My lord, Do remember me. Do Lord, My Lord, Do remember me. Do Lord remember me. (She hums it.)

Pokie: Aint Mamie?

Mamie: Do you think he gon remember me, Pokie?

Pokie: Who?

Mamie: The Lord.

Pokie: He don't forget nobody.

Mamie: I keep telling myself that, but I done begun to wonder—

Pokie: The Lord don't forget, Aint Mamie.

Mamie: I wonder why folks got to get old?

Pokie: For the same reason they be born, I guess.

Mamie: They get old and they can't do for theyselves no more. It's hard for them to walk 5 yards, it's hard for them to laugh like they usta or talk like they usta. Voice get slow and cracked. Your breathing changes. Your mind wonders. It gets hard for you to remember how old you is, or what your face looks like. It's like going back to being a baby...but your mama ain't no where round-

Pokie: I read somewhere that getting old was a blessing—

Mamie: Don't let nobody fool you. The person who wrote that was probably young and getting ready to die.

Pokie: Just think about all your friends that didn't live this long...

Mamie: They lucky.

Pokie: Aint Mamie, don't say that.

Mamie: (Singing.) Do Lord, Do Lord...

Pokie: You all right?

Mamie: In a minute, Lemuel. The time ain't just right yet....

Pokie: Aint Mamie, this is Pokie. This is me.

Mamie: I know who it is. (Laughs.) I was just thinking, Pokie, Just thinking.

Pokie: About what?

Mamie: About me and when I was your age. I was married.

Pokie: You got married when you was 15, didn't ya?

Mamie: Yeah. In Eunice, Louisiana. That's way down south. We usta have to cut sugar canes almost every day of the week even if we was little.

Pokie: Could you eat all that you wanted?

Mamie: We'd sneak and do it. Us little folks would make off with three or four canes and sit under the levy and eat it.

Pokie: Betcha that was fun, huh?

Mamie: Unless we got caught. Then it was all hell.

Pokie: What happened when you got caught?

Mamie: The worse whupping you ever had. My daddy had a belt made of leather. It had about nine or ten little-bitty straps tied together at the top with another piece of leather. So when you got one lick, you got ten.

Pokie: Ooowee! Couldn't stand that!

Mamie: Couldn't help but stand it if you was caught. And I got caught at least four times a week.

Pokie: Poor Aint Mamie....

Mamie: But Lemuel never got caught. That boy would steal the bitter cut of a lemon and never hear high tail of it.

Pokie: Was he a bad boy?

Mamie: Bad? That ain't the word for it. Lemuel was sinful. But he was a dependable fella. He took care of his blind daddy until the day he died.

Pokie: Blind? I didn't know his daddy was blind, too.

Mamie: I ain't too much on doctorin', but I reckon he had bout got the same thing his pappy had.

Pokie: I didn't know that...

Mamie: But Lemuel stay right by that man. Sometimes I wondered when we was really gon be married. He always put his papy before me. But that's the way he is—if he got something he got to do, he do it.

Pokie: Did his daddy stay with you?

Mamie: Old man died in this house. Funny thing, though, I was happy he had finally passed on. It don't do a soul good to see him sufferin' like that. He was 97 when he finally left this life. (Pause.) No, mam, it ain't good to live a long time. Folks start wishin' you dead and hopin' something bad happens to you. I don't want to live this long. If there is a heaven let me see it soon. Let me see what it's like to walk straight through the streets of gold, let me stand tall like I used to, let me put my own clothes on my back, and take care of my own aches and pains, let me think and keep my thoughts strong, let me cry and know the reason I'm cryin'....

Pokie: Aint Mamie, please. Stay with me. This is Pokie.

Mamie: I want to wipe my brow. Lemuel, it's time for him to go. It's time for him to pass on. Let him go, Lemuel! He don't want to stay here and you trying to make him stay. Let him leave his life behind. Let him be!

Pokie: (Going to embrace Mamie.) Aint Mamie, come back to me.

Mamie: Pokie, Lemuel won't let him go.

Pokie: He will Aint Mamie. He lettin' him go right now. Look around. Do you see him? He's gone.

Mamie: Is he gone?

Pokie: Yes.

Mamie: Then he's happy. He told me he was ready to die. He told me.

Pokie: He surely did.

Mamie: Where's Lemuel?

Pokie: He's back in his room.

Mamie: Lemuel, Lemuel. That man is a great man, Pokie. Good man.

Pokie: I know.

Mamie: Sometimes you don't understand him. He is hard to understand sometimes.

Pokie: He treats me like I'm a little baby.

Mamie: He tryin' to protect you.

Pokie: From what?

Mamie: What he had to go through.

Pokie: Things ain't like that no more. There's a lotta things I have to do and he won't let me. I think he don't want me to graduate.

Mamie: Aw, Pokie...

Pokie: Every time I ask him for something I need, he tells me that I don't need it.

Mamie: You got to try real hard to make him see.

Pokie: I told him I needed a white dress—

Mamie: He's always been like that. Like the time I told him I needed some new shoes for my sister's wedding...

Pokie: I wouldn't ask him for the dress if I didn't have to have it...

Mamie: All the time before that, all the money had to be spent on things for his pappy.

Pokie: Do you think he'll let me buy it?

Mamie: "Lemuel, the shoes don't cost but $2. And I'll take good care of them. You won't have to buy me no more..."

Pokie: I saw a dress that cost only $12 up at the Woolworth...

Mamie: He told me that we didn't have the money. But I knew we had the money cause I had worked five days straight down to Miss Belma's store that week and I gived him all the money...

Pokie: Aint Mamie, will you listen to me?

Mamie: So I tells him I had the money and he gets mad at me. "You ain't grateful for all I done for you. Who else gon marry a woman like you?" You be thankful for me marrying you..."

Pokie: Will you listen to me?

Mamie: I told him that he didn't have to marry me. If he had to wipe my brow with it, he didn't have to marry me.

Pokie: I got problems, too! But nobody around here never listens to me talk...

Mamie: It was just like talkin' to myself. You told me you didn't make no mind about children. You told me I was just as much a woman cause I couldn't make babies. Lotsa women can't make babies. I ain't the only one, Lemuel.

Pokie: (Unable to control her moment of disgust.) For once can't you hear me? Come back and talk to me!

Mamie: I love you, Lemuel. I love Jesus, too. Jesus is the Savior! Save me, Lord! Take this curse from my womb...

Pokie: Come back and talk Aint Mamie!

Mamie: Too old now. Life done creeped up on me. It done snatched my breath from my lungs. I'm still a woman.

Pokie: Listen to me!

(Mamie burst into a fit of tears. Pokie goes to her and starts to shake her.)

Listen! You come back here and listen!

Mamie: Turn me loose! Jesus gonna remember me! Turn Jesus aloose! Take the cross from his back! He's the son of God! Turn the Lord aloose!

Lemuel: (At door.) Mamie, what's the matter? (Seeing Pokie.) Pokie, let her be! You trying to kill her? What you doing? Stop hollin' at her! Turn her loose!

Pokie: (She releases Mamie and stands back staring at Lemuel.) You saw that?

Lemuel: It's alright Mamie. All right.

Pokie: How did you see what I was doing to her?

Lemuel: She was hollin'...

Pokie: No, you saw it. Joretta was right. You can see.

Lemuel: Girl, stop that barking and help me get her to bed.

Pokie: Do it yourself.

Lemuel: What you say?

Pokie: Do it yourself. You saw well enough a minute ago...

Lemuel: Go get the alum so you can rub her down.

Pokie: I ain't gonna do it!

Lemuel: Is this the thank-you we get after all we done for you? You musta forgot we didn't have to take you in...

Pokie: I'm leaving Uncle Lemuel.

Lemuel: Pokie, shut up that noise.

Pokie: Me and Joretta going up north to college.

Lemuel: Help me get Mamie to bed.

Pokie: I ain't coming back here. You done all this to keep me here, but I'm going to college. And I'm gonna be an artist!

Lemuel: Then what we suppose to do?

Pokie: You can move to town.

Lemuel: This is my land.

Pokie: You can sell it and buy somewhere in town.

Lemuel: Who gon take care of Mamie? She's your ainnie and you talking about leaving her. A decent girl would stay as close to her kin as she could—

Pokie: I ain't willing to sacrifice my life—

Lemuel: You know we can't take care of ourselves. We subject to die in this house.

Pokie: I can't stay here. I won't.

Lemuel: If you think I'll let you leave—

Pokie: How you gon stop me? You can't see remember? All I got to do is walk out of here.

Lemuel: You shut up! (He comes toward her.)

Pokie: I'm leaving. I don't owe nobody nothing but me.

(Lemuel tries to grab her. Pokie dashed out of the way. Lemuel stumbles on the chair. Pokie rushes to the door and exits.)

Lemuel: Pokie! Come back here! Pokie!

(Pokie runs toward the tree, lays her head against it and cries. Lemuel looks after the door.)

Mamie: Lemuel, we need to get Pokie a white dress to graduate in. A nice white dress, with ruffles and a big collar. Lemuel, Pokie needs a white dress...

(Lights dim)

End of Scene 1

Mirror
Mirror

by

Gayle Weaver Williamson

SETTING/TIME: Downstairs portion of Neicey Smithers and Jerome Underwood's
home in the inner city.

CHARACTERS: 5 women, 3 men

Neicey: Mid 20's light skinned black woman
Karen: Early 30's black woman, gallery owner
Cissy: Late 50's black woman
Jewel: Late 50's black woman
Noella: Mid 20's black woman
Booker: Late 20's black man
Jerome: Late 20's black man, Neicey's lover & neighborhood "revivalist"
Kyle: Mid 20's white man

Blacks in this inner city neighborhood attempt to define what, exactly, is the black
experience as one light-skinned black woman struggles to find the answer within
herself. This realistic drama examines the expectations placed on Blacks by Blacks,
how their perceptions and mis-conceptions affect their relationships and how when
they work together, a beautiful experience can be formed.

Start Scene

KAREN

Fine. (*There is a pregnant pause as* KAREN *and* NEICEY *assess their next words*)
I can't do it. I've got to ask.

NEICEY

What?

KAREN

Where you got this black enough theory?

NEICEY

I told you, Jerome wants somebody who knows more about what it means to be blacker than me.

KAREN

Jerome wants who understands that this (KAREN *goes to the window and spreads her arms out*) doesn't have to be, and who's willing to fight for that.

NEICEY

But I do believe in what he's fighting for.

KAREN

From a comfortable distance.

NEICEY

I'm down here, aren't I?

KAREN

With four locks on the back door and an attitude that won't quit.

NEICEY

Who said I had to feel safe? And I do not have an attitude.

KAREN

Yeah you do.

NEICEY

You don't understand.

KAREN

See, there you go again. Everytime the finger points at you you start cryin about how nobody understands you.

NEICEY

There's more to me than meets the eye.

KAREN

So what?!

NEICEY

You've told me yourself that my art isn't black enough.

KAREN

I have a clientele that demands a certain message from their art. Yours just doesn't convey that message.

NEICEY

Translation: My art isn't black enough.

KAREN

You can feel sorry for yourself if you want, but I'm not going to help you.

NEICEY

I am not feeling sorry for myself.

KAREN

It's just like this neighborhood. It's not that you're not black enough, you're just approaching it from the wrong attitude.

NEICEY

Well, I'm taking care of all of it.

KAREN

What does that mean?

NEICEY

It means I'm going back to where I came from.

KAREN

What?

NEICEY

You heard me.

KAREN

Going back?

NEICEY

Yes.

KAREN

But what about Jerome?

NEICEY

What about him?

KAREN

He loves you.

NEICEY

Oh yeah? Then where is he?

KAREN

He just has to figure things out.

NEICEY

What about me?

KAREN

You should be trying to work things out, too.

NEICEY

I have.

KAREN

No you haven't.

NEICEY

I've figured out that there is no place for me down here.

KAREN

I thought you wanted to find out what was happening with our people.

NEICEY

I do.

KAREN

Well, this is it.

NEICEY

I don't think I need to live down here to find out what I've found out.

KAREN

You don't.

NEICEY

Then why are you giving me so much shit?

KAREN

Because you wanted to come down here.

NEICEY

Jerome asked me to come with him.

KAREN

But you came. Why?

NEICEY

Because I love him.

KAREN

Is that the only reason?

NEICEY

I'm going back to where I'm comfortable, so don't try and stop me.

KAREN

Then go.

NEICEY

I'm going.

KAREN

Why aren't you willing to let this neighborhood become a part of you?

NEICEY

I'm an outsider, Karen. They don't want what I have to offer.

KAREN

Who is this 'they' you keep holding up like a brick wall?

NEICEY

Do you know what it's like to be on the outside?

KAREN

Oh yeah.

NEICEY

Then you understand?

KAREN

Yeah. But it's not a crutch, Neicey.

NEICEY

They don't want to accept my ideas because I'm not one of them and they can sense it.

KAREN

You wear it like a banner.

NEICEY

What did you do to make them accept you.

KAREN

I didn't have to make them accept me.

NEICEY

Then what happened?

KAREN

I was myself.

NEICEY

So when did they finally treat you like a person?

KAREN

When I stopped apologizing for who I am.

NEICEY

You make it sound so simple.

KAREN

It's not, believe me.

NEICEY

I'm not as strong as you.

KAREN

If you say so.

NEICEY

Don't give me that.

KAREN

I call them as I see them. When are you leaving?

NEICEY

As soon as my ride gets here.

KAREN

That soon?

NEICEY

There aren't a lot of reasons for me to stay any longer.

KAREN

Who's your ride?

NEICEY

A friend from college.

KAREN

(KAREN *looks at* NEICEY *suspiciously*) Male or Female?

NEICEY

What difference does it make?

KAREN

None.

NEICEY

Male.

KAREN

I see.

NEICEY

No you don't.

KAREN

You gonna try to make things work with the white boy?

NEICEY

I don't know.

KAREN

Why did you break it off with him in the first place?

NEICEY

I felt that I was better off with a black man.

KAREN

MmHm.

NEICEY

Oh don't even start with that judgmental little MmHm thing you do.

KAREN

I don't judge.

NEICEY

Then what is all this crap I'm taking from you?

KAREN

I'm just asking some questions.

NEICEY

You're being nosey.

KAREN

Whatever. So you really think you can keep in touch with our people from the other side of the fence?

NEICEY

There you go again putting words in my mouth.

KAREN

I'm just saying that knowing what's happening with our people isn't always comfortable.

NEICEY

I never said it was.

KAREN

But you're doing what's comfortable for you. Pretty soon it'll be even more comfortable not to even think about it.

NEICEY

I"m not going to forget I'm black.

KAREN

But you're gonna try?

NEICEY

You're getting as cruel as Jerome.

KAREN

Because you seem to think this is something that will go away just because you don't want to deal with it.

NEICEY

You're judging something you know nothing about.

KAREN

Okay, look, it's obvious you're not giving in to the hard sell. So what are you going to do?

NEICEY

I don't know yet.

KAREN

Can I ask you a personal question?

NEICEY

How personal?

KAREN

Very.

NEICEY

Go ahead.

KAREN

What attracted you to this white guy?

NEICEY

I didn't see him as white or black. He was just a guy I thought was nice and nice looking.

KAREN

So what color did you think he was when you looked at him?

NEICEY

I didn't look at color.

KAREN

I hate when people say things like that.

NEICEY

Why?

KAREN

Because I don't see how you can say something like that, especially being a black woman.

NEICEY

It's true.

KAREN

You have always had to be conscious of who and what you are.

NEICEY

My parents taught me that we're all the same color when you turn out the lights.

KAREN

I guess your mama and daddy spent a lot of time walking around in the dark, too bad the rest of the world had their lights on.

NEICEY

There comes a time when you have to stop being color conscious.

KAREN

Who raised you?

NEICEY

Look, none of this means squat anymore.

KAREN

I guess.

NEICEY

(NEICEY *looks out the window, then checks her watch*) I wonder if I should call Moselle's grandmother and make sure she's okay.

KAREN

Moselle's a survivor. She's been getting around this neighborhood all her life.

NEICEY

Yeah, maybe.

KAREN

In any case what's it to you? Soon as your ride gets here this will all be a good story for the girls at your weekly bridge meeting.

NEICEY

It's not like that, Karen, and you know it.

End of Scene

Mother Spense

by

Olivia Hill

SETTING: Mother Spense's house, a small home in a poor neighborhood; evening

CHARACTERS: Mother Spence, a religious woman in her late 60's
              that heads her household

              Jo, Mother Spense's 28 year old granddaughter. She
              is unmarried and the mother of two children from
              different men. She along with her two children live
              in Mother Spense's household.

Jo's pregnancy provides the tension between the two women as they struggle to assign responsibility and blame for their many problems. "Both women live in a world that reveals the deterioration of family—the absence of men, the abundance of children, the lack of money and the unhappiness perpetuated through the

Scene 2

The scene opens with Jo lying on the sofa In a house robe. Mother Spense is ironing her white dress for church. It's a week later, Saturday night.

Mother Spense

Jo put your legs down. I just don't like that. One of the kids walk in and you got all your business up in the air.

(Jo doesn't answer; just sits up)

Mother Spense

When you gonna get to that kitchen? I know them kids done went through like a tornado and you been lyin' there doin' nothing all night.

Jo

Alright mama I'm going to clean it up in a minute.

Mother Spense

You said that twenty minutes ago.

Jo

Mama leave the iron out: I'm going church with you tomorrow.

Mother Spense

For what?

Jo

What do you mean, for what?

(Mother Spense starts to put the iron away)

Mother Spense

Girl you know good and well you not gettin' up In the morning.

Jo

Just wake me up, when you get up.

Mother Spense

Oh, hush, I ain't foolin' with you in the morning. You know you ain't gettin' up for no church. You ain't been to church since I could make you.

Jo

Mama, just wake me up. I'll go. I need to. Maybe sister Harris will let me sit with the choir. I know the songs. I saw her the other day.

Mother Spense

You ain't told me you talked to somebody at the church.

Jo

I saw her a minute. She talked me into going.

Mother Spense

I tried to get you to go. I've been trying for years now; you talk a minute to somebody else, now you goin'. Who's gonna get them kids ready. I'm not foolin' with 'em. They ain't got nothin' ready to wear. You not makin' me late, draggin' around. You wanted to go you should've said something 'fore now. I got to be there early in the morning. It's pastor's anniversary and all the church mothers got to get things together. I can't be bothered.

Jo

Mama you sound like you don't want me to go.

Mother Spense

I ain't stoppin' you from goin'. Just said you wanted to go you should've been gettin' ready 'fore now. Had all week. Instead, set round here mopin' 'bout that ole boy and hardly said boo to nobody—need to be thinking about another mouth to feed. You change too much 'fore me. One minute it's one thing, then look around it's something else. Now all of a sudden you goin' to church and nothin' ready.

Jo

Alright forget it; you don't want me to go with you. I thought as a church mother you'd be glad. They're still in the business of bringing In the sheaves.

Mother Spense

Don't be tryin' to put something off on me. Be blamin' me next for keepin' you out of the church. I didn't say for you not to go. Just wondered why. Why you wait so late to get your things together. Here it is almost bed time and them kids not even in yet and had a bath.

Jo

I'm going to do the dishes and get the kids in.

(Jo goes out the kitchen, to the back door and calls for the children. Mother Spense speaks out loud to herself)

Mother Spense

Ain't talked to me 'bout nothing. Got no business puttin' family matters in the street. Didn't ask me a thang. Cat a kill a whole litter, nobody don't know why that happens, maybe she know something wrong with 'em...my sweat and tears kept us goin'....papa said better to drown' now then to to have bunch of mouths to feed nobody wants... Lord, how it going to look, what'a say...girl, you trying to pull me down where I can't see; take It away from me. Lord, how I'm goin' to walk ..'

Jo

What? (*Jo Interrupts, and startles Mother Spense as she goes to look out the front door*)

Jo (*continued*)

I told them kids to stay around this house. They're catching lighting bugs; probably pulling the light off 'em. You talking to me? I didn't hear you.

Mother Spense

I be bless', I can't speak out loud to myself, without somebody eavesdropin'.

Jo

I wasn't eavesdroping. I thought you were talking to me.

Mother Spense

Maybe I'll stay home tomorrow, sence you look like you not feeling well any way. That way, I can go through those kids clothes and see what they got to wear for next time.

Jo

Stay home, you? You ain't never missed church, especially Pastor's anniversary; unless one of us look like we dying. I'm fine mama, don't stay on mine and them kids' account. Sister Harris said she and some of the other sisters would come by if they didn't see me at services.

(*Jo goes over to the front door and calls to the kids*)

Mother Spense

I don't want nobody in this house, with it filthy like this. It's got to get cleaned up around here first.

Jo

They coming to try and save me, not the house.

Mother Spense

I done told you. Jo; got to get this place in order, I wont have it in my house. Things like this. You ain't told me people comin' in here, like this. I got to stay home and....

Jo

Mama.

Mother Spense

I said...you ought to eat something before you start on the kitchen. That baby come out with rickets or something.

Jo

There ain't no baby; we don't have to worry about that.

(The voices of children laughter filters in from the yard)

ma

Mother Spense

Alright then...

(She looses control, then pauses. The sounds of the children stop)

havin' a miscarriage happens sometimes. It's just God's will, and maybe your blessin'. Ain't a thang to be shamed of. You alright now? Get everythang checked out.

Jo

Right, everything's fine.

Mother Spense

Good. That's what counts, you in good health. Could've told me. You should be taken it easy. Give your body chance to heal. They say you can have more? I mean it ain't messed you up? You know some woman loose a baby, infection set in, that kind of thing.

Jo

Don't worry mama, all parts In place. I can have twenty more babies.

Mother Spense

You better be tryin' to get the two you already have in here. Next thang we know Sandy draggin' a baby.

(Mother Spense starts to the kitchen to do the dishes)

Mother Spense

I'll do the kitchen. I don't want to get blamed for you keelin' over. I hope this is it and you learnt something cause I'm too old for this stuff. I'm tired, and not goin' through it no more. Else you got to do something else. I'll tell sister Harris that you restin' up; no need to come here. God done took that little baby on, we got to just pray now. Maybe in a week or so, you feel like comin' to church; you still want to.

(*Jo walks over to Mother Spense*)

Jo

Well ain't this a... That's what you worried about, what them old bible blabbin' hypocrites that's done and doing as much Saturday night before Sunday morning roll call, as I ever thought about. I got a news flash for you. You want to sit there and pretend you don't know what's up. Well, I did it and you wanted me to. You sat right there and said it. No more babies in your house.

Mother Spense

I didn't tell you to get or not to get a baby. I don't know what you talkin' about and I ain't interested in it. That's 'tween you and God. But I know I'm tired, tired of your mess. You done got on your feet maybe it's time to do somethin' different. Keep brin' children into the world unwed—God spells it out plain and simple; it's a sin. But if they here, I've always done what I could.

Jo

I didn't want it, or the other two. Maybe I would if he had wanted me. Shit I thought having a baby was like painting a picture. Turning around in me, with invisible ink. We'd both stand back and look at what we've done. I was the damn fool looking, looking with you. Why this happen to me? Now you, want me to live it by myself. Wiping your hands off me, so you can say see "I knew she was gonna be just like that woman no matter what I did. It's just born in them. Sinner, murderer, bastard maker, streetwalking trash born from the same." Right, right mama.

(*Mother Spense hits Jo across the face. Raises her hand to hit her again, stops, tightens her fist, pulls away, starts to cry a moment then stops*)

Mother Spense

What's the matter with you. I don't understand; what you tell me? You just actin' crazy and I'm not lis'enin' to this mess. I don't know what you done did. I don't want to know. I've been raisin' babies all my life. This one's baby; that one's baby. I had to help raise my mama's kids, some of theirs, mine, you. I'm tired; I don't want to raise no more babies. I could've been somethin' instead of.... What you wantin' from me?

Jo

Nothing mama, forget it.

Mother Spense

Forget my foot, you hardly say two words around here for almost a week and then you drop this and start rantin' and ravin' at me. Well little sister you better come again, you think I'm gonna keep puttin' up with this mess, don't offer up no kind of apology and you just say nothin'.

Jo

You want an apology. I'm sorry. I'm sorry that when she found out she was pregnant with me, she didn't reach in and rip my little lump of nothing out. I'm sorry that you, you didn't take this bible and put it between your legs so there wouldn't be no sorrys.

(Jo Is crying, screaming)

Jo *(continued)*

I got rid of it, mama. I let them cut it out of me, can you hear that, Mother Spense, church mother. No more bastards in your house. Just like that, there won't be. I sent It back. To wait, wait wherever they wait. No more of them eyes looking at me. Wanting, expecting. You've seen them eyes, black children's eyes; look at you even slightly with dark endless, forever eternity. I couldn't. God damn it, them little eyes.

Mother Spense

I won't take your trash, you hear me. What you did, you did all by yourself. Don't think you gonna dust it off on me. 'Cause we don't walk in the same places, girl. What, you think–you God? That you got a right to give life and take it away? Well you don't. There ain't no right, no kind of rights. Oh. father, father in heaven what we goin' to do with this. I don't know what to do. I prayed and prayed. Now look. She wouldn't lis'en till it came to this. I had to. That's the onliest way I made it through. What could I do? Oh, Jesus set my feet upon the path and have mercy on my soul.

(Silence)

Mother Spense *(continued)*

Now you got to get yourself up from there, ain't no point and lettin' them chil'ren see you like that. They need to be gettin' in this house. We just turn it over to God, he knows what's best. Woman lose babies all the time, ain't no shame in that. Just give it to God.

Jo

Mama, God's not listening. He's just, watching us and waiting, with all the other waiting, watching little faces.

End of Scene

Movie Music

by

Shay Youngblood

copyright © MCMXCIV
by Shay Youngblood
THE DRAMATIC PUBLISHING COMPANY

All Rights Reserved
Printed in the United States
(**TALKING BONES**)

All inquiries regarding performance rights should be addressed to Dramatic Publishing Company, 311
Washington St., Woodstock, IL 60098

SETTING/TIME: Ancestors' Books and Breakfast, a half empty bookstore in a small
southern town.

CHARACTERS: 3 women, 2 men.

Ruth: Aristocratic, bohemian mother/grandmother; early 60's
Baybay: Ruth's gaudy, slightly out-of-step daughter; early 40's
Eila: Ruth's daughter caught between the two worlds of her mother
and grandmother; early 20's
Mr. Fine: Business man and in early 40's
Oz: Hip, homeless young man in his 20's

THE STORY: A family of women feel trapped in their lives where voices and visions
guide them. Each interpret the signs differently. The two men who
enter their lives are seen as signs of change.

SCENE THREE

The Bookstore, two weeks later (There are bunches of dead flowers all around the stage. RUTH is ripping newspaper into strips. ElLA is sitting on the sofa reading a book. BAYBAY enters and watches ElLA for a while.)

RUTH

Grand daughter, you got sense enough to use protection? Do you understand the implications of social intercourse?

ElLA

What do you mean Grammie?

RUTH

You think I'm talking about conversation? You got to protect yourself baby. You're like a little sponge trying to sop up the sea.

ElLA

What am I supposed to do? People are hungry out there. I can feel them.

RUTH

You can feed them one by one, a day at a time.

ElLA

How can we do that if we don't have a place Grammie?

RUTH

The bones can't be disturbed. Your mama is chasing rainbows.

BAYBAY

And I'm gonna catch one. I can feel things out there. (*Reading from a notebook*) We kissed a whole season. I surrendered. We were swimming on the horizon. I felt a hurricane coming, we were pulled by the undertow, split open, devoured, licked clean. After the storm the most exquisite calm. Our flesh parted in dreams. We woke up this morning clinging to each other. (*To Ruth*) Last night I saw things I've never seen before. (RUTH *begins to clang pans together to drown out Baybay*) Mr.Fine loves me. He promised me a real life out there.

ElLA

When do we get to meet this Mr. Fine?

BAYBAY

Soon enough. Where is the messenger boy? Does he know why he's here?

ElLA

He had soup this morning. I fed his soul. (TRANCE) When I step off the train all I can see and feel is suffering, hunger and broken people.

(MUSIC up. ElLA acts out the scene as documentary FILM footage of homeless people run on her body)

ElLA

People ask me for money and I give because it is criminal to look away. I try to eat but I see hungry minds in the window. I put the leftovers from the Chinese restaurant on top of a garbage can and leave a pair clean chopsticks and a napkin for the woman I see. She is chewing on bread she peels from cracks in the sidewalk. I take off my shoes and walk up to women and men I don't know and I kiss them on the lips in broad day light. I kiss a woman with holes in her shoes. I kiss her on the mouth. I kiss a man missing teeth and the third finger of his left hand. A man is lying on the steps of a church. A policeman comes to wake him up and move him on. The man says that he has nowhere to go and wants to go to jail. The policeman tells the man that he can't take him to jail unless he commits a crime. The man says, "What crime do I have to commit to be given some food to eat. I'm cold and tired. The policeman says "Any crime will do." When the policeman turns his back the man throws a rock and breaks a stained glass window in the church. I don't eat or sleep for 3 days. On the fourth day I have a vision. That the world is a watermelon and everybody can eat from its juicy pink flesh and drink the sweet juice. The seeds are large warm cocoons for sleeping. I keep asking myself, what can I do?

BAYBAY

Keep dreaming baby.

RUTH

Give the messenger an honest love. A good fine excellent love. (FINE *knocks then enters with a large bunch of flowers*)

MR. FINE

Good evening pretty ladies.

RUTH

Ain't no pretty ladies in here. We all women in here. Baybay look at what he got in his hands. Some more of them damn flowers.

(BAYBAY rushes over to take the flowers. FINE kisses her hand)

BAYBAY

Good evening Mr. Fine. You are such a gentleman.

MR. FINE

Is this your lovely daughter?

RUTH

Take your eyes off my grand daughter. Baybay, will you stop all this foolishness. You had this man come all the way over here for you to tell him we ain't selling this place. It just ain't for sale.

BAYBAY

Mama that is not true.

RUTH

How dare you sell something that don't belong to you?

BAYBAY

I bought this place with my own money. Bought it with money I won in Las Vegas.

RUTH

That don't mean squat. Who bought the ticket to get you there? Who told you the numbers to play? You bought temporary time here. Who do you think was here before you?

BAYBAY

That crazy civil war hero trying to sell bait for well fishing.

RUTH

I mean before that. Long before that the Indians lived here. Their spirits are here. How will we hear them if we leave? The sound is clear and strong in this place. They ain't going nowhere and neither am I. Neither are you.

MR. FINE

Ma'am your daughter and I have plans for our future. Is there a deed to the property?

BAYBAY

Eila be a good girl and bring the lock box from under my bed. (*Eila doesn't respond defiantly*)

RUTH

You can't pave over bones.

BAYBAY

(*Goes to kneel by* RUTH *pleading*) Mama don't spoil my second chance. I don't want to dry up and blow on the wind like dust. I want to live, this once. Please mama. I don't want to hear them anymore. I'm dying here mama.

RUTH

Tell that man standing there we can't leave baby. You promised me you'd never leave.

BAYBAY

Things are gonna change mama. I'm not happy.

RUTH

You wouldn't be happy in heaven. Who needs happiness? I need you.

MR. FINE

I see why you want to get out of this place.

BAYBAY

I want to make a new start with you. There's some things I need to tell. Some things Eila don't even know. When mama's hearing aid broke, she started hearing them voices in her ear piece. I thought she was crazy but they was telling her things that were gonna happen, things like Eila being born. Sometimes they talked to me too. I'm forgetting my manners. I invited you to dinner and here I am running off at the mouth.

RUTH

I ain't eating with no stranger trying to take my daughter and run me outta my own place.

MR. FINE

Those papers are really important sugar.

BAYBAY

Not more important than eating. Come help me Eila.

(BAYBAY *begins setting up a bridge table, Eila helps set the table for four.* EILA *sets up tv table for* RUTH)

RUTH

(*To Mr. Fine*) When I was a little girl I used to dream about them. Tall pipe smoking medicine men and healing women wrapped in blankets. Sometimes I be sleeping in my bed and they'd come to me four, five, six of em all talking at once waking me up with conversations. Sometimes they'd tell me stories. They left me for a long time. Didn't come back til I was grown right before Boston hurt Baybay. It snowed that night. Look like it's gonna snow tonight.

MR. FINE

I'm afraid we're not in a position to get snow. It would be something of a miracle for it to snow.

RUTH

You a weather man? I tell you it's gonna snow tonight

BAYBAY

Last time it snowed round here, they helped me make Eila.

MR. FINE

I can hardly believe...

BAYBAY

Then how do you think I got her?

MR. FINE

The regular way women get them.

BAYBAY

Eila was made in the desert on an island under a blanket of stars and snow. It was after midnight when I heard them outside my window. They were chanting and beating drums. I walked out the backdoor and stepped into the desert to look for them. They said, "Open your eyes." And I did and everything was soft blue and lavender. I could still see a thin slice of moon and one bright morning star. They were a tall handsome people with feathers in their hair. They came and possessed me. They drew me to them and snow began to fall all around us. When I woke up, I knew Eila was with me, growing inside of me. She is the one who is of this world and the other, keeper of desert snowflakes and dreams. They promised me love. Mr. Fine you are an undeniable sign.

MR. FINE

You said you used to write fiction didn't you?

BAYBAY

I wrote a book...

MR. FINE

Look here Barbara...

BAYBAY

My name is Baybay. Baybay.

MR. FINE

Yeah, Baybay, I can't stay for dinner tonight. I've got a meeting with some cash money business men who might be interested in investing in the club. Baybay, honey. Listen, could we sign these papers. I got to get going.

RUTH

Hissss. Hissss. Hissss. You ain't nothing but a two legged snake. This is my place and will be even after I'm dead. You wanna take a chance I won't hain't you?

MR.FINE

I'm willing to take that chance since I don't believe in ghosts or spirits and shit. What I believe in is M-O-N-E-Y And we gonna be bringing home lots of it when we get the club in full swing.

BAYBAY

You don't believe me?

MR. FINE

That's beside the point. Now lets get on with business. I'm quite ready to be generous with you.

RUTH

Baybay won't you think about this? I don't have long. Let me leave this world knowing I still have my place?

EILA

Mama why can't you just go if you want. Leave me here with Grammie.

BAYBAY

Who needs this old, broken down place. We can still go all those places can't we? We can open a club in New York, L.A. or Paris. Let me get my hat we can leave right now.

MR. FINE

Hold up baby, it's gonna take a little time. I've got to build my reputation.

BAYBAY

You can build a night club anywhere. There ain't nothing holding me back.

MR FINE

Sweetheart, this is my town. I told you, I got friends here, I know people. I'm just getting my career started. I can't leave now. Aretha's got a concert at the Civic Center next month.

RUTH

(*Sarcastic and unbelieving*) Aretha.

BAYBAY

You know Aretha Frankin?

MR. FINE

Know her, we grew up in the same neighborhood. I know all her brothers. Matter of fact the one I used to shoot pool with is now her business manager. Me and him go way back. I figure it like this, Aretha could make a guest appearance for the grand opening at Mr. Fine's Hideaway. Fine dining, dancing and entertainment 24 hours a day, just like I said.

BAYBAY
You sure? You talking about Rescue Me-Spanish Harlem-Chain of Fools- Amazing Grace-Natural Woman-Pink Cadillac-Aretha Franklin?

MR. FINE
The one. Her brother owes me. Tina Turner coming for Christmas and Smokey Robinson just might bring the Miracles back together in time for Valentines Day. I'm telling you we got to move on this now. I got a call from the architect this morning, the blue prints are ready. All we got to do is sign these papers, get a few more investors and BAM. BOOM. We gonna be making history and enough money to go all them places you want to go. Once my divorce is final its just me and you baby. I got it all planned.

RUTH
(*Repeats after Fine*) Tina Turner. (*Repeats*) Divorce, uh huh.

BAYBAY
You didn't say anything about a divorce last night when you were making me bed full of promises. You've got a wife?

MR. FINE
Yeah, I just told you. Do you think your lovely daughter has found the deed yet?

BAYBAY
You don't want me do you? I've been dreaming about you...(BAYBAY *takes out gun points at* FINE)Get out Take your stinking flowers and get the hell out of here. (*She throws the flowers after him, beats him with bunch*)

MR. FINE
You're all crazy. Listening to voices and shit. You can't let something you can't even see tell you what to do. You could take the money and go anywhere, do anything, be anybody you want . You can star in your own movie.

(BAYBAY shouts after him Os. He yells as if hit OS)

(*The* SAINTS *open their umbrellas and dance on stage.* RUTH *sees them and opens her own umbrella and dances off with them happily.* EILA *enters and sees the bunch of fresh white carnations or calla lilies in* RUTH's *wheelchair. She watches the* MOVIE *of the* SAINTS *dancing with black umbrellas in the cemetery*)

BAYBAY
Happy now mama? I'm all yours. We'll wait together.(BAYBAY *realizes Ruth is not there. She sees the flowers and continues to call out* "MAMA") Where's mama? (*runs through house screaming*) 'Mother.' Don't go yet! Don't leave me mama!

EILA

She's gone mama, but we're here. Others will come and we're gonna feed their souls and honor the ancestors. We'll get more books, we'll make our own movies.

(BAYBAY wanders around the space crying as she puts books back on the shelves. OZ enters carrying the yellow umbrella. He and EILA hug like old friends. OZ opens the umbrella and dances around with EILA. They encourage BAYBAY to dance with them. They embrace.)

End of Scene

Oh Oh Freedom

by

Erwin Charles Washington

CHARACTERS

ISADORA STONE: 40ish black woman; great singer; modest, kind, a peace keeper; somewhat tired and beaten down, but with a spark of life left. Medium build. Pretty.

TERRANCE STONE: 45. Isadora's husband. strong, firm, factory worker with a deep pain inside. A giant.

ALICE STONE: 23; oldest daughter of Terrance & Isadora. College educated; liberated; slender, pretty, somewhat refined; but bold & sassy. Strong.

BIRD STONE: 17; oldest son of Terrance & Isadora. He is becoming a man & trying to stay straight in the ghetto, but having a hard time of it.

PHYLLIS STONE: 15; next to the youngest child of Terrance & Isadora; She is becoming a woman. She is saucy, very hip, with a fast mouth, ghettoish.

DANNY STONE: 10; baby of the family; spoiled; a good boy; very nice.

THEO: 25ish Impetus; free; selfish; cocky; a rebel with big dreams; full of idealism; naiveté, etc; son of a wealthy music industry big shot.

JANITOR: 25ish; hip; street type; proud.

FREEMAN: 16. Black youth; Phyllis' boyfriend. The type of kid who wears big glasses. Never made love before.

NATE: Off stage voice of teen-ager; black ghetto type

FOREMAN: 65ish. White. A good guy, but an old fashioned, no nonsense supervisor type.

Start Scene

TERRANCE
(BEWILDERED, HURT, ENRAGED, PLEADING) Issie, you're destroying us. You're destroying the whole family.

ISADORA
Do you think we would be going through this if you had let me go sing that first night?

TERRANCE
Yes.

ISADORA
...if you had helped me with my singing, instead of doing everything in your power to stop me?

TERRANCE
Yes. Yes I do.

ISADORA
Well I don't! It's you whose destroying this family. Not me.

TERRANCE
No...

ISADORA
These kids are doing wrong because you have acted a fool ever since I started singing. You've been drinking every day, cursing me every day, calling me names, accusing me of horrible things. No wonder they're confused.

TERRANCE
What kind of mother are you to talk like this? You don't care.

ISADORA
I do care. I've tried to teach them right from wrong. That's all I've done every day, day in and day out. Teach them over and over. Don't be too fast with boys; don't run with thugs; do your homework. They know what's right. But what happens when I want to do something for me? Do you step in and help? Do you tell 'em the things I had to tell them every day? No. You get drunk. No wonder they're acting a fool.

TERRANCE

You don't care do you? You actually don't care about your own children. And you call yourself a mother.

ISADORA

I don't care if I'm the worst mother in the world. It doesn't give them an excuse to mess up their lives and blame it on me. It's their own fault, because they know right from wrong, we taught them, remember.

TERRANCE

Issie, something's got to give.

ISADORA

Alright, now that its getting down to that. Let's talk about what's got to give. My audition is finally over. They loved me. Theo says I'll get all kinds of offers. Records, tours. Everything... But I was planning on spending some time here to get my family together, first.

TERRANCE

You're going to give it up?

ISADORA

And do what? Go back to being a maid? Turn down $500 a week for $100 a week? Well I'm not. I just want to spend the next few weeks at home with you and the kids to get you to accept what I'm doing, because I love you. In spite of how you treat me, I love all of you. And when I start going out and singing and making records, I want you all to share in my happiness.

TERRANCE

Naw, it can't work that way, Issie.

ISADORA

But ...

TERRANCE

I said it can't work that way. You have to be here.

ISADORA

Then what do you suggest, Terrance?

TERRANCE

Give it up.

ISADORA

I can't. They loved me. They cheered and applauded. I have not felt that good in I don't know how long. I can't give that up, Terrance.

TERRANCE

Then get outta my house, before I do something I'll regret.

ISADORA

I had hoped — But I see now, it won't work. You are obsessed with putting things back like they were, and I can never go back to that. So, even if I stayed home all year it wouldn't do any good. You'd start right up again as soon as I started to sing again. You have to have me locked up like a bird in a cage. Only I can't stand being in cages anymore Terrance. So there's nothing left for me to do, but leave. At least that way the kids won't be around a whole lot of fighting and arguing. They'll be better off. New schools, new friends. And that is the important thing anyway. Isn't it? That the kids be better off? (SHE LOOKS SAD) Good-bye, Terrance. (SLOWLY STARTS OUT)

> (ISADORA EXITS TO THE BACK BEDROOM. TERRANCE IS CRUSHED. HE FLOPS WEAKLY DOWN ON A CHAIR. HE IS IN GREAT PAIN AND AGONY)

> (HE LOOKS SKYWARD, BUT CAN'T SPEAK. HE'S DEFEATED. TERRANCE TAKES OUT THE GUN. HE AIMS IT AT HIMSELF)

> (ALICE ENTERS, SEES WHAT HE IS DOING. SHE'S IN WHITE)

ALICE

Daddy, no.!

TERRANCE

Stay away from me Alice. Don't come near me.

ALICE

Daddy please, don't do it daddy.

TERRANCE

I ain't shit no more, Alice. Ain't got no job, the kids all messed up, and Issie, God, Issie's leaving. I just want to end it.

> (TERRANCE PULLS THE TRIGGER. THERE IS A COLD, LOUD, METALLIC CLICK, BUT NO BLAST. ALICE GRABS HIS HAND AND IS WRESTLING FOR THE GUN)

ALICE

Daddy, daddy, no! No, Daddy.

> (ALICE GETS HIM TO LOWER THE GUN. HE STILL HAS IT GRIPPED IN HIS HANDS, BUT SHE HAS GOT THE GUN POINTED AT THE FLOOR.)

TERRANCE

Tell me how I can make it back like it was, Alice. Tell me how to be a man again. (HE IS WEEPING)

ALICE

I'll help you, Daddy. I'll help you, just give me the gun.

(TERRANCE REFUSES TO FREE THE HANDLE. HE SHAKES HIS HEAD)

ALICE

Daddy, please, we need you too much and we love you too much for you to do this.

TERRANCE

She's going to take the kids, Alice. And she's going to leave. Where's the love in that, Alice? Bird threatened to kill me. My own eldest son.

(RISING. STILL HOLDING GUN. ALICE'S HAND ON HIS)

It's all falling down, Alice. My kingdom is falling down.

ALICE

Then Daddy, build a new one.

TERRANCE

How am I supposed to do that? No job. No family. How Alice?

ALICE

I don't know, Daddy. You have to find the way. All I know is, you just aimed a gun at your head and you pulled the trigger, at point blank range. But for some reason, what reason I don't know. But for some reason, that gun didn't fire. For some reason, God reached his hand down into this house and put his finger in the barrel of this gun and saved your life. By rights, you should be dead, Daddy. There had to be a reason for it. Daddy, you're being given a second chance. I think you should act as if the old Terrance T. Stone died when you pulled that trigger. From this moment on, you should live as though you're a whole new person. Free from everything that's behind you. And if you don't, Daddy. Then this gun should have fired... the kids should be left with no father; ...Mama should be alone. And she should blame herself for your death, and be miserable forever. The family should fall apart. Everything you worked for should be lost because you don't want mama to sing.

TERRANCE

We were happy before your mama started singing, again.

ALICE

No, Daddy. And I'm saying this because I want to help you. Daddy, mama wasn't happy. You were. Only you were happy... Mama was miserable.

TERRANCE

That's not true —

ALICE

You bullied mama. Even the kids. You bullied us, so that sometimes we all hated you. But we hated you more when you stopped mama from doing what she wanted and needed, to make her happy.

TERRANCE

No, that's not true. The kids respected me. They always respected me.

ALICE

We feared you Daddy. And we feared that somehow mama wouldn't be able to hide all our problems from you, and we'd have to answer to you. We lived in fear of that. Mama made us look real good for you Daddy. So you could be happy. But we were all living a lie, trying to be perfect for you.

TERRANCE

I never knew. Alice is it true that Bird's been running around with the wrong crowd for a long time? And Phyllis, has she been flirtin' with boys since before your mama was singing?

(ALICE NODS YES)

TERRANCE

Why didn't I see it? (HURTING) I thought my house was safe. I thought that world out there couldn't come in here. This was the castle where white folks couldn't hurt us, and where black folks couldn't pull us down into the muck and the mire. But it happened here, anyway.

ALICE

Daddy, you might have seen this as a castle. But it wasn't that to mama. It was a bird cage. And we were all inside, and you had the key. You built a cage for us, and you called it a kingdom. Why did you do that Daddy? I don't understand. And, to tell you the truth. I don't know how mama took it as long as she did. Because if it had been me, I would have left your butt. I would have left your butt, or broke it, one.

TERRANCE

What?

ALICE

I said, if it'd been me, I would have left yoe butt, or broke it one.

TERRANCE

Where do I know that from?

(THEY HUG)

TERRANCE

Thank you, Alice, you've been honest. I guess I needed some honesty —

ALICE

You were always honest with me. The things you told me about James, they were honest. I listened to you, and now, we're back together.

TERRANCE

Good.

ALICE

He's going down South to start his business. I'll finish my masters. I'll pass on all my job offers, but I'll help him. We'll work together to build something for the both of us. And we're not having any children right away. We're going to wait and see how everything works out first.

TERRANCE

I'm happy for you, Alice. At least I did something right.

ALICE

You did a lot right. You supported your family, helped me through school, paid for my wedding, remember? You sacrificed a lot for me, for all of us.

TERRANCE

Alice, I quit my job. I ain't going back, no matter what. I might have to send the kids down to stay with you a while, is that okay?

ALICE

Sure, Daddy. And I'm glad you quit, because you can do better. You could even start your own business.

TERRANCE

Me? Old as I am? You forget, I ain't been to college, like you.

ALICE

You don't need to. All you need is a dream, Daddy.

(ISADORA ENTERS).

ISADORA

I thought I heard voices in here. What's going on? Did he try to hurt you?

ALICE

No mama. Everything's fine. We were just talking.

ISADORA

Alice, can we stay at your place a few days? We're moving out.

ALICE

Sure mama. I'll go help the kids get their things. (EXITS)

TERRANCE

Issie...

ISADORA

Don't try to stop me, Terrance.

TERRANCE

I just want you to know, I never meant to hurt you.

ISADORA

You didn't mean to, Terrance, but you did.

(ISADORA HEADS BACK TO THE BACK.)

TERRANCE

Isadora... I'm sorry.

End of Scene

The Ballad of Charlie Sweetlegs Vine

by

Farrell J. Foreman

SETTING/TIME: Inner City Pool Hall

CHARACTERS: 1 woman, 5 men

       Charlie: Pool hall owner and business man
       Zeke: Charlie's partner in crime
       Scott: Charlie's "honest" brother
       Jimmy: Charlie's 16 yr. old brother
       Blind Man: Sage and singer
       Mikaela: Charlie's woman

       Scene 1: Mikaela has it out with Charlie as the pressures mount
       Scene 2: The brothers, Charlie, Scott and Jimmy, discover painful truths
              about themselves as Zeke and the Blind man witness.

A pool hall provides a framework for much of the action of this realistic drama about a black dope peddler, and numbers runner and other members of his family and community who are doomed to pay for all the crimes that surround them.

Scene 1

Mikaela
(Mikaela enters. Charlie is drinking from a bottle of champagne) Hi.

Charlie
Where you been? You wuz supposed to be here by twelve.

Mikaela
I called and told you that I'd be late. Don't you remember?

Charlie
I don't remember no call....drink?

Mikaela
Yes please.

(He gets up and gets another champagne glass from behind the counter and pours the champagne into it. He hands her the glass)

Thank you.

Charlie
Well time to open another.

Mikaela
You been drinkin a lot lately.

Charlie
I always drink a lot.

Mikaela
I mean especially since your momma's death.

Charlie
So what!

Mikaela
I just made a statement.

Charlie
And I said what I had to say so drop the shit?

Mikaela

Baby I'm worried about you.

Charlie

Aw shit! Here we go. FIRST BEN COMES IN HERE TALKIN SHIT ABOUT THE PEOPLE, THEN SCOTT MY LONG LOST BROTHER COMES IN HERE MOUTHING A WHOLE LOTTA SHIT ABOUT JIMMY AND NOW YOU 'RE WORRIED ABOUT ME. I WISH SOMEBODY WOULD TELL ME WHAT THE HELL IS GOIN ON HERE...GOTDAMN!

(*He pours another drink. There is a momentary pause.*)

Mikaela

I know you used to drink before. But it was different. You seem driven by somethin. Like somethin is eatin your insides out or somethin. What is it Charlie? ...you been snappin at me, at Jimmy, at Zeke, at everybody.

Charlie

I don't know. The business is doin fine. Everythin is happenin just like I want, I don't know. I just never thought of momma diein, I guess.

Mikaela

You knew she was diein.

Charlie

Yeah.

Mikaela

I guess knowin it and internalizin it are two different things.

Charlie

Yeah.

Mikaela

Why you keep pushin me away?

Charlie

I ain't pushin nuthin.

Mikaela

Somethins botherin you Charlie but you won't spill ya guts. Tell me what it is. Tell me what it is. TELL ME WHAT IT IS!!

Charlie

Just leave me be. I'll be alright.

Mikaela

Not by the looks of things. Every day you drink more and every day you seem to close up inside yourself more....strikin out at everythin and everybody...

Charlie

I ain't strikin out at nobody. I just got some things to sort out that's all.

Mikaela

What things Charlie? What things? For the last few weeks that's all you been sayin....THINGS TO SORT OUT...WHAT DAMN THINGS?!!

Charlie

You pushin woman just let me be.

Mikaela

Just let me be. (Sarcastically) What the hell am I supposed to do in the mean time....drop dead?

Charlie

That's up to you.

Mikaela

Maybe you're right. Maybe it is up to me. Well

(*getting up*)

I ain't gonna stand around and watch a man fall apart. Feel sorry by yo'self nigger

(*she exits*)

Charlie

Feel sorry

(*running after her, opening the door*)

...bitch you ain't gotta feel sorry for me. BITCH YOU HEAR ME. YOU AIN'T NEVER GOTTA FEEL SORRY FOR ME. .NEVER!!! NEVER!!!

(*goes over to the phone and dials a number*)

Yeah..how you doin baby...yeah come on over...dats right, come on sweet thing...

(*the lights fade out*)

Scene 2

(The set is dark. Jimmy opens the door with a set of keys and he and Scott enter. It is about twelve noon. Scott and the blind man enter behind him. The blind man sits on the benches next to the wall.)

Scott
How'd you get keys to the pool room. Don't tell me Charlie trusts you with the keys to his livelihood? (mockingly)

Jimmy
Sometimes he lets me open up. I'm workin for him ya know.

Scott
In what capacity?

Jimmy
Huh?

Scott
What do you do for Charlie?

Jimmy
Sometimes he lets me collect from the bars. Sometimes I just run messages for him. You wanna play some pool?

Scott
Why not? Straight pool?

Jimmy
Okay. How much a ball?

Scott
Nuthin. You ever play anything just for the sheer enjoyment of doin it?'

Jimmy
Nope..

Scott
You should try it sometime. You might find that you'd like it.

Jimmy

What's the use playin for nuthin. Only chumps play for nuthin. If you're good you ain't scared to put your money behind ya.

Scott

Suppose you don't have any money?

Jimmy

Then you really a chump. Shit if you ain't got no scratch you ain't got nuthin.

Scott

You really believe that?

Jimmy

Name me somethin that don't cost money.

Scott

Happiness...peace of mind.

Jimmy

How you goin to be happy with no money?

Scott

If I listen to you that means that only people that are rich can be happy.

Jimmy

That's right.

Scott

You got a lot to learn.

Jimmy

I don't know big brother. Seems to me the other way round. Charlie says money is the only thing that keeps us on an equal stance with the white man. Without money we can't do shit.

Scott

What about your self respect?

Jimmy

What about it?

Scott

Don't you think it matters how you get your money?

Jimmy

Hell no. As long as you hold onto it and it keeps comin in...that's the only thing that matters. You gonna keep talkin or are you gonna shoot pool?

Scott

(*moves toward the table*) What about dope?

Jimmy

What about it?

Scott

You think it's a good way of makin money?

Jimmy

Good as any I guess.

Scott

(*movin closer to Jimmy*) What you mean good as ANY I GUESS!

Jimmy

(*scared*) Just what I said, what's wrong with you?

Scott

AIN'T THIS SOME SHIT! A LITTLE SHITASS PUSHER!

Jimmy

What the fuck you talkin bout pusher!

(*surprised*)

Scott

You 're the punk that's been selling junk at the schools. You're the reason why eight kids have been showin up dead in the last six months. You little punk, my gotdamn kid brother...Charlie give you the shit. HUH ANSWER ME GOTDAMNIT.

(SLAPPING HIM LOUDLY ACROSS THE FACE)

ANSWER ME GOTDAMNIT!

(SLAPPING HIM AGAIN)

Jimmy

(*breaking the cue stick*) You crazy or sumpthin. You better stay back Scott. You ain't slappin me no mo'.

Scott

You right I ain't slappin you no more.

(*taking off his jacket*)

I'm gonna whip your ass.

(*going over to the door and locking it, Scott comes back over to the table, Jimmy is on the other side tryin to find someplace to run. He tries one side and then the other. The blind man strikes up a song fast and loud on his guitar almost as if he realizes Scott will need some sound to cover the noise he will make. He finally grabs Jimmy and slaps him once, twice across the face. Jimmy falls down and tries to get behind the counter because there's a gun there. Scott cuts him off and slaps him again. He holds him by the collar and says*)

Did Charlie give the shit to you? Did he gotdamnit!!? ANSWER ME! DID HE!!?

Jimmy

No. I stole it from him.

Scott

What?

Jimmy

I said, I stole it from him.

(*The blind man stops playin*)

Scott

(*throws him away*)

Oh mv God! Mv God.

(*holding his face in his hands*)

I'm too late momma. I'm too late.

(*Jimmy runs to the door and tries to get out. Scott goes after him and then slings him in the seat next to the blind man*)

I should kill you. I should kill you eight damn times for the kids you killed.

Jimmy

I ain't killed nobody. I ain't put no needles in nobody's arms. THEY WANTED IT, THEY BOUGHT IT CAUSE THEY WANTED IT.

Scott
SHUT UP LITTLE BROTHER. JUST SHUT UP WHILE I FIGURE OUT WHAT TO DO WITH YOU.

Jimmy
You ain't gonna do nuthin. Charlie ain't gonna let you do nuthin. What do you think he's gonna do when he finds out what you did to me. He's gonna kick your ass.

> *(Scott walking toward him like he's going to hit him again. The blind man intervenes)*

Blind man
Killin him ain't gonna do no good son.

> *(Scott just looks at him and turns and leans on the pool table)*

Scott
I really shouldn't blame you. I should've known. I should've known.

> *(Charlie enters with Zeke. He seems to be in a good mood laughing and talking with Zeke.)*

Charlie
What's happenin gentlemen? What's wrong with you youngblood?

Scott
(grabbing his coat) ASK 'EM WHAT HE'S BEEN STEALIN. ASK 'EM.

> *(he exits)*

Zeke
What's goin on?

Charlie
Well.. .what the fuck happened? Somebody tell me what happened?

> *(Jimmy looks at the blind man and then back at Charlie)*

Look slim go down to the diner and get somethin to eat.

> *(giving him some cash)*

Blind man
Sure Mr. Vine, sure.

(he exits)

Charlie

Well....I'm waitin.

(goes behind the counter and pours a drink—there is a pause)

Jimmy

It wasn't nuthin.

Charlie

Looks to me like nuthin just whipped your ass.......well.

Jimmy

Me and Scott was playin pool.

(Zeke is picking up the busted cue pieces)

All of a sudden he went off....like he was crazy or somethin. He accused me of killin eight kids. He started rantin and ravin and slappin me around, so I picked up a cue and tried to bust his head with it.....

Zeke

Didn't have too much success youngblood.

(Jimmy just looks at Zeke)

Jimmy

Well...I missed. Then he started shoutin oh my God...somethin about momma and then you walked in.

Charlie

Seems like you leavin out somethin. Start it again this time without the beatin... just what was it that you said that made our mild-mannered brother go off.

Jimmy

I don't know what.....

Charlie

Don't lie to me. Cause I'll make what he did to you look like Sunday picnic time. Now tell me this time, what was it?

Jimmy

I was sellin stuff at school.

Zeke

What you say boy.

Charlie

You been pushin at the school.

Jimmy

I don't push the stuff. I sell to one dude and he takes the stuff and sells it or does whatever he wants with it.

Charlie

Where you gittin the stuff.

Jimmy

From you.

Charlie

You been stealin from my warehouse?

(*Jimmy says nuthin*)

WEll???

Jimmy

Yeah.

Charlie

How much you makin a week?

Jimmy

Four to six hundred dependin on the week.

Charlie

Come here.

(*Jimmy is apprehensive*)

Come here!

(*Jimmy walks over to him*)

From now on you work for me. All your shit is checked through Zeke. You pay him for it. He sets the wholesale prices. You give him sixty percent of your take each week. Don't miss a week.

Jimmy

Okay.

(he turns and walks away)

Charlie

C'mere.

(He turns back and walks to him. Charlie slaps him hard across the face).
The next time you steal from me you're dead. Now git the hell outa my sight.
(Jimmy exits)

Zeke

I think you might be makin a mistake. He'll steal again.

Charlie

What choice I got. Either we take him in or I got a scared kid brother who might start runnin his gotdamn mouth. He wants to be a man...well we'll see.

Zeke

I still say it's wrong.

Charlie

I don't give a shit what you say. I SAY. YOU HEAR ME?!!   I SAY.

Zeke

So be it. But don't say I didn't warn you.

End

Afterword

by

Dr. Margaret Wilkerson

More than three decades have passed since I saw A *Raisin in the Sun* on Broadway and cheered with so many others the eloquence of Lorraine Hansberry's voice and the extraordinary performance of that gifted cast. I never suspected that I would spend a decade studying her life and work, and writing her biography. It has been an extraordinary journey, filled with challenges of all kinds, but one constant remains for me — the ability of Hansberry's life and work to inspire young writers of each generation everywhere. On the heels of her success in 1959, young people wrote to her from all over the world asking her advice, congratulating her, but always proclaiming how inspirational her play and her public statements were to them. My own experiences as a teacher parallel this fact. From the high school production of A *Raisin in the Sun* that I directed in Watts just after the Revolt of 1965, to the University seminars at all levels that I have taught at Berkeley, the response has been the same. Her piercing insights into our confused world, her fighting spirit, and her fearless inquiry appeal especially to young people.

Hansberry was only twenty-eight years old when she won the New York Drama Critics Circle Award for her first play produced on Broadway. The meaning of her success was many-layered. It salved the conscience of a nation whose racism was displayed daily on the front pages of newspapers with pictures of southern Blacks and their northern supporters marching to end segregation and discrimination. This young Black woman had written a play that gave voice to a whole group of people determined to be free in the land of their birth, and the craft was so excellent that those who saw it came to realize that they, too, belonged to the human family. For her many friends in the Left, it brought national and international attention to their political and social values without off-putting jargon that would diminish her message. And for young people throughout the nation and world, her success validated their voices and their aspirations.

Close friends like Douglas Turner Ward, who later founded the Negro Ensemble Company, attribute to Hansberry their motivation to write for the theatre. If she, a young adult, could attain this success, then that possibility existed for them as well. And Hansberry fed this perception with every talk that she gave, every luncheon she addressed, every school she visited. She mirrored the promise and energy of youth who risked their lives for the highest of principles in the Civil Rights Movement. Her unpublished papers are filled with letters, cards and scripts from the many people influenced by her work. Some achieved distinction of their own and moved on to make their artistic contributions to American theatre, while others became loyal members of an expanded audience.

Of the many factors that influenced Hansberry two are particularly important: Her family and her early life in New York. Hansberry had the pioneering spirit of her parents who challenged housing discrimination in Chicago by moving their family into a white neighborhood. A brick thrown through a window by an angry mob almost hit the eight year old Lorraine. But Mrs. Hansberry patrolled her house with a loaded pistol and Mr. Hansberry pressed their right to live in a house they could afford all the way to the Supreme Court. He won his case against restrictive covenants, setting the precedent for later cases to come. They cultivated in Lorraine and their other children a sense of independence, telling them that they could achieve whatever they cared enough to strive for. Lorraine took them at their word and chose to attend the University of Wisconsin for its journalism program, becoming the first in her family to attend a predominantly white university rather than a Black one. Although aspiring to be a journalist at that time, she began to find her voice in the visual and performing arts — and in progressive politics. As president of the Young Progressives Association, she worked hard on Henry Wallace's unsuccessful run for the U.S. Presidency and developed a season of plays performed by the group — already signaling the wedding of art and politics that would inform her social and artistic vision.

After two years, she left the University and headed for New York City to seek "an education of a different kind." Here she entered a life of political activism and intellectual development judged not by grades or college credits, but by the sheer force of her ideas, and she studied with some of the greatest minds and mentors of the Twentieth Century. She took a seminar on Africa taught by W.E.S. Dubois, was Associate Editor of Paul Robeson's monthly newspaper Freedom, and developed a literary friendship with Langston Hughes whose poetry would inspire her writing. In the political and highly literate circles of the New York Left, she met other young people who, like herself, wanted to make a better world. Hansberry read avidly, voraciously the journals and publications of the Left. The fiery eloquence and incisive thought of "Dubois and Frederick Douglass became the foundation for her analysis of Black and American life and culture, and the radically profound book The Second Sex by French existentialist Simone de Beauvoir shaped her perspective on the status and potential of women.

Having worked as a journalist, she began to realize that the details demanded in news articles sometimes obscured the truths that lay behind the story and suppressed the role that the imagination could play in exploring an issue or a principle So in the early 1950's, she decided instead to be a writer and focused her attention on drama and, to a lesser extent, short stories.

The playwriting award established in her name by the American College Theater Festival, celebrates the work that emerged from her life and the ideas that informed her dramatic writing. In Hansberry's dramas, the experiences of African American people have a universal aspect. The deterred dream, of the Younger family in A Raisin in the Sun are the experience of people everywhere who worked hard for subsistence wages and who struggle to improve their lives despite social predators. The hollow aspirations of George Murchison, whose wealth and class deaden his humanism, reflect a bourgeois mentality rampant in the industrialized world. In The Sign in Sidney Brustein's Window, she poses the dilemma of intellectuals of her time — the perception of powerlessness in the face of corruption. Her television play, What Use Are Flowers? not only condemns an arms race that ends in a nuclear holocaust, but forces the audience to reflect on the use of such intangibles as beauty and truth, love and respect. And that most definitive and horrifying experience of

Black Americans — slavery — becomes in Hansberry's *The Drinking Gourd* a prism through which to examine fundamental myths of American culture. Throughout her work, the roles to which women are relegated are implicitly questioned by the women themselves and the men who benefit from them.

"Art is social," she argued, whether it persuades you to act or puts you to sleep. Hansberry embraced the political and Social import of her subjects, digging deep to find the human elements that connect people's experiences. She found in the life of the most *ordinary* human beings the stuff of high drama — articulating a fundamental principle of her dramaturgy. The kings and queens of classical drama were no more complex and contradictory than the people who often go unnoticed in every day life. Hansberry's vision was broad and comprehensive. She did not confine her imagination to what is, but insisted on exploring what is possible — a compelling definition of realism and a call for vision in the theatre. At the same time, she believed that the work must be honest and willing to expose the brutality of which humans are capable, but always within a context that affirms life.

The winners of the play writing award bearing Hansberry's name reflect her breadth as the dramas range from folk to historical to documentary. They are serious as well as comedic and depict the diversity and complexity of African American life and experience. They take, as Hansberry urged, the stuff of life at its dramatic height. In the spirit of this great playwright, these writers do not confine themselves to a particular style, but rather go where the material and their vision leads them. So the plays in this anthology are not slavishly attentive to a particular style of theatre, but rather explore various forms that can be used to depict human life on the stage, and the forms are many.

Hansberry knew that great writing is a defiant act that rails against the ignorance and misery and corruption and bigotry of its time. It is an act of faith, especially in the theatre, that presumes that the literary, the imaginative can move and persuade and change the course of history. It is this large view of art that gives spirit and definition to the work of the playwrights in this volume. Hansberry believed that "If man is as small and ugly and grotesque as his most inhuman act, he is also as large as his most heroic gesture — and he is therefore a hero many fold. It is this experience of being human, of being black, that should be written large on the page of history." She firmly believed that "The human race does command its own destiny and that destiny can eventually embrace the stars."

But despite this elevated view of humankind's potential, she was well aware of human shortcomings and the challenge to those who would transcend those limitations. In a speech delivered two weeks before the opening of A *Raisin in the Sun*, she said:

I think of Leonardo, contemplating man in the sky — and finding about him demons of ignorance and intolerance insisting that if man had been meant to fly, God would have given him wings. I think of Leonardo, nonetheless patiently filling his notebooks with geometric studies and algebraic equations and anatomical diagrams, literally writing his exercises and conclusions backwards — and I think: Ah, but it is still the dark ages ... and while it is true that the figurative descendants of his persecutors do not hesitate to get on an airplane to go and torment his spiritual descendants — true that there never will be enough light in these shadows — the fact is that it is still the dark ages. And because now at last on the upward ladder toward human enlightenment, we find that man's relationship to man seems by far the most precarious, the most dangerous, and in that sense the newest of our terrors, we fear for the future itself. [Emphasis mine.]

Hansberry wrote out of a time of crisis when Blacks demanded that this nation honor its claims of freedom and equality. That crisis continues in our own time with the spread of poverty and misery, the fear and desensitization of people across classes, and the dominance of an unbridled, socially unresponsive economic system that benefits only the privileged. Hansberry had a word even for this time, a call to writers to visualize and conceptualize what is possible.

Let us take courage. Once physics overwhelmed the minds of men. And it came to pass, that he who had no wings came to command the air at speeds no bird can manage. Surely then, as we turn our full attention to the hearts and minds of men, we shall see that if man can fly — he can also be free.

But that freedom must be grasped and nurtured by our writers and artists. Our visionaries must set the course and help us to navigate the rough waters.

Because Hansberry died too soon, her voice is forever young, filled with the vitality, the hopes and beliefs of youth — and, yes, the wisdom.

Dr. Margaret Wilkerson
University of California at Berkley

Credits

Credits

This page constitues a continuation of the copyrights page.

The Plays

Bulldog And The Bear © Richard Gordon and Irvin S. Bauer

Second Doctor Lady © 1980, Endesha Ida Mae Holland

Silent Octaves © 1979, Brenda Faye Collie

Strands © Eric Wilson

Union Station © 1990, Marta J. Effinger

The Scenes

A Star Ain't Nothin' But A Hole In Heaven © 1977, Judi Ann Mason

Mirror Mirror © Gayle Weaver Williamson

Mother Spense © Olivia Hill

Movie Music © Shay Youngblood The Dramatic Publishing Company

Oh Oh Freedom © 1975, Erwin Charles Washington

The Ballad of Charlie Sweetlegs Vine © Farrell J. Foreman